TRANSAFRICA

TRANSAFRICA

The Languages of Postqueerness

Edited by Chantal Zabus and Chris Dunton

ZED

LONDON · NEW YORK · OXFORD · NEW DELHI · SYDNEY

ZED
Bloomsbury Publishing Plc
50 Bedford Square, London, WC1B 3DP, UK
1385 Broadway, New York, NY 10018, USA
29 Earlsfort Terrace, Dublin 2, Ireland

BLOOMSBURY, Zed and the Zed logo are trademarks of Bloomsbury Publishing Plc

First published in Great Britain 2025

Cover design by Adriana Brioso
Cover image: Reflections on the Road, Logan February
photographed by Gbenga Smith, 2017, Nigeria

A catalogue record for this book is available from the British Library.

A catalog record for this book is available from the Library of Congress.

ISBN: HB: 978-1-3504-0075-7
         PB: 978-1-3504-0076-4
         ePDF: 978-1-3504-0078-8
         eBook: 978-1-3504-0077-1

Typeset by Integra Software Services Pvt. Ltd.
Printed and bound in Great Britain

To find out more about our authors and books visit www.bloomsbury.com
and sign up for our newsletters.

CONTENTS

Part I
CASE STUDIES

ISLAMIC AFRICA

WEST AFRICA

CONTRIBUTORS

Omar Boukhatem holds a PhD in postcolonial studies from Sorbonne Paris Nord University in Paris, France, and a certificate in sociology from the University of Sydney, Australia. Born and raised in Fez, Morocco, he completed his education from primary school through to his master's degree at Sidi Mohamed Ben Abdellah University. Dr Boukhatem's academic interests span cultural studies, gender and sexuality, as well as Arab and Islamic studies. He is also a passionate flamenco guitar player and music composer, finding inspiration and creative expression through his musical endeavours.

Johann De Lange is an award-winning Afrikaans poet (winner of the prestigious Hertzog Prize) and editor of the AVBOB poetry project. He is a well-known short story writer and translator of Wilma Stockenström, Antjie Krog and others. A number of his translations have been published in *The Penguin Book of Southern African Verse* (1989) and *Breaking the Silence – A Century of South African Women's Poetry* (1990).

Naminata Diabate is an associate professor of comparative literature at Cornell University and a member of the Advisory Board of the African Institute in Sharjah in the United Arab Emirates. A scholar of gender, sexuality, race, biopolitics and neoliberalism with linguistic expertise in six languages, her work engages multiple cultural productions and oral traditions from Francophone and Anglophone Africa, Black America, Afro-Hispanic America and the French Antilles. Her most recent provocations on defiant disrobing, erotic pleasure, freedom and the impact of internet media on queerness have appeared in peer-reviewed journals, collections of essays and podcasts, as well as in a monograph, *Naked Agency: Genital Cursing and Biopolitics in Africa* (2020), which was awarded the African Studies Association (ASA) 2021 Best Book Prize and the African Literature Association (ALA) 2022 First Book Award. Diabate just completed her book *Pleasure and Displeasure: An Interdisciplinary Investigation* and is currently working on a monograph, 'Digital Insurgencies and Bodies'.

Chris Dunton, born in the United Kingdom and an Oxford graduate, worked at universities in Nigeria, Libya and South Africa, and was most recently Professor and Dean of Humanities at the National University of Lesotho. He is the author of, for example, *Make Man Talk True: Nigerian Theatre in English since 1970* (1992), with Mai Palmberg *Human Rights and Homosexuality* (1996), and *Nigerian Theatre in English* (1998). Dunton was the first Anglophone scholar to publish work on homosexualities in African literature.

Logan February is a nonbinary Nigerian poet, songwriter and graduate student at Purdue University's MFA programme in Creative Writing. Their writing has appeared in *Berlin Quarterly*, *The Poetry Project* and *The Rumpus*, among other publications. They are the author of the poetry collection *In The Nude* (2019) and three poetry chapbooks. In 2020, February received the Future Awards Africa Prize for Literature.

Joan Hambidge is a poet, theorist, novelist and currently Fellow and Senior Researcher at the University of Cape Town, South Africa. Her latest novel is entitled *Stasies* (2023), a campus novel. Her novels navigate the relationship between theory and creativity.

John C. Hawley, Professor Emeritus at Santa Clara University, is author or editor of a number of books on postcolonial and queer theories and their intersection. He has also contributed chapters to books on these topics, and articles in journals that also deal with religion. He was a Fulbright Fellow in Berlin and a former resident at the Bellagio Center, and member of three MLA executive committees and the delegate assembly. He has served on the executive council of the African Literature Association, as President of the South Asian Literature Association and of the US chapter of the Association for Commonwealth Literature and Language Studies, as President of the Faculty Senate and twice as chair of his department. He is currently writing on the literature of migration.

Katlego K. Kolanyan-Kesupile is a Motswana trans performing artist, impresario, poet and independent researcher. She is one of the pioneers of trans activism in Botswana and has been researching African trans issues since 2007. She is the founder and director of Queer Shorts Showcase, an annual LGBTQ theatre festival in Gaborone. Her first collection of poetry was published by Bahati Books in 2016. A Chevening Scholar, Katlego graduated from Goldsmiths College, University of London, in 2016 with a master's degree in human rights, culture and social justice.

Francois Lion-Cachet is a PhD student in the Centre for Rhetoric Studies, Faculty of Law, University of Cape Town, where he received the Dikgang Moseneke Fellowship and an AW Mellon-UCT Rhetoric Studies scholarship. He is employed as Curator: Public Engagement of the Constitutional Court Art Collection, by the Constitutional Court Trust. He is also editor and chairperson of the Afrikaans arts and culture journal *Klyntji*. His research and work revolve around queer literature, legal theory, South African visual culture and art, spirituality, and environmentalism.

Belinda Qaqamba Makinana is the Legal & Policy Programme Manager at Gender Dynamix. A civil society organization based in South Africa that promotes, protects and advance the human rights of trans and gender diverse persons in Southern Africa. They (preferred pronoun) are finishing a master's degree in education policy studies at Stellenbosch University focusing on modalities of resistance employed by transgender learners in township schools. They describe themselves as a gender fugitive with an interest in artivism, policy studies, and sexuality and gender justice work in Africa.

John McAllister retired from the University of Botswana in 2015. He has published widely on colonial and postcolonial African literature and on queer activism in Botswana and has written or edited a broad range of materials for LGBTQ rights organizations in Botswana, South Africa, Kenya, Senegal and Burkina Faso. He was one of the founders of *Q-zine*, a pioneering online magazine of African LGBTQ arts and culture, and served as its managing editor from 2011 until 2015.

Alyette Rajaofera Andriamasinalivao graduated from the University of Antananarivo, Madagascar before completing her PhD at the University of Paris (Paris 7 – Paris Diderot). Her transdisciplinary work investigates the interplay between gender, discourses on female empowerment and postcolonial studies in Madagascar. Her most recent publication explores the influence of the French colonial system on the construction of Malagasy culture and identity through the analysis of school manuals during the colonial period. Her manuscript project considers the challenges faced by Malagasy female orators who engage in the performance of the traditionally masculine art of oratory. It questions the possibilities for the constitution of a female, postcolonial subject in contemporary Madagascar. Her other research areas include critical studies of men and masculinities, queer and feminist theory, and critical race and ethnicity studies.

Todd W. Reeser is Professor of French and Gender, Sexuality, and Women's Studies, Chairperson of the Department of French and Italian, and former Director of Gender, Sexuality, and Women's Studies at the University of Pittsburgh, USA. For spring 2022, he was an external fellow at the University of Strasbourg Institute of Advanced Study (USIAS). His research lies at the intersection of French and gender/sexuality studies, with a focus on politics, identity and cultural representation. He has published *Moderating Masculinity in Early Modern Culture* (2006), *Masculinities in Theory* (2009), *Setting Plato Straight: Translating Ancient Sexuality in the Renaissance* (2015) and *Queer Cinema in Contemporary France* (2022). His most recent edited volume is *The Routledge Companion to Gender and Affect* (2023). He is working on a monograph 'Transgender France: Universalism and Sexual Subjectivity' studying how the inception and development of the category of transgender/transsexual in France starting in the 1950s relates to political ideas on the 'universalist' citizen.

Philippe-Joseph Salazar was born in 1955 in Casablanca, then part of French Morocco. A rhetorician and philosopher, he is currently Distinguished Professor of Rhetoric in the Faculty of Law, University of Cape Town. He was a founder member and President of ARCSA (the Association for Rhetoric and Communication in Southern Africa). Amongst his books are *An African Athens: Rhetoric and the*

Shaping of Democracy in South Africa (2002) and *Words as Weapons: Inside ISIS's Rhetoric of Terror* (2017).

Adriaan van Klinken is Professor of Religion and African Studies at the University of Leeds and Extraordinary Professor in the Desmond Tutu Centre for Religion and Social Justice, University of the Western Cape. His research focuses on religion, gender and sexuality in contemporary African contexts. He is the author, among other titles, of *Kenyan, Christian, Queer: Religion, LGBT Activism, and Arts of Resistance in Africa* (2019).

Chantal Zabus is Professor of Postcolonial and Gender Studies at the University Sorbonne Paris Nord. She is the author of, for example, *Tempests after Shakespeare* (2002), *The African Palimpsest* (1991; 2013; 2018), *Out in Africa: Same-Sex Desire in Sub-Saharan African Literatures and Cultures* (2014) and *Between Rites and Rights* (2007; 2016). Her last two edited books are *Transgender Experience* (2014) and *The Future of Postcolonial Studies* (2015). She is currently working on a monograph titled *Post-I.D.: Relationalities in the Literatures of the Late Anthropocene*. She is the Editor-in-Chief of *Postcolonial Text*.

ACKNOWLEDGEMENTS

Chantal Zabus would like to thank the Université Sorbonne Paris Nord (USPN), formerly known as Université Paris 13, for the *Bonus qualité recherche,* a €20,000 bonus for excellence in research. This allowed her to carry out semi-structured interviews in several locations on the African continent to flesh out her project, *Transafrica,* which picks up where her monograph, *Out in Africa: Same-Sex Desire in Sub-Saharan African Literatures and Cultures* (2013) left off. Warm thanks also go to USPN again and the University of Chicago Center in Paris and its academic director, Professor Daisy Delogu, for helping bring together scholars and artists around 'the transnational languages of postqueerness' conference in May 2022, which spurred us on to wrap up the *Transafrica* project, born in 2014, a decade later.

Having retired from the National University of Lesotho, Chris Dunton has no institutional affiliation or support to acknowledge, but in the context of the current project he is profoundly grateful for the learning experience he enjoyed in the 1990s working with MATRIX, Lesotho's LGBTQ+ support organization, and at the conference on contesting homophobia organized by the Open Society Initiative for Southern Africa (OSISA) in Centurion, South Africa. Would that similar experiences had been available during earlier times in Nigeria and Libya.

INTRODUCTION

Chantal Zabus and Chris Dunton

… as doors are shut and bolted it seems the hammering on those doors grows louder

Chris Dunton (2023)

The Bolted Doors …

Eighty-seven United Nation member countries have laws that criminalize same-sex relations; some thirty-seven African countries, along with Middle Eastern countries, constitute a majority of these.[1] Average citizens, religious authorities and heads of state alike have contributed to entrenching the belief that homosexuality, itself a slippery category, is un-African. Even such an eminent scholar as Toyin Falola can state without qualification that 'for Africans at large, the idea of homosexuality is un-African' (2023: 55). A spectacular illustration of this was to be found on placards outside the Johannesburg Supreme Court during the 1991 Winnie Mandela trial: 'HOMOSEX IS NOT IN BLACK CULTURE'. This *ad populum* logical fallacy is often used as a means of controlling gender variance, and punitive behaviour includes beating, rape, imprisonment and, in some contexts, aversion therapy, forcible sex-change and even murder. Murder was the fate of gay and lesbian rights activists such as Sierra Leonean Fanny Ann Eddy in 2004 and Ugandan David Kato in 2011, three years before the amended 'Kill the Gays' bill was voted on, shortly after Nigeria enacted similar legislation. However, some individuals who have been indicted for 'crimes against nature' such as in the Tamsir Jupiter Ndiaye case in Senegal in 2012, have turned down help from LGBTQ+[2] organizations, and others, as in the 2010 Malawi trial, have accused such organizations of suffering from the 'white saviour' syndrome (see Dunton and Hoad 2014: 477–97).

The African continent wavers between two extremes in the legal spectrum: on the one hand, it issues the most stringent reforms in terms of criminalization of sexual dissidence, as in Uganda and Nigeria in 2014 and again in Uganda in

2023. On the other hand, it boasts the most innovative jurisdictions and liberal legislations in the world regarding gender nonconformity and sexual orientation. For instance, the post-apartheid, 1996 South African Constitution boasts an unprecedented bill of rights (Clause 9/3), and Botswana decriminalized same-sex relations in 2021. In February 2023, the Supreme Court of Kenya struck down a government decision to ban the registration of an LGBTQ+ community rights organization, which however triggered off mass protests against the court ruling. The African continent, with its extremes, thus provides the ideal testing terrain for examining gender nonconformity and sexual dissidence. The Republic of South Africa Bill of Rights led the way. The first country to follow suit outside of Africa was Canada.

In the face of official narratives by medical doctors, legal and religious authorities that have often been prioritized over a gender-variant (queer, trans, nonbinary) individual's lived experience in a kind of systemic disempowerment, the present collection of essays attempts to identify the new vocabularies that queer and transgender Africans have used in the first two decades of the twenty-first century to refer to themselves and narrativize their desire.

At the cross-roads of the humanities and the social sciences and across a broad geographical, religious and legal spectrum, *Transafrica*, through thirteen essays and testimonies, addresses the cultural production and the lexical production that gender nonconformity and sexual dissidence on the African continent have produced. As some of the contributors show, this lexical culture lies at the crossroads of western discourse and local African naming practices.

The volume explores this new lexical culture in cultural materials (novels, poetry, testimonies/life stories, interviews, film, visual art) in English, French, Arabic and other African languages, and the meanings which Africans have transnationally conferred upon 'queer' and 'transgender' – from north to south – in the first two decades of the twenty-first century. The following countries are therefore represented: Morocco, Egypt, Cameroon, Somalia, Nigeria, Botswana, Madagascar and South Africa, with occasional references to other African countries (e.g. Kenya) and their diasporic (e.g. Somali) offshoots.

It is fitting to take stock of those narratives which are autobiographical or autofictional. 'Narrativizing the self' (Najmabadi 2014) involves African selfhoods as 'open-ended' forms of personhood-in-becoming typical of African thought, countering the dominant conception of a self-determining autonomous individual (Wiredu and Gyekye 1992; Masolo 2010), as well as 'modern selves' (Wahrman 2004) lately enhanced by digital selves 'out online' (Raun 2016). These selves function as sites of both vulnerability and empowerment in identity formation in a 'participatory culture' (Burgess and Green 2009) and a 'convergence culture' (Jenkins 2006). This narrativization connects cultural production's 'fields of force' (Bourdieu 1991), with its articulation in often religiously, societally and legally hostile milieus or 'fields of struggle'. The more rigid those 'fields of struggle' become, the more creative the 'fields of force'. The more bolted the doors, the louder the hammering.

The Louder Hammering on Those Doors

In order to understand the loud banging on the doors of those penal postcolonies, it is necessary to provide a short detour through the early moments of embryonic voicing as they later galvanize into a loud polyphony in the first two decades of the third millennium, when homosexuality in Africa has moved from being treated as an occasional or ritualized practice to being claimed as an *identity* in an *outing* process of sorts in postcolonial societies (see Zabus 2013). We then hope to answer Chris Dunton's question at the end of 'Tuning into the Polyphony: the Emergence of LGBTQ+ Writing in Africa' (2023): 'Are we in a time of transition or borne along by a tidal polyphony?'

Ato Quayson proposes the concept of postcolonial literature as calibration to advocate for a method of 'reading *for* the social', which embraces 'the ideological notion of using the literary as means towards social enlightenment' (Quayson 2003: 4). The first two scholars to trace the literary aetiology of same-sex desire in African literature are French critic Daniel Vignal (1983) and British Chris Dunton (1989). Even though writing in French, when Dunton knew Vignal, the latter was Head of the Alliance Française office in Zaria, Northern Nigeria and was up to scratch with Nigeriana. Both pioneers tapped into the ideological mood of the 1980s, with the first Lesbian and Gay Pride march in Johannesburg, South Africa on 13 October 1990, and the emergence of an epidemiological discourse around HIV/AIDS. Unlike Vignal, Dunton considers female same-sex desire when male same-sex desire had prevailed in the early European ethnographic imagination.

In this early literary aetiology, the novel takes centre stage, possibly because of its capacity for dialogic amplification and its polyphonic aesthetics. Contrary to anthropological discourse, which establishes exclusive links between homo-sexuality and initiation rites, and colonial discourse, which often documents unequal relationships between partners (due to age, social status, pecuniary means), present-day literature, especially the novel and, more recently, the autobiographical or the autofictional genre, have successfully projected homosexuality as a lived experience, based on the Plutarchan *charis* or reciprocal obligingness.

In *Out in Africa* (2013) Chantal Zabus has outlined developments regarding gender and sexuality in three stages: (1) from the mid-nineteenth century and the *fin-de-siècle* European sexual imaginary to the sexual initiation models of the 1970s in African countries as well as diasporic milieus, such as in France at a time when philosophy is imbued with Sartrean existentialism, and the United Kingdom with its first 'Afro-Queer' protagonists (Zabus 2013: 83–124); (2) from the late-twentieth-century narratives of sexual emancipation to the turn of the millennium to the contemporary moment culminating in transgenderism (125–250); on to (3) new vocabularies and new subjectivities created via the new media in the first two decades of the twenty-first century (251–68; see also Zabus 2021).

Naminata Diabate (in this volume) updates Zabus' 2013 account with more recent francophone African LGBTQ+-themed writing. Likewise, in 'Tuning into the Polyphony' (2023), Chris Dunton updates the account of such writing that has been emerging in English most recently on the African continent and which continues to grow, the more entrenched homophobic legislation has become in the majority of African countries. As a 'Postscript: All Shall Have Prizes', Dunton mentions 'a more affirmative take on the reception of LGBTQ+ writing from Africa':

> In 2023 US-based Nigerian author Arinze Ifeakandu was awarded the Dylan Thomas prize for his gay-themed short story collection *God's Children are Little Broken Things* (the prize, administered by the University of Swansea, Wales, is for writers under the age of 39). And in 2022 Nigerian poet Romeo Oriogun (also US-based) became the first openly gay author to win the prestigious Nigeria Prize for Literature for his collection *Nomad*. As that prize is awarded by Nigeria LNG (Liquified Natural Gas) Ltd., the honour given Oriogun's work can be regarded as a significant case of mainstreaming.
>
> (Dunton 2023: 11)

In the two years leading up to the publication of the present volume significant developments took place on the Nigerian literary scene. After repeated postponements, the reason for which the present authors have not been able to ascertain, Cassava Republic published in 2023 a volume of testimonies edited by Olumide F. Makanjuola and Jude Dibia and titled *Love Offers No Safety: Nigeria's Queer Men Speak* (in 2018 the same press had published *She Called Me Woman: Nigeria's Queer Women Speak*, edited by Azeenarh Mohammed, Chitra Nagarajan and Rafeeat Aliyu). An instructive exercise is to go through these volumes, roughly quantifying how many of the narratives express a positive outlook on the prospects of survival, fulfilment and happiness for African LGBTQ+, how many a negative outlook, and how many are equivocal. In the case of the Makanjuola and Dibia volume, a remarkable number of the testimonies are optimistic and resilient, though the tenor of these is not so much akin to a hammering on doors as to finding an adjacent window through which to climb.

There have also been significant developments in the field of fiction. Earlier works had largely focused on the stigma LGBTQ+ individuals faced from their family, peer-group and employers; this is the case from the pioneering Nigerian gay-themed novel, Jude Dibia's *Walking with Shadows* (2005) through to a novel such as Chinelo Okparanta's *Under the Udala Trees* (2015). It remains true largely of a more recent work such as Arinze Ifeakandu's already mentioned, prize-winning collection *God's Children Are Little Broken Things* (2022). For example, in the most substantial of the stories, 'What the Singers Say About Love' (Ifeakandu 2022: 131–68), which details the breakdown of a relationship because the record company of one partner, a successful musician, places pressure on him not to be revealed as queer. Yet the stories can take on a more lethal tenor, as when one character exclaims: "'This country eats people alive, and only the strong and sharp can make it'" (111). And the reality of violence – the homophobic violence unleashed by the 2014 Same Sex Marriage Prohibition Act – is depicted with horrifying impact in two very recent novels, Ani Kayode Somtochukwu's heart-rending *And Then He Sang a Lullaby* (2022) and Chukwuebuka Ibeh's *Blessings* (2024), the concluding thirty pages of which are on the passing of the 2014 bill prohibiting same-sex marriage and its agonizing consequences – through the homophobic violence this unleashed – for the novel's LGBTQ+ characters. One especially striking feature of this section of the novel is Ibeh's emphasis on (the then) President Goodluck Jonathan's motivation for implementing the bill, namely its appeal to Nigerian homophobes, in an attempt to salvage his own failing political career.

Some idea of the scale of this proliferation of African queer-themed texts in recent years can be seen in the fact that on 21 February 2024, *The New York Times* carried as the lead item in its Arts Section an article titled 'The Needle Has Been Moved', in which the author, Abdi Latif Dahir, begins: 'Queer literature is booming all across Africa as authors push boundaries, win major awards and find eager audiences' (Dahir 2024: 1).

If developments in sub-Saharan Africa can be regarded as promising despite severe implementation of constrictive laws, an inquiry into the Maghreb and the Mashreq reveals that LGBTQ+ characters need to be vigorously retrieved, for they are consistently obscured by legal and religious discourses.

Doors Ajar for Desiring Muslim Africans

In the Arab-Muslim world, the banging on bolted doors may prove at first to be less loud, more muffled, but writers have designed their own perception of same-sex desire, starting with changing the language inherited from the vocabulary of deviance. The Arabic word *al-mithliyyah-al-jinsi* (المثلية الجنسي) is a recent invention patterned on the Arabic word for 'same' or 'identical' (مماثل) to convey homosexuality whereas *ghayriyah* (غيرية) after 'other' or even 'altruist' renders heterosexuality. They have come to gradually oust *al-shudhuudh al-jinsi* (الشذوذ الجنسي – literally 'deviance of sex') and, according to a 2012 survey carried out by Justin McGuinness on the use of *mithly* on a Moroccan site, it is gaining ground but was already in use in Lebanon as of 2000 (McGuinness 2012: 125, 119). In that respect, George Massad's *Desiring Arabs* (2007) remains such an alternative, Arabic-inflected contribution to opening doors, if only by leaving them ajar. Massad discusses early novels, especially emanating from the Mashreq, here Egypt.

In an early novel such as Egyptian Naguib Mahfuz's *Zuqaq al-Midaq* (1947; *Midaq Alley*), *shudhuudh* is used to refer to the married café owner Kirshah's sexual practices with young men but also general social misconduct, recoded in English by a Sufi ascetic customer as 'Homosexuality and is spelled, h-o-m-o-s-e-x-u-a-l-i-t-y, but it is not love. True love is only for the family and descendants of the prophet' (quoted in Massad 2007: 277). In *Al-Sukkariyyah* (*Sugar Street*, 1957) Mahfouz re-introduces male same-sex desire as an 'illness', combined with a 'disgust' for women (quoted in Massad 2007: 287), reflecting the influence of European medical terminology. Another Egyptian novelist Sun'allah Ibrahim, who had already dwelled on same-sex and castration in *That Odor* (1966), stages in *Sharaf* (1997) the attempted rape of a young man called Sharaf (شرف means 'honour') by an Englishman, which functions as the symbolic rape of Egypt by the West. 'Ala' Al-Aswani in *'Imarat Ya'qubyan* (2002; *The Yacoubian Building*, 2004) links 'sexual deviance' to 'postcolonial degeneration' (389). Overall, Massad laments the discursive, Occidentalist transformation of practitioners of 'same-sex contact' in the Arab-Muslim world into subjects who identify as homosexual or gay, following the hegemonic pull of the Gay International, 'where all same-sex desire must lead to the romantic ethos of coupling' (2007: 345). It is in this Massadian light that Boukhatem's contribution to this volume on Egyptian novelist Muhammad Abdelnabi's *Fi gurfat al-'ankabūt/In the Spider's Room* (2017) has to be understood.

What Hayes has called 'the homopast' needs to be retrieved as it has been neglected by official Maghrebi discourses (Hayes 1997: 523). Outside of Muhammad Shukri's polymorphous novelistic autobiography *Al-Khubz al-Hafi* (1956, *For Bread Alone*, 1972), which can be argued to re-orientalize the Orient, such a retrieval can be observed in, for example, Moroccan Rachid O. in *L'enfant ébloui* (1995) and *Chocolat chaud* (1998); and Franco-Tunisian writer Eyet-Chekib Djaziri in *Un poisson sur la balançoire* (2001).

Franco-Algerian Nina Bouraoui problematizes a process of identity formation that incorporates same-sex desire in *Garçon Manqué* (2000)/*Tomboy*, (2007): 'Every morning, I check my identity: French? Algerian? Girl? Boy?' ('Tous les matins je vérifie mon identité. J'ai quatre problèmes. Française? Algérienne? Fille? Garçon?' 163). As a woman cross dresser who desires other women, she writes in *Poupée Bella* (2004), without once using the French word 'lesbienne': 'I am in the time of my homosexuality' ('Je suis dans le temps de mon homosexualité'; Bouraoui 2004: 16–17), a stance she furthers in *Mes Mauvaises pensées* (2005). Interestingly, Nigerian novelist Chinelo Okparanta in her 2015 novel, *Under the Udala Trees*, also manages to sketch a relationship between two girls (one Igbo, the other Hausa) in post-civil war Nigeria without mentioning the word 'lesbian', as Van Klinken and Makinana observe in this volume.

Likewise, English-Somali Diriye Osman writes about his alter ego in his short story 'The Other (Wo)man' (2013): 'He didn't belong to just one society. … He was Somali first, Muslim second, gay third'. This is echoed by Somali Afdhere Jama in his book *Being Queer and Somali* (2022), which contains three chapters – (1) 'Queer', (2) 'Somali' and (3) 'Muslim' – and is discussed by John C. Hawley in this volume along with more recent works by Diriye Osman and by, for example, Tofik Dibi, who was born in the Netherlands to Moroccan parents. This three-tiered approach to identity finds a suitable, scholarly equivalent in Hassan J. Ndzovu's discussion of the three-pronged onslaught of undermining sexual freedom in Kenya: 'Un-Natural, Un-African and Un-Islamic' (2016: 78–91).

As Gopinath has argued, 'queer desire reorients the traditionally backward-looking glance of diaspora' (2005: 3). In other words, Osman, who lives in exile in the United Kingdom and has broken off with his Somali family, has initiated a forward-looking conception of diaspora by being a Somali, Muslim, gay yet relocated subject. Outside of the diaspora, South African Muhsin Hendriks, the imam and head of a queer mosque, the Inner Circle in Cape Town, deems that this hierarchization of identities can be toppled: he feels *at once* Muslim and queer.[3]

Moroccan Abdellah Taïa, who, in *Une mélancolie arabe* (2008), had already recounted his tribulations as a queer child, shows, in *Le jour du roi* (2010), one boy Omar, who wears the other boy's underwear and has put on lipstick: 'I am neither boy, nor girl. I am in desire' ('Je ne suis ni garçon, ni fille. Je suis dans le désir'; Taïa 2010: 179). Taïa had confided in 2008 to Jean Zaganiaris (2008), the author of *Queer Maroc* (2013), that he wished to go 'beyond heterosexuality and homosexuality'; 'towards transgender, transformation' ('au-delà de l'hétérosexualité et de l'homosexualité ... vers le transgenre, la transformation'). However, as Zabus has argued, 'transgender here remains a metaphor in a homosexual space' (2021: 392).

Already in *Le livre du sang* (1979) Moroccan sociologist Abdelkebir Khatibi had portrayed androgyny but more in an eighth-century Sufi sense than in the contemporary understanding of transgender. Moroccan Berber novelist Abdelhak Serhane in *Messaouda* ([1983] 2002), which features a young man's rape by older men in a hammam and his anal 'rupture' ('déchirure') by the *fqih* in the Qur'anic school, also describes the eponymous prostitute as a 'solitary hermaphrodite' (43, 45, 11). In *Au bonheur des limbes*, Moroccan Mohamed Leftah portrays Jeanne the transvestite's male-to-female (MTF) body as 'mutilated' with 'acid and glass' so as to create a vagina (Leftah 2006: 69–70). This barely revealed penectomy recalls the surgery, which, as of 1956, French gynaecologist Georges Burou carried out in his Clinique du Parc in Casablanca, on mainly French MTFs such as Coccinelle; *pied noir* Bambi aka Marie-Pierre Pruvot; but also, British Jan Morris, who relates in semi-Orientalist fashion her transitioning in *Conundrum* (1974).[4]

It is against such a rich proliferation of Moroccan characters that Todd Reeser in this volume approaches Moroccan filmmaker Daoud Aoulad-Siyad's French-language film *Bye-Bye Souirty/Adieu Forain* (1998). The film's main character, Rabii, was inspired by Moroccan artist-actor Bouchaib El-Bidaoui, who dressed as a woman and who appeared as such at events and on television. Reeser concludes that 'Rabii is ... not living like an LGBTQ+ global northerner ... defined by linguistic tags such as *transgenre*, *homosexuel*, or even queer .... At the end of the film ..., linguistic signifiers will be left behind in favour of localized ones.' In this film, which foregrounds what Reeser calls 'a twenty-first-century form of transgender on the horizon' – a horizon, however, located, in the Maghreb rather than in the diaspora, Aoulad-Siyad opts for a line of flight in visual language and a lack of directionality, which goes against the grain of a south–north queer migration.

Banging on Virtual Portals

Outside of the traditional literary canon, blogs can contribute to the popularity of gay, lesbian and bisexual characters from novels, which would otherwise be known only to a restricted readership. Such is the case with a blog posted on 6 May 2015 by the UK-based social scientist Zahrah Nesbitt-Ahmed, founder of Bookshy

Blogger. Together with Dele Meiji Fatunla, the Administrator of the Caine Prize as of 2018, Nesbitt-Ahmed published a list of ten 'gay' characters, including the Black bisexual South African woman Nonceba, in Lindiwe Nkutha's 'The Glass Pecker' (2005); the young gay activist Tendeka from Cape Town in Lauren Beukes' 2008 cyberpunk, dystopian novel *Moxyland*; Nigerian 'straightest gay' Chinedu in Chimamanda Ngozi Adichie's 'The Shivering' from her short-story collection *The Thing Around Your Neck* (2009); and Tendai Huchu's Dumisami in *Hairdresser of Harare* (2010).[5]

Various online collections and literary forums such as *StoryTime*, *Author-Me*, *NigeriansTalk* as well as pan-African electronic magazines and sites such as *Q-Zine* and HOLAA! regularly publish the work of 'queer' Africans, who also help 'circulate different kinds of affects' in the blogosphere (Macharia 2013: 108). Brittle Paper's second Anniversary page on Facebook (2017) reads: 'Unsilencing Queer Nigeria: The Language of Emotional Truth'; and Otosirieze Obi-Young's response (2023) reads: 'Dear Mr. Brittle: queer African Literature is not a trend, has always existed.' Elnathan John, the author of, amongst other relevant work, 'Barna and I' (2014) and *Born on a Tuesday* (2015), confessed his embarrassment in Elnathan's Dark Corner blogspot in 2013: 'I cannot give a definition beyond whom I have or have not had penetrative sex with.' Two years after Kenyan founding editor of *Kwani?* Binyavanga Wainaima declared that he was gay,[6] he tweeted in 2016 to World Aids Day that he was 'HIV+ and happy' ('I'm HIV+ and happy' 2020).

On YouTube, Nigerian MTF founder of TransValid Ms SaHHara testified that she 'left Nigeria to save her life'. She had earlier taken Adichie to task for belittling her experience growing up as a transgender boy and called Adichie a TERF (Trans Exclusionary Radical Feminist), thereby pointing to a clash between African feminisms and transfeminism. Blogs and vlogs continue to contribute to new identity formations such as datafied and digitized selves as a result of being a member of a 'queer' space or a trans-'imagined community'. Such is the case with Nigerian Akwaeke Emezi's Tik Tok video #*TheOpulentogbanje* discussed by Zabus in this volume, which occasioned an Ibibio follower to respond in 'A Letter to the Opulent Ogbanje' (on 25 December 2018): 'I may not be an ogbanje [a spirit child], but I know I'm not human. I'm probably a spirit, trapped in a body.'[7] But on African soil, these blogs and media selfies are under surveillance and remain volatile ways of countering deep anxieties about same-sex desire in the sub-Saharan African postcolonies.

Transsahara, Transnational, Transgender

As indicated in the Acknowledgements, the Transafrica project was born in 2014 in the aftermath of Zabus's publication of *Out in Africa*. This exploration of same-sex desire in literatures and cultures had a specific geographical coverage as it concerned sub-Saharan Africa. The concluding chapter gestured towards 'Trans-Sahara', that is, the necessity to dare the trans-national crossing across the Sahara and contemplate queerness in the Maghreb and the Mashreq; it also pointed to the penury of transgender-focused writing, both scholarly and creative. The *Transafrica* project was born.

The 12 May 2022 conference at the University of Chicago in Paris may be considered a step towards the present volume. However, the conference included papers that covered the Caribbean – for instance, papers by Katheen Ghyssels, Josiane Ranguin and Johan Mijail – but we narrowed our focus to confine ourselves to the African continent, as otherwise we would have been taken further afield. However, the transnational aspect of *Transafrica* soon imposed itself as its pan-African focus and spatial spread, from the Maghreb to Southern Africa, provides a branching topiary of connections.

Of the array of meanings of the word 'trans', we could catalogue the following: translation/transliteration/transgender (Boukhatem; Rajaofera Andrianasinalivao); trans migration, transing language, transing media (Reeser, Zabus); nonbinary gender identities (Dunton; Rajaoefra Andriamasinalivao); and translects (Zabus; Andriamasanalivao; February). The 'trans' as in transgender *Trans-Africa* was simply ignored on the African continent, until the 2010s. In 2012, Geoffrey A. Jobson et al. wrote a short article entitled 'Transgender in Africa: Invisible, Inaccessible, or Ignored?' which acted as a trigger of visibility for African transgender, albeit in the medical field. Taking his cue from Sausa, Keatley and Operario (2007), Jobson, a researcher with Anova Health Institute in Cape Town, focused on 'people whose gender identity and/or gender expression is different from the sex which they were assigned at birth, regardless of their sexual orientation' (Jobson et al. 2012: 161). He and his co-authors wished to alert activists and health specialists to the relevance of gender identity for HIV risk.

In this type of research carried out a decade ago, transgender people were included as subcategories of MSM (Men Who Have Sex with Men) and, to a lesser extent, WSW (Women who have Sex with Women). It soon appeared that the team did not receive 'straight' answers to the three basic questions in the questionnaire: the first was: 'What is your sex or gender? (check all that apply)', with response options including: Male, Female, Transgender Male, Transgender Female, Genderqueer, Additional sex or gender (to be specified); the second question read: 'What sex were you assigned at birth? (choose only one)', with response options: Male or Female; and the third question concerned sexual orientation. The research tools proved to be blunted, for a biological male with female gender identity who is sexually attracted to men, could answer: female to the first question; male to the second; and heterosexual to the third. Jobson et al. concluded that 'the questions and response options need to be adapted to local country terminology' (Jobson et al. 2012: 162). This 'local country terminology' lies at the heart of *Transafrica* and what we have ventured to call 'postqueerness'.

Postqueerness: Four Characteristics

'Postqueerness' is a space-clearing gesture to point to a future beyond 'queer'. 'Queer' itself has been seen as an 'addiction' (Hoad 2011). Hoad's irritation with the word 'queer' may be seen in his frenzied but erudite dithyramb:

> Aikane, arse-bandit, baby, baby-dyke, bear, bent, berdache, bugger, bulldagger,
> butch, carpet-/rug-muncher, catamite, chaser, cherry-sister, chubby, cub, dandy,
> dinge-queen, dyke, femme, floozie, friend of Dorothy's, fudge packer, gay,
> heterosexual, high-femme, hijra, homosexual, hungochani, husband, invert,
> jimbanda, john, kathoey, khawal, kiki, lesbian, libertine, light in the loafers,
> mahu, man, maricon, mary, member of the church, molly, MSM, nanshoku,
> otter, pederast, pervert, pillow-biter, poofter, postop, pre-op, queen, queer,
> quimbanda, rice-queen, Sapphist, shirt-lifter, slob-femme, slut, snow-queen,
> sodomite, soft-butch, stibane, stone-butch, straight, stud, that way, trade,
> trannie, tribadist, uranist, urning, wife, women, xanith, and so on ….
>
> (Hoad 2011: 128)

In western academe, 'queer' is thus seen as having run its course. As James Penney has remarked in *After Queer Theory*, 'the injunction to (be) queer tends to have perversely normalizing effects. This is the case, for example, with the various types of queer vangardism that wish to normalize promiscuity, inveigh against same-sex marriage, or impose regimes or aesthetically conceived forms of alternative social being' (2014: 6).

It might seem Eurocentric at first to imagine a move beyond a term or label such as 'queer', which is itself an import from Euro-American academic circles and therefore Eurocentric in origin. It was originally used as an alternative to 'gay' with the extra dimension of openness, the blatant refusal to conform, acting-up.[8] Moreover, 'queer', unlike 'gay', which has been incorporated in some African languages, as seen in the term *magai* in Kenya, has not found a fertile terrain to grow as a noun, adjective or verb in everyday African discourse. However, the proponents of the queering of the African continent are both African and non-African scholars writing in the second decade of the twenty-first century as in some sort of academic trickle-down effect from western academe.

Examples of such 'queering' include but are not limited to the already mentioned Imam Muhsin Hendricks of the Inner Circle and author of *Hijab: Unveiling Queer Muslim Lives* (2009); Solarin Ekine and Hakima Abbas' edited volume, *Queer African Reader* (2013); Karen Marten and Xala Makhosozana's edited volume, *Queer Africa: New and Collected Fiction* (2013); Zethu Matebeni's *Reclaiming Afrikan: Queer Perspectives on Sexual and Gender Identities* (2014); Brenna Munro's article, 'Locating "Queer" in Contemporary Writing of Love and War in Nigeria' (2016); Taiwo Osinubi and Neville Hoad's guest issue, *Queer Valences in African Literatures and Film* (2016); the 36th volume of *African Literature Today, Queer Theory in Film and Fiction* (2018); Mohamed Azeenarh's edited volume, *She called me Woman/ Nigeria's Queer Women Speak* (2018); S. N. Nyeck's edited *Routledge Handbook of Queer African Studies* (2021); and, more recently, Kwame E. Otu and Adriaan van Klinken (also in this volume) in their article 'African Studies Keywords: Queer' in *African Studies Review* (2023); as well as Sybil Fekurumoh, '25 Queer Books from African and African diasporan Writers' (2023).

Pre-queer terms operating before the 2010s include 'homosexuality' as in Dunton and Palmberg (1996); 'dissident sexuality' (Epprecht 2004); 'sexual diversity' as in Nyeck and Epprecht (2013); 'intimacies' as in Neville Hoad (2007); and 'same-sex desire' as in Zabus (2013).[9] The suspensive aspect of 'queer', as in David Halperin's (1995) definition and the general signalling through the flames in the 1990s, then seem to have captured the evanescence of sex and gender identities on the African continent. However, 'post-queer', which seems to emerge as the pendant to 'pre-gay', takes stock of more recent developments on the African continent.

We distinguish four characteristics of 'postqueerness'.

1. To us, the first characteristic of postqueerness is that it comes to best designate both a cultural production and a lexical production that often take their roots in African cultures and languages and are oftentimes 'calqued', 'loan-translated', 'transliterated' or 'relexified' (Zabus 2007: 111–74) into English. As Peter Jackson argues about Asian homoeroticism, 'Western gay/lesbian styles and terminology have often been appropriated as strategies to resist local heteronormative strictures and carve out new local spaces'. Yet, these appropriations, whether in Asia or in Africa, do not reflect 'a wholesale recreation of Western sexual cultures' (Jackson 2001: 6). Just as with Asian erotic identities, some are 'pre-gay' while others are 'post-queer' in the sense that 'they exist outside Eurocentric understandings of sexual and gender difference' (7).

   Stella Nyanzi seems to have anticipated 'postqueer' without spelling it out in her 2014 book chapter 'Queering Queer Africa' in Zethu Matebeni's volume, *Reclaiming Afrikan*. The 'reclaiming' project is fraught with 'two non-negotiable strategies': one must simultaneously 'reclaim Africa in its bold diversities and reinsert queerness' (Nyanzi 2014: 65). Nyanzi further advocates thinking beyond 'the loaded Westernized frame of the LGBT[Q]+ acronym' to explore and 'articulate local nuances of being non-heteronormative and non-gender conforming. … Cultural indigenous understandings of gendered spirits of ancestors who may possess individuals offer socially appropriate notions of handling fluid, transient gender identities. Queer Africa must reclaim such African modes of blending, bending and breaking gender boundaries' (67). Ancestor worship is, as Zabus shows in the present volume, generative of erotics that cannot be explained through a western lens and its corollary terminology.

2. The second characteristic of 'postqueer' is that it takes into account the post-secular turn, and its corollary religious and spiritual complexity on the African continent. African and Africanist scholars have recognized the need to address a pan-African yet culture-specific and history-specific type of gender diversity outside of western epistemic borders while confronting Euro-American models, which are fundamentally secular and based on a liberal concept of human rights.

Such rights have even been perceived as part of human rights fundamentalisms (Epprecht 2013), which vie in complexity with Islamic and Christian fundamentalisms (Chitando and Van Klinken 2016) as well as the influence of the US Christian right (Kaoma 2012). The religious and spiritual complexity of the African continent from north to south needs to be addressed. This complexity covers indigenous cosmogonies; the religious beliefs held by Africans prior to Christian and Islamic colonization (Mbiti 1969; Olupona 2014); and the relevance of 'witchcraft' (Geschiere 2010); as well as the emergence of such controversial Christian and Islamic organizations that are hospitable to gender variance such as the House of Rainbow Church in Lagos, Nigeria, founded by Reverend Jide Macaulay,[10] and the Inner Circle in Wynberg, Cape Town, South Africa, headed by the already mentioned queer Imam Muhsin Hendricks. Another queer Imam is the Somali Imam, Nur Warsame, whom Afdhere Jama, discussed by Hawley in this volume, meets during his travels and who is now the first openly gay Imam in Australia. While citing these examples, one must bear in mind the caveat: 'there is no facile link between for instance and therefore'.

In their discussion of three recent Nigerian 'narratives of deliverance' traversed by the adverse effects of Pentecostal Christianity – Elnathan John and Àlàbá Ònájìn's *On Ajayi Crowther Street*, Buki Papillon's *An Ordinary Wonder* (2021) and Chinelo Okparanta's *Under the Udala Trees* (2015) – Van Klinken and Makinana argue that these novels 'move beyond, and present alternatives to, a Eurocentric secular frame of understanding sexual and gendered embodiment'. More generally, here and elsewhere, Van Klinken et al. have argued that Eurocentric models 'do not allow for spiritually enchanted perceptions of the body, sex and sexuality'. Hawley concedes that authors such as Tofik Dibi and Lamya H, who, in *Hijab Butch Blues* (2023), has the additional merit of portraying Allah as trans, interpret 'queer' via a prior, pre-diasporic cultural lens, that is, the djinn.

The djinn, the *mami wata* figure, or the spirit-child (the Yoruba Abíkú or the Igbo ọgbanje) definitely hark back to pre-colonial indigenous belief systems that are being 'reclaimed' or reinvoked in the twenty-first century. Researching the *sarimbavy*, often described as same-sex desiring and gender nonconforming male-bodied spirit mediums in Antananarivo, Madagascar, Alyette Rajaofera Andriamasinalivao concludes that further research in spirit possession may explain some facets of the *sarimbavy*. Zabus in this volume investigates Zulu gender-differentiated spiritual possession cults among South African *male women*, and also shows how Igbo cosmology involving the figure of the ọgbanje is invoked by Akwaeke Emezi to reckon with her trans status. Likewise, the Mami Wata or 'Mammy-water', a water spirit with many devotees and shrines in Nigeria, is used to make sense of the intersexed condition of a character in Buki Papillon's *An Ordinary Wonder* (2021) and in Chinelo Okparanta's *Under the Ulala Trees* (2015).

The indigeneity of these myths is, however, not always ascertained. For instance, as Henry John Drewal has shown, the original chromolith picture of a snake charmer known as Mamy Water was printed in Germany around 1885, then copied and widely circulated in India, England, and West and Central Africa where in less than eighty years it became the key image of mami wata (Drewal 2008: 60–83). Not all belief systems are quintessentially African although they shed light on contemporary sexual and gender identities. In this volume, Chris Dunton proposes a Tantric take on Logan February's poetry and February gives an account of the non-gender-specific nature of Yorùbá pronouns in relation to the poet's nonbinary identity.

3. As mentioned above, 'postqueer' is characterized by (1) its resorting to indigenous African languages; (2) its documenting a post-secular turn through looking at escape routes within non-indigenous belief systems such as Pentecostal Christianity and through indigenous, often pre-colonial belief systems around specific mythical figures and ancestor worship; and (3) its embrace of an autobiographical, and oftentimes autofictional, stance, which reveals a desire to narrativize the self and, through narratives that include digital-born texts, foreground gender variance and experientiality.

   In that respect, we have privileged not only testimonies documenting early, pre-queer events (Salazar and Hambidge in this volume) but also contemporary postqueer ones such as Logan February's essay on pronouns and power among the Yorùbá and John MacAllister and Katlego's 'conversation' about today's Bostwana after the decriminalization of homosexuality in 2021. Unfortunately, we were not able to include testimonies from 'Islamic Africa'. Zabus' own recordings of trans individuals in Moroccan *darija* while doing fieldwork in Casablanca in 2018–19 have not been transcribed nor translated, but a future project called *TransMaghreb* in collaboration with the University of Hassan II in Casablanca and the University of Tunis is in the works and will, we hope, provide the Derridean 'dangerous supplement' to the testimonies in this volume.

4. The fourth and last characteristic of 'postqueer' lies in its dialogue with 'postcolonial ecocriticism' (Huggan and Tiffin 2015). An example of this dialogue is provided by Lion-Cachet in his 'eco-queering' of the symbol of the tree in post-apartheid South African constitutionalism. Future postcolonial ecocritical approaches are bound to embrace not only better interspecies living and a sustainable biodiversity but also gender diversity.

   Transafrica therefore augurs a turn-of-the-third-millennium post-secular, postqueer set of African open-ended gender identities, which, like the inaugural South African Truth and Reconciliation Commission, will spread 'like a bush-fire in the harmattan' (Achebe 1958: 3) and burn down all those hammered doors with a crash.

Sequence

The first three chapters in the collection focus on Islamic Africa. Omar Boukhatem examines the naming and categorization of same-sex sexuality and relationships in the Arab world, his key text being *In the Spider's Room* by Egyptian novelist Muhammad Abdelnabi. There is an increasing tendency to examine African film alongside fiction (see, for example, *African Literature Today* 36: *Queer Theory in Film and Fiction* and Lindsey Green-Simms's *Postcolonial Automobility* [2017]) and the second chapter is on film. Here Todd W. Reeser analyses the exploration of transgender experience in Daoud Aoulad-Syad's *Bye-Bye Souirty*. This film is notable in that it explores migration but advances beyond the familiar narrative of Mahgrebi migration to the Global North, being entirely set in Morocco. To adapt the term Nigeriopolitanism, coined by Olanike Lawore (2021), it could be said to explore Moroccopolitanism. The section concludes with a chapter by John C. Hawley that examines the language used in the exploration of identity in novels from East Africa (notably Somalia) that depict migrant experience.

The volume then turns to West Africa, with a chapter by Chris Dunton that discusses the work of nonbinary Nigerian poet Logan February, with special emphasis on the influence on their work of Tantric art. Nigeria is the powerhouse of contemporary African literature and, in the following chapter, Adriaan van Klinken and Belinda Qaqamba Z. Makinana explore novels that expose the influence of Pentecostal churches in Nigeria and the rhetoric employed in their onslaught on same-sex relationships, their 'demonization of queer sexuality and … culture of deliverance of the queer body'. The section concludes with Naminata Diabate's chapter '(Non)Genealogical Radical Queerness', focussing on Cameroonian writer Frieda Ekotto's extraordinary and innovative novel *Chuchote pas trop*.

As the collection turns to Southern Africa, a chapter by Chantal Zabus bridges this and the preceding section, focussing on three works of autofiction – one from Nigeria and two from South Africa – that are concerned with 'translects', that is, transnational transgender terms employed in self-naming. This process and that of categorization are the concern also of Alyette Rajaofera Andriamasinalivao, on the *sarivambary* of Madagascar. Then comes a chapter on the visual arts, Francois Lion-Cachet's 'The Eco-Queer Tree of South African Constitutionalism'. As this chapter is predicated on South Africa's groundbreaking defence of LGBTQ+ rights in its Constitution, it ends the first three sections of the volume on a positive note, a strategic move on the part of the book's editors.

The volume concludes with a section subtitled 'Testimonies', though the first of these, by Philippe-Joseph Salazar, synthesizes personal narrative with academic discourse. Salazar's account of his convening in 1995 the first colloquium of gay and lesbian studies in Southern Africa explores various aspects of the event including its reception. Following this, South African poet and scholar Joan Hambidge contributes an autobiographical piece, in both prose and poetry, tracking the author's self-identification and her commitment to gender studies. In a piece that resonates with this volume's concern with naming and categorization, Logan February writes on their own self-identification as nonbinary in relation to the gender-neutral status of Yorùbá third-person pronouns. And the volume ends on an affirmative note, as a dialogue between John McAllister and Katlego K. Kolonyane-Kesupile focusses on the impact on the LGBTQ+ community of the decriminalization of same-sex sexual activity in Botswana in 2021.

The Cover

Last but not least, the cover photograph for this volume is by Gbenga Smith and is of Nigerian poet Logan February, who is the author of one of the chapters in the collection and whose work is the subject of another chapter. We have chosen this photograph (1) because of the heightened alertness revealed in the subject's expression as they lean out of a car, and (2) because, when combined with the frontal image, their reflection in the rear-view mirror, here seen in profile, suggests the future, panoptical vision of genders implied in postqueerness.

Notes

1 Around the world, sixty-seven countries still criminalise same-sex relations, with ten imposing the death penalty. Twenty countries criminalize gender diversity. See UNAIDS 2023.

2 Throughout the Introduction, we have used the acronym LGBTQ+ for short for longer acronyms discussed by Zabus in this volume.

3 Chantal Zabus carried out an informal interview with Muhsin Hendriks on 31 May 2017 at the Inner Circle, Cape Town, South Africa.

4 See Zabus 2021; more specifically on Bambi, see Zabus 2019. Women authors have also explored bodies-in-transition. A case in point is the Algerian author Fériel Assima in *Rouhlem ou le sexe des anges* (1996), which chronicles the Black decade spanning 1988 to 1998. Through Assima's intersex character raised as a boy, the repressed feminine genders and the discursive erosion of male genitalia, *Rouhlem* augurs the 'transing' of the Algerian nation-state, away from a traditional engendering of the nation-state as male (see Zabus 2019). For broader approaches to Maghrebi literature, see, among others, Hayes (2000) and Zaganiaris (2013).

5 Among the other characters, one could number: Marija in Ama Ata Aidoo's *Our Sister Killjoy* (1977); Tshepo in K. Sello Duiker's *The Quiet Violence of Dreams* (2001); the two girls in Monica Arac de Nyeko's 'Under the Jambula Tree' from *African Love Stories* (2006); Hatim Rasheed and Abd Rabbuh in Alaa Al-Aswany's *The Yacoubian Building* (2007); Sethunya in Wame Molefhe's 'Sethunya Likes Girls Better' from *Go Tell the Sun* (2011); and Boniface in Diriye Osman's 'Shoga' in *Fairytales for Lost Children* (2013). See Nesbitt-Ahmed and Fatunla 2015.

6 'I am a homosexual, mum', he titled the confessional 'lost chapter' from *One Day I Will Write About This Place*.

7 Accessed on Medium.com on 1 November 2023.

8 When Dunton produced an essay for *Wasafiri* exploring the sexuality of the character Professor in Wole Soyinka's *The Road*, the editor queried his title, 'Professor as Queer' on the basis that, one might argue, not that Professor is queer but, if anything, a closeted gay (of course, he does act up in all sorts of other ways)'.

9 An exception is Andy Carolin's use of 'same-sex desire' in his recent book on South Africa (Carolin 2021).

10 Now UK-based, Macaulay is the author of the *Pocketbook Devotional for Lesbian, Gay, Bisexual and Transgender Christians* (2005).

References

Achebe, Chinua. 1958. *Things Fall Apart*. London: Heinemann.

Al-Aswani, Alaa. 2002. *'Imarat Ya'qubyan*. Cairo: Mirit Lil-Nashr wa al-Ma'lumat.

Al-Aswani, Alaa. 2004. *The Yacoubian Building*. Translated by Humphrey Davies. Cairo: American University in Cairo Press.

Bouraoui, Nina. 2000. *Garçon Manqué*. Paris: Stock.

Bouraoui, Nina. 2004. *Poupée Bella*. Paris: Stock.

Bouraoui, Nina. 2005. *Mes Mauvaises pensées*. Paris: Gallimard.

Bouraoui, Nina. 2007. *Tomboy*. Translated by Jehanne-Marie Gavarini and Marjorie Attignol Salvodon. Lincoln and London: Bison Books/University of Nebraska Press.

Bourdieu, Pierre. 1991. *Language and Symbolic Power*. Translated by G. Raymond and M. Adamson. Cambridge, UK: Polity Press.

Burgess, Jean and Joshua Green. 2009. *YouTube: Online Video and Participatory Culture*. Malden, MA: Polity Press.

Carolin, Andy. 2021. *Post-Apartheid Same-Sex Sexualities: Restless Identities in Literary and Visual Cultures*. London and New York: Routledge.

Chitando, Ezra and Adriaan van Klinken, eds. 2016. *Christianity and Controversies over Homosexuality in Contemporary Africa*. London: Routledge.

Dahir, Abdi Latif. 2024. 'The Needle Has Been Moved'. *New York Times*, Arts Section, February 21: 1, 4.

Dibia, Jude. 2005. *Walking with Shadows*. Lagos: Blacksands.

Drewal, Henry John. 2008. 'Mami Wata: Arts for Water Spirits in Africa and Its Diasporas'. *African Arts* 41–2: 60–83.

Dunton, Chris. 1989. '"Wheyting be Dat?" The Treatment of Homosexuality in African Literature', *Research in African Literatures* 20 (3): 422–48.

Dunton, Chris. 2023. 'Tuning into the Polyphony: The Emergence of LGBTQ+ Writing in Africa', *Research in African Literatures* 53 (4): 1–14.

Dunton, Chris and Neville Hoad. 2014. 'African Literatures', in E. L. McCallum and Mikho Tuhkanen, eds. *The Cambridge History of Gay and Lesbian Literatures*, 477–97. Cambridge: Cambridge University Press.

Dunton, Chris and Mai Palmberg. 1996. *Human Rights and Homosexuality in Southern Africa*. Uppsala: Nordic African Institute.

Ekine, Sokari and Hakima Abbas, eds. 2013. *Queer African Reader*. Dakar: Pambazuka Press.

Epprecht, Marc. 2004. *Hungochani: The History of a Dissident Sexuality in Southern Africa*. Montreal: McGill-Queens University Press.

Epprecht, Marc. 2013. *Sexuality and Social Justice in Africa: Rethinking Homophobia and Forging Resistance*. London: Zed Books.

Falola, Toyin. 2023. *Memories of Africa: Home and Abroad in the United States*. Jackson: University Press of Mississippi.

Fekurumoh, Sybil. 2023. '25 Queer Books from African and African Diasporan Writers', May 2023. Available online: https://www.afrocritik.com/25-queer-books-from-african-and-african-diasporan-writers/ (accessed 28 August 2024).

Geschiere, Peter. 2010. *Witchcraft and Modernity: Perspectives from Africa and Beyond*. Chicago: University of Chicago Press.

Gopinath, Gayatri. 2005. *Impossible Desires: Queer Diasporas and South Asian Public Cultures*. Durham, NC: Duke University Press.

Green-Simms, Lindsey B. 2017. *Postcolonial Automobility: Car Culture in West Africa*. Minneapolis: University of Minnesota Press.

Halperin, David. 1995. *Saint Foucault: Towards a Gay Hagiography*. New York and Oxford: Oxford University Press.

Hayes, Jarrod. 1997. 'Rachid O. and the Return of the Homopast: The Autobiographical as Allegory in Childhood Narratives by Maghrebian Men', *The Journal of Twentieth-Century/Contemporary French Studies* 1.2: 497–526.

Hayes, Jarrod. 2000. *Queer Nations: Marginal Sexualities in the Maghreb*. Chicago: University of Chicago Press.

Hoad, Neville. 2007. *African Intimacies: Race, Homosexuality, and Globalization*. Minneapolis and London: University of Minnesota Press.

Hoad, Neville. 2011. 'Queer Theory Addiction', in Janet Halley and Andrew Parker (eds), *After Sex? On Writing Since Queer Theory*, 128–39. Durham, NC and London: Duke University Press.

Huggan, Graham and Helen Tiffin. 2015. *Postcolonial Ecocriticism: Literature, Animals, Environment*. London and New York: Routledge.

Ibeh, Chukwuebuka. 2024. *Blessings*. London: Viking Penguin.

Ifeakandu, Arinze. 2022. *God's Children Are Little Broken Things*. London: Weidenfeld and Nicolson.

'I'm HIV+ and happy, says Binyavanga Wainaina'. 2020. Nation, 2 July. Available online: http://www.nation.co.ke/news/I-m-HIV–and-happy-says-Binyavanga-Wainaina/1056-3479162-9bpnfm/index.html (accessed 7 December 2023).

Jackson, Peter A. 2001. 'Pre-Gay, Post-Queer: Thai Perspectives on Proliferating Gender/Sex Diversity in Asia', *Journal of Homosexuality* 40 (3–4): 1–25.

Jama, Afdhere. 2022. *Being Queer and Somali*. Self-published. Las Vegas, Nevada.

Jenkins, Henry. 2006. *Convergence Culture: Where Old and New Media Collide*. New York: New York University Press.

Jobson, G. A., L. B. Theron, J. K. Kaggwa and H. J. Kim. 2012. 'Transgender in Africa: Invisible, Inaccessible, or Ignored?' *SAHARA-J: Journal of Social Aspects of HIV/AIDS*, 9 (3): 160–3. https://doi.org/10.1080/17290376.2012.743829.

Kaoma, Kapya John. 2012. *Colonizing African Values: How the U.S. Christian Right is Transforming Sexual Politics in Africa*. Somerville, MA: Political Research Associates.

Khatibi, Abdelkebir. 1979. *Le livre du sang*. Paris: Grasset.

Lawore, Olanike. 2021. 'A Critique of Afropolitanism: Toward the Formation of a New Reading Model—Nigeriopolitanism', *Research in African Literatures* 52 (1): 139–55.

Leftah, Mohamed. 2006. *Au bonheur des limbes*. Paris: La différence.

Macaulay, Jide. 2005. *Pocketbook Devotional for Lesbian, Gay, Bisexual and Transgender Christians*. London: RBM Consulting.

Macharia, Keguro. 2013. 'Blogging Queer Kenya', *Journal of Postcolonial and Commonwealth Studies* 1 (1): 103–8.

Makanjuola, Olumide F. and Jude Dibia, eds. 2023. *Love Offers No Safety: Nigeria's Queer Men Speak*. Abuja and London: Cassava Republic Press.

Masolo, D. A. 2010. *Self and Community in a Changing World*. Bloomington and Indianapolis: Indiana University Press.

Massad, Joseph A. 2007. *Desiring Arabs*. Chicago and London: University of Chicago Press.

Matebeni, Zethu, ed. 2014. *Reclaiming Afrikan: Queer Perspectives on Sexual and Gender Identities*. Athlone: Modjaji Books.

Mbiti, John S. 1969. *African Religions and Philosophy*. London: Heinemann.

McGuinness, Justin. 2012. 'Représentation et résistance sur mithly.net: analyse du discours d'un site communautaire marocain', in Sihem Najar (ed.), *Les nouvelles sociabilités du Net en Méditerranée*, 117–42. Paris: Editions Karthala & IRMC.

Mohammed, Azeenarh, Chitra Nagarajan and Rafeeat Aliyu, eds. 2018. *She Called me Woman: Nigeria's Queer Women Speak*. Abuja and London: Cassava Republic Press.

Munro, Brenna. 2016. 'Locating "Queer" in Contemporary Writing of Love and War in Nigeria', *Research in African Literatures* 47 (2): 121–38.

Najmabadi, Afsaneh. 2014. *Professing Selves: Transsexuality and Same-Sex Desire in Contemporary Iran*. Durham, NC: Duke University Press.

Ndzovu, Hassan J., 2016. '"Un-natural", "un-African" and "un-Islamic": The three pronged onslaught undermining homosexual freedom in Kenya', in Adriaan van Klinken and Ezra Chitando (eds), *Public Religion and the Politics of Homosexuality in* Africa, 78–91. London and New York: Routledge.

Nesbitt-Ahmed, Zahrah and Dele Meiji Fatunla. 2015. 'Ten Gay Characters from African Literature That Everyone Should Know', Whats_On Africa [blog], 6 May. Available online: http://whatsonafrica.org/ten-gay-characters-from-african-literature-that-everyone-should-know/ (accessed 7 December 2023).

Nyanzi, Stella. 2014. 'Queering Queer Africa', in Zethu Matebeni (ed.), *Reclaiming Afrikan: Queer Perspectives on Sexual and Gender Identities*, 61–6. Athlone: Modjaji Books.

Nyeck, S. N., ed. 2021. *Routledge Handbook of Queer African Studies*. London and New York: Routledge.

Nyeck, S. N. and Marc Epprecht, eds. 2013. *Sexual Diversity in Africa: Politics, Theory, and Citizenship*. Montreal and Kingston: McGill-Queen's University Press.

Obi-Young, Otosirieze. 2023. 'Dear Mr. Brittle: Queer literature in Africa is not a trend, has always existed'. Online https://brittlepaper.com/2017/12/dear-paper-queer-literature-trend-africa/. Accessed 7 December 2023.

Okparanta, Chinelo. 2015. *Under the Udala Trees*. London: Granta.

Olupona, Jacob Kehinde. 2014. *African Religions: A Very Short Introduction*. Oxford: Oxford University Press.

Osinubi, Taiwo and Neville Hoad, eds. 2016. 'Queer Valences in African Literatures and Film', special issue of *Research in African Literatures*, 47 (2).

Otu, Kwame E. and Adriaan van Klinken. 2023. 'African Studies Keywords: Queer', *African Studies Review* 66 (2): 509–30.

Penney, James. 2014. *After Queer Theory: The Limits of Sexual Politics*. London: Pluto Press.

Quayson, Ato. 2003. *Calibrations: Reading for the Social*. Minneapolis: University of Minnesota Press.

Raun, Tobias. 2016. *Out Online: Trans Self-Representations and Community Building on YouTube*. London and New York: Routledge.

Sausa, L. A., J. Keatley and D. Operario. 2007. 'Perceived Risks and Benefits of Sex Work among Transgender Women of Color in San Francisco', *Archives of Sexual Behavior*, 36 (6): 768–77. https://doi.org/10.1007/s10508-007-9210-3.

Serhane, Abdelhak. [1983] 2002. *Messaouda*. Paris: Points.

Somtochukwu, Ani Kayode. 2022. *And Then He Sang a Lullaby*. London: Grove Press.

Taïa, Abdellah. 2008. *Une mélancolie arabe*. Paris: Seuil.

Taïa, Abdellah. 2010. *Le jour du roi*. Paris: Seuil.

UNAIDS. 2023. 'UNAIDS urges all countries to decriminalise homosexuality as a vital step in ensuring health for all', 15 May. Available online: https://www.unaids.org/en/

resources/presscentre/pressreleaseandstatementarchive/2023/may/20230517_idahobit (accessed 7 December 2023).

Vignal, Daniel. 1983. 'L'homophilie dans le roman négro-africain d'expression anglaise et française', *Peuples noirs, peuples africains* 33 (May–June): 63–81.

Wahrmann, Dror. 2004. *The Making of the Modern Self: Identity and Culture in Eighteenth-Century England*. New Haven, CT: Yale University Press.

Wiredu, Kwasi and Kwame Gyekye. 1992. *Person and Community: Ghanian Philosophical Studies*. Washington, D.C.: Council for Research in values and Philosophy.

Zabus, Chantal. 2007. *The African Palimpsest: Indigenization of Language in the West African Europhone Novel*. Amsterdam & New York: Rodopi/Brill.

Zabus, Chantal. 2013. *Out in Africa: Same-sex Desire in Sub-Saharan Literatures and Cultures*. Woodbridge, Suffolk and Rochester, New York: Boydell & Brewer/ James Currey.

Zabus, Chantal. 2019. 'Transing the Algerian Nation-State: Textual Transgender and Intersex from Independence to the Black Decade', *Acta Neophilologica* 52 (1–2): 69–97.

Zabus, Chantal. 2021. 'Outing Africa: On Sexualities, Gender and Transgender', in Olakunle George (ed.), *A Companion to African Literatures*, 381–98. Hoboken, NJ: John Wiley & Sons.

Zaganiaris, Jean. 2008. 'Jean Zaganiaris interviews Abdellah Taïa', The Institut français de Casablanca on 12 June.

Zaganiaris, Jean. 2013. *Queer Maroc: Sexualités, genres et (trans)identités dans la littérature marocaine*. Paris: Des Ailes sur un Tracteur.

Part I

CASE STUDIES

ISLAMIC AFRICA

Chapter 1

POWERS OF RESISTANCE AND THE LEXICON OF POSTQUEER SEXUALITY IN MUHAMMAD ABDELNABI'S *IN THE SPIDER'S ROOM*

Omar Boukhatem

Introduction

During a visit to Cairo in 2021, I was staggered by the proliferation of sexual expressions used by Egyptians in their daily speech. Cairenes display a propensity for selecting words that are apt in specific contexts, notably in the spheres of religion, politics and sexuality. Thus, the linguistic register pertaining to these undergoes incessant metamorphosis. The language of queer sexuality in Egypt is no exception, for it represents the only means by which queer individuals can exercise their agency and assert their sexual identities.

In Egypt queer individuals have been the objects of persistent hostility, with their very existence strongly denounced. This can be attributed to the influence of cultural power dynamics and the strict enforcement of the androcentric foundations that are held to define 'Arabness'. As a result, Egyptian society hierarchizes patterns of behaviour, action and language based on their level of acceptance within the patriarchal power structure. In Egypt, patriarchal norms lead to the classification of queer sexuality as a violation of masculinity.

Dhukura (ذكورة; masculinity) and *rujula* (رجولة; manhood) are concepts representing fundamental qualities that patriarchy upholds. In the context of an Arab society, being suspected of homosexuality results in immediate social rejection, as the individual is no longer considered a true *rajul* (رجل; man). Patriarchy views men as figures of power and authority over women, and through such structures, heterosexual relationships further reinforce these imbalances of power. The gender roles in heterosexual relationships often mirror the power dynamics of these systems. Masculinity, for Arabs, requires a set of characteristics to be owned. Regarding sexuality, an Arab man is and must inevitably be the active partner in sexual encounters. When a man becomes the insertee, he incurs an enduring social stigma as he no longer behaves according to the Arab codes of masculinity.

In *Desiring Arabs* (2007), Joseph Massad contends that during the mid-twentieth century, Arab translators of psychology books, along with Arab behavioural psychologists, embraced the European term 'sexual deviance' and directly translated it as *al-shudhudh al-jinsi*, a term that is still the prevailing expression used in academic works, media and polite conversations when discussing the western concept of 'homosexuality' (Massad 2007: 172). Nowadays, the term *shudhudh* (شذوذ) itself has gradually lost its original meaning and has become predominantly associated with queer sexuality. When nowadays an individual is described as being *shadh* (شاذ), this means *he* is non-heterosexual. *Shadh*, occasionally transliterated as *shath*, is an adjective that categorizes what is deviant or abnormal, signifying a departure from the usual. This implies that the term *shudhudh*, outside the sexual realm, means 'deviance'.

Al-shudhudh al-jinsi (الشذوذ الجنسي) is not accepted by Arabs who defend and militate for the rights of homosexual individuals. It has a derogatory connotation propagating the marginalization of non-heterosexual Arabs, thereby confirming their 'abnormality'. The term that is used in Arab circles to name a homosexual subject is *mithli* (مثلي). *Al-mithliya* (المثلية) is an Arabic term meaning 'sameness'. *Al-mithliya al-jinsiya* (المثلية الجنسية), 'sexual sameness', only describes the same-sex sexual attraction that a subject feels for another, and has, in Tina Dransfeldt Christensen's words, 'gained ground as a term contesting homophobia' (2021: 24). By using this term, its pejorative connotation is erased.

The queer community in the Arab world is often referred to as *mujtama' al-meem* (مجتمع الميم; the 'meem' society). 'Meem' (م) is the Arabic pronunciation of the letter *m* in the Arabic alphabet. The term *mujtama' al-meem* serves to cover an array of queer identities resonating with the initial 'm', including *mithli* (homosexual), *mutahawil jinsi* (متحول جنسي; transgender), *muzdawij al-jins* (مزدوج الجنس; bisexual), and *mutahayyir* (متحير) or *mutasa'il* (متسائل; questioning). Yet, beneath the surface lies a subtler disdain, as the term *mujtama' al-meem* perpetuates a veiled condescension, underestimating the diversity of queer individuals by denoting them with a single letter. Yet the essence of 'queer' itself remains untranslatable in Arabic. The inexhaustible depth and nuances of the queer experience elude its formulation within linguistic confines.

Homosexuality has a rich and well-documented history in Arab culture and literature. However, its logical progression has been obscured by many historical, political and cultural obstacles. This chapter aims to examine the representation of homosexual characters in a contemporary Arab novel, aiming to connect queer Arab literature to the modern, present-day register of queer sexuality. I have chosen the Egyptian author Muhammad Abdelnabi's novel *In the Spider's Room*, for it provides the most relevant case study for us to focus on. First, it is a novel that comprises two geographical areas, namely the Arab world and Africa, both represented by Egypt. Second, it was published in 2017, in the midst of international calls for the rights of queer individuals. Third, it is a novel in which Abdelnabi uses transliteration as a means to assert the 'Egyptianness' of the homosexual protagonist and his striving for sexual freedom. In the following subsections, we will explore the perceptions of homosexual individuals in Egyptian society; the ways in which hegemonic, patriarchal power oppresses them in order to uphold heterosexual dominance; the role of language used by the 'oppressor' in stigmatizing homosexual subjects; and how these subjects themselves employ language to construct their own homosexual identity.

The Author, the Text and the Incident

Muhammad Abdelnabi Muhammad Gomaa[1] was born in 1977 in Dakahlia Governorate, Egypt and received an Azhari education, graduating from the Department of English Studies in the Faculty of Languages and Translation. After graduating, he worked as a full-time translator and later as a freelance translator to devote more time to writing. Abdelnabi is the founder of *Al-Hikaya Wa Ma Fiha* (الحكاية وما فيها; The Story and What it Contains) workshop, which focuses on developing literary writing skills. Abdelnabi wrote several collections of short stories, and his novel *Ruju' Ashshaykh* (رجوع الشيخ; *The Sheikh's Return*; 2014) earned him the Sawiras Cultural Award for Best Novel by a Young Author. In 2019, Abdelnabi's *In the Spider's Room* won the Arabic Literature Prize established in France by the Arab World Institute and the Jean-Luc Lagardère Foundation.

In the Spider's Room was originally published in Arabic in 2017 and translated into English by Jonathan Wright in 2018. The story takes place in Cairo in 2001 and focuses on the arduous journey of Hani Mahfouz, an Egyptian homosexual man coming to terms with the pervasive oppression that reigned in Egyptian society at the beginning of the twenty-first century. Inspired by an event known as the 'Queen Boat' incident that received widespread media attention in Egypt in 2001, Abdelnabi crafts a narrative that sheds light on the challenges faced by fifty-two men, arrested and imprisoned under section 9c of the Anti-Prostitution Act No. 10 of 1961 on charges of engaging in homosexuality, which Egyptian society views as *fujur* (فجور; debauchery). In the early 2000s, there was no specific legislation criminalizing homosexuality and the arrests were made under the laws that prohibited promiscuity and prostitution (see Golia 2004: 182). *In the Spider's Room* is recognized as being the first Egyptian novel to take up the 'Queen Boat' incident and to feature a homosexual man as its protagonist.

Several books in French and English have addressed this incident, with the most recent being the second edition of Brent L. Pickett's book *The Historical Dictionary of Homosexuality* (2022), where he records:

A floating discotheque in Cairo popular with gay men, the Queen Boat was raided by police (on Friday, 11th of) May of 2001. Ultimately, fifty-two men were charged under Egypt's penal code. While the country has no formal anti-sodomy law, it does have provisions against 'debauchery' that the courts interpret as forbidding same-sex sex acts. Authorities used police harassment and torture, including savage beatings, in the Queen Boat and other cases in the first decade of the twenty-first century.

(Pickett 2022: 233)

Subsequently, the court issued a verdict that led to the imprisonment of twenty-three individuals who had been charged, with the most severe sentence being five years. Joseph Massad mentions that in May 2002, the government, taking into account President Mubarak's refusal to endorse the rulings, overturned a total of fifty verdicts out of the original fifty-two (Massad 2007: 185). Despite President Mubarak's decision to revoke the verdicts, two defendants remained charged with *izdira' al-adyan* (ازدراء الأديان; defamation of religions).[2] Following this case, American-born activist Scott Long and Human Rights Watch published a book in 2004 titled *In a Time of Torture*, where they contended that the Egyptian government routinely detained and subjected men suspected of engaging in homosexuality to acts of torture. Moreover, Long and Human Rights Watch hold that the arrest and torture of hundreds of men reveal the fragility of legal protections of individual privacy and legal process for all Egyptians.

Hani, the novel's central character, ends up being declared innocent, yet bears the indelible marks of psychic fragmentation. Bereft of the power of speech, he finds within himself the solace of writing, an avenue that proves itself to be the most efficacious means to mend his wounded soul. Sequestered in a hotel room, accompanied only by a diminutive spider, Hani willingly embraces seclusion as a sanctuary for inner exploration. Through writing, Hani begins a personal journey to discover himself, reflecting on his family, his preferences, the loss of enchantment on night-time streets and the struggles during his imprisonment. This introspective quest leads him to discover profound significance behind the wreckage of his experiences. However, this journey lacks the predictability of a linear trajectory; instead, it mirrors the artful complexity of a spider's web. Hani finds himself drawn along different paths, each connected to another by a single, tenuous thread that reaches from the depths of his being to the hearts of those he encounters.

The Arab Penis and the Beginning of Homosexuality

The novel comprises thirty-nine parts, arranged in a fragmented order that alternately draws the reader closer to and then away from Hani's narrative. The story begins with Hani and Abdelaziz walking hand in hand to a bar near Falaki Square in Cairo. Unfortunately, this act marks the beginning of a nightmare that extends throughout much of the novel, after the police arrest them on suspicion of a homosexual relationship. The arrest is Hani's first exposure to how he will commonly be described:

> The man in charge looked at me. 'Are you *gay*?' he asked, using the English word and speaking rapidly in order to confuse me. 'What does that mean?' I answered in a trembling voice. 'Okay, come along with us, my dear, and we'll tell you what it means'.
>
> (Abdelnabi 2018: 8)

Hani's lack of self-awareness becomes even more pronounced when he is suddenly confronted with an unfamiliar English term that relates to his sexuality. Such a circumstance can be attributed to the prevailing stringent restrictions enforced in Egypt, aimed at stifling any openness to western influences and to the universal dimensions of human sexuality. Abdelnabi wrote the term 'gay' in English, indicating that the authorities in Egypt possess a level of knowledge that the general public lacks. The police represent the dominant power that is aware of a *shadh* translating as 'gay', while the *shadh* himself remains unaware that his sexual orientation is universal, albeit articulated in English.

Hani's discovery of his sexuality begins at an early age. His nurturing environment is shaped by the presence of his loving grandfather, the proprietor of a tailor's workshop. Following his grandfather's demise, the workshop passes into the ownership of Hani's father, with its space now engulfed by a bustling marketplace, alongside other similar workshops. In this newly established public market, Hani's father actively engages with fellow workshop owners, thereby cultivating an extensive network of workers and friends. Throughout this time, Hani often finds himself by a window overlooking a urinal, concealing himself from his father and the other men who frequent it. This clandestine position allows him to voyeuristically observe these interactions without being noticed. Thus, this peculiar vantage point serves his burgeoning awareness and exploration of his own sexual identity: 'That window allowed me to play my secret game' (20). The game Hani is talking about is sniffing at men urinating and looking at their penises. 'Furtively I looked at all these hamamas, doves, as they called them, and wondered what lay behind the name. Did they fly like doves?' (21).

Throughout the novel, the penis is presented as a hegemonic device, endowed with the exclusive power to evoke desire. This construction of masculinity, heavily reliant on the penis, helps perpetuate a phallocracy. It should be noted that while the penis is socially accepted as the primary sexual organ for Arabs, it should not be regarded as the sole origin of pleasure and arousal. The narrative voice of the novel reinforces a limited conception of masculinity, where gender identity becomes narrowly defined by the presence of the sex organ. This portrayal of masculinity fails to recognize the multifaceted nature of male identities and their associated experiences.

Hani's voyeurism is noticed by Ra'fat, who is happy flaunting his penis in front of him:

No one noticed me spying except Ra'fat. Ra'fat worked as a cutter [...]. He was the only one who noticed me snooping. In fact, he liked me looking at his penis but he pretended that he couldn't see me [...] His hamama inflated as though it were going to take off. Would it coo like the doves in the light well at home? On one occasion, he unexpectedly looked at me and caught my eyes feasting on the sight of his penis. I had been discovered. I anxiously expected he would complain to my father, but he never did.

(21)

Ra'fat plays a central role in shaping Hani's understanding of sexuality since he is the only individual who openly discusses with him the pleasurable nature of masturbation (33). Additionally, Ra'fat becomes the first person whom Hani kisses (34) and experiences penetration (38). Thus the common associations of the penis, hinting at an unchecked power to control, possess and influence other physical attributes. Although the name Ra'fat originates from the Arabic word *ra'fa* (رأفة), meaning compassion or clemency, Abdelnabi's selection of the name does not align with the traits exhibited by Ra'fat. Ironically, Ra'fat is assigned such a name and portrayed as the epitome of the typical Egyptian man, emphasizing the masculine attributes that are crucial to heteronormative society. Hani's homosexuality is predominantly rooted in the masculinity embodied by Ra'fat. David M. Halperin emphasizes this link, stating: 'Masculinity represents not only a central cultural value – associated with seriousness and worth, as opposed to feminine triviality – but also a key erotic value for gay men' (Halperin 2012: 306).

In Arab culture, the penis emphatically symbolizes a man's *dhukura* (masculinity), *rujula* (manhood) and *fuhula* (فحولة; virility). In Arabic, the term *fahl* (فحل; stallion) denotes the male of any animal that exhibits strength. *Fuhula* encapsulates notions of power, dominance and is primarily tied to one's *rujula*. In *Sexuality in the Arab World* (2014), Samir Khalaf and John Gagnon point out that:

> [...] the penis itself becomes the site of a condensation of all that signifies patriarchal masculine social power, whether in the realm of the sexual (men's domination over women), the familial (men's domination within the family) or the social (men's domination within a society). Thus, the penis comes to *embody* social power, not just *signify* it.
>
> (Khalaf and Gagnon 2014: 143)

Khalaf and Gagnon provide a comprehensive examination of the societal ramifications entwined with the penis, which assumes the role of a potent emblem of male authority. This perception transcends the realm of mere sexual connotations and materializes in the manifestation of male dominion not only within the familial unit but also on a broader scale. Thus the magnitude attributed to the penis as a focal point of power serves as a tangible embodiment and symbol of the overarching social supremacy sustained by patriarchy. Such emphasis foregrounds the social proclivity to fortify traditional gender roles and norms, through which masculinity becomes intricately enmeshed with conceptions of dominance and control. Any transgression of these entrenched patriarchal norms is met with grave censure and is branded as *eib* (عيب).[3]

In Egypt and throughout the Arab world, queer sexuality finds itself restricted to the notion of *eib* (shame). An exploration of the terminologies employed by Egyptians assumes paramount significance in elucidating their stance towards queerness. The term *eib* is a recurrent part of daily Egyptian speech, serving as both a noun synonymous with 'shame' and an adjective meaning 'shameful'. It refers to an individual or collective sentiment that emerges within a social and cultural framework, while simultaneously functioning as a normative mechanism to delineate what is regarded as 'shameful', operating as a code of social sanction. Even in the current era of globalization, the term *eib* continues to be used and is adapted to various contexts in Egypt, with sexuality being one of its strongest connections.

Abdelnabi confronts the reader with the concept of *eib*, which is all too often ingrained in the experiences of queer individuals. The exploration of two distinct forms of masculinity unfolds through the portrayal of the penis. Hani's subconscious attraction to Ra'fat is juxtaposed with Ra'fat's deliberate act of exposing his penis in front of Hani. Hesitant to allow Ra'fat to reveal his voyeuristic inclinations to his father, Hani's actions demonstrate that he has internalized the Egyptian social codes of *eib*. Conversely, Ra'fat's behaviour transgresses this norm, as exposing one's penis in the presence of others, particularly children, is widely regarded as unbecoming:

> The next time he stood there, as soon as I could control myself and look at him, he gave me a slight smile and made a little nod as if inviting me to carry on playing with him, but I looked away, my heart beating violently.
>
> (Abdelnabi 2018: 21)

Young Hani becomes entangled in a complex relationship with Ra'fat, who embodies all that Hani considers culturally *eib*, yet finds sexually arousing. The quote subtly alludes to Hani's yearning for profound intimacy and emotional rapport with Ra'fat, juxtaposed with his unyielding resolve to resist succumbing to his voyeuristic tendencies. The phrase 'my heart beating violently' serves as confirmation of Hani's heightened excitement and arousal when confronted with Ra'fat's exposed penis.

Ra'fat is the first man whose penis is described by Hani, but the latter speaks more broadly about the other men whom he has met before:

> Even before Ra'fat, and before I started peeping at the penises of urinating men, I often imagined some man, a man I made up out of my fantasies. I tried to bury myself inside him. I curled up into a ball on my bed, as tightly as possible. I wanted to make myself so small that I could slip inside my imaginary man [...]. On a few occasions this man was my father [...]. His penis had extended a little with the flow of urine. I took hold of my own little hamama and tried to imitate him, but only a few feeble drops came out and fell right between my feet. He noticed that I was looking back and forth between my hamama and his elongated penis. He gave a little laugh. 'Don't worry, Hannoun, when you grow up it'll get bigger', he said with confidence.
>
> (31)

The penis holds a central and privileged role in the sexual encounters of Hani and other male characters, becoming a vessel for physical pleasure and power. The use of phallic descriptors, employing language linked to authority, reinforces the prevailing cultural belief that masculinity aligns with dominance, conquest and force.

In the Egyptian dialect, a plethora of words are used to refer to the penis. The three most prevalent formal terms, used in Egypt and all Arabic-speaking countries, are *dhakar* (ذكر; male); *al-qadib* (القضيب; *el-qadib* in Egypt, as the Arabic definite article *al* is pronounced *el* in the Egyptian dialect), a non-scientific word signifying 'penis' 'rod', 'rail' or 'splint'; and *al-'odw at-tanasuly ad-dhakary* (العضو التناسلي الذكري; the male reproductive organ), with *al-'odw* meaning both 'member' and 'organ', and *at-tanausly* denoting both 'reproductive' and 'genital'. The penis is frequently referred to as *al-'odw ad-dhakary* (العضو الذكري). The word *hamama* means 'dove' in Arabic; however, Egyptians humorously use it to refer to the penis, especially in memes and social media trolls. This choice originates from the belief that the penis resembles a dove in that both are perched on two eggs.

Arabic, whether expressed in its classical form or diverse in dialects, abounds with a plethora of vocabulary signifying the penis. Remarkably, all of these words carry masculine connotations. Recently, certain names which Egyptians have traditionally reserved for men, such as *'am Ezzat* (uncle or Mr Ezzat) and *Bulbul*, have also taken on the additional meaning of referring to the penis. Therefore, in the context of an Egyptian street conversation, a sentence such as 'am Ezzat is sick' acquires a dual meaning, leaving the listener uncertain whether it is about a real man named Uncle Ezzat or alludes to the penis.

Hani's Homosexuality: Resisting Oppression, Resisting Language

In *In the Spider's Room*, a compelling portrayal of power, oppression and resistance unfolds, evoking themes extensively explored by Michel Foucault. The dynamics of life and resistance are profoundly bound together with strategic relationships, where opposing forces emerge.

The concept of resistance, as elucidated by Michel Foucault in an interview titled 'Non au sexe roi' ('The End of the Monarchy of Sex'), transcends conventional notions of substance and chronological precedence vis-à-vis opposing power structures. Foucault asserts that resistance and power are contemporaneous. Contrary to being a mere inverse reflection of power, resistance exhibits the same inventive, dynamic and productive qualities as power itself (Foucault 1977: 224). Indeed, both resistance and power find their existence in the realm of action, as they manifest through the complex interplay of forces, often culminating in confrontation. Foucault urges us to perceive resistance not only as negation but also as an intricate process involving metamorphosis.

In the course of Abdelnabi's novel, the protagonist Hani recognizes his homosexuality. Nevertheless, he encounters formidable challenges arising from both the sphere of political authority, symbolized by the police force, and cultural dominance, embodied by heterosexual society. In *Imagining Queer Methods* (2019), Amin Ghaziani and Matt Brim discuss power and domination in relation to queer sexuality:

Social scientists, and gender scholars in particular, have been charged to [*sic*] conceptualize power and domination in ways that recognize how heteropatriarchy and cisnormativity disadvantage queer people and privilege straight folks.

(Ghaziani and Brim 2019: 164)

The forces of oppression level accusations against Hani and other individuals presumed to be homosexuals, as they are charged with engaging in practices viewed as depraved. Abdelnabi's narrative accentuates the older Hani's profound trepidation towards an external world that perceives him and other homosexual men as aberrant and marginal subjects. Concurrently, it highlights Hani's resolute determination to confront this world, embracing his *shudhudh*. While en route to meet his partner, Abdel Aziz, Hani candidly acknowledges:

Suddenly I had a whimsical desire to hold his hand. Something may have sent a shiver of fear up my spine, and I wanted to cling to him. It might have been the first time I had held his hand in front of people in the street, and the strange thing was that he didn't move his hand away or discourage me, as I had expected. We held each other's hands and my fear, which had no known cause, evaporated.

(Abdelnabi 2018: 7)

This quote describes a moment of Hani's vulnerability and fear and his desire for physical connection as a means of comforting him and making public his display of affection. His surprise at Abdel Aziz not refusing the gesture but letting him hold his hand also demonstrates Abdel Aziz's resistance to the heterosexual power that has long controlled them. This act of physical connection, though fleeting, has a calming effect on both of them.

Egypt has always been a heteropatriarchal society that criminalizes homosexuality, whether through *fatwas* decreed by the prestigious Islamic institution, Al-Azhar, or by the Egyptian Coptic Church. Hani's acute awareness of the potential peril that he faces adds an element of intrigue to the process of challenging it. Holding hands with Abdel Aziz is so dangerous a step that Abdelnabi titles the first chapter 'I clearly remember how the nightmare began'. The cessation of Hani's fear when he holds Abdel Aziz's hand is a telling indicator of the emotions he anticipates should he embark on the risk of revealing his homosexuality openly. On the psychological level, this is substantiated by Avi Sion, who states in *Logical and Spiritual Reflections*:

Moreover, if a person *believes* he or she has no power of resistance to some impulse, his or her power of resistance is proportionately diminished. To act decisively, one has to believe the action concerned to be possible or useful. The beliefs one has *influence* one's will to act; one's beliefs are among the forces that affect (though do not determine) one's course of action.

(Sion 2008: 371)

Hani and Abdel Aziz are arrested by the police as suspected homosexuals. Hani admits: 'For a moment I felt guilty: maybe they had appeared out of nowhere to punish us just because I had reached out my hand to my friend and he had held it' (Abdelnabi 2018: 7). Although Hani is guilty of holding Abdel Aziz's hand, he shows no regret for it. In the Arab world, guilt and shame form implicit associations to Arab ethical principles. Talib Kafaji, in *The Psychology of the Arab* (2011), contends that Arab society is distinguished by a shame-based culture. Individuals are compelled to exercise caution and avoid actions that might engender shame upon their families and communities. Moreover, the culture is also permeated with a sense of guilt due to the profound adherence to deeply ingrained ritualistic practices, cultivated over millennia (Kafaji 2011: 73). The conflation of diverse systems gives rise to Hani's torn persona, with distinct and intense emotions. These include a vehement rejection of the cultural and social constraints that suppress his identity and his fervent affection for men. As a consequence, the notion of 'difference', mostly when related to homosexuality, assumes heightened significance in Arab society, where identities are subject to ongoing contestation, thereby paving the way for the emergence of novel and evolving 'postqueer' identities.

Upon Hani and Abdel Aziz's arrest on suspicion of homosexuality, Hani keenly observes how Abdel Aziz resorts to bribing the police in order to secure the privilege of making phone calls. This move cannot be made by all Egyptians, for power, financial means and strong social connections are only enjoyed by those who belong to upper-class Egyptian society. Abdel Aziz contacts a lawyer who skilfully resorts to implicit threats during his client's interaction with the police. This exchange escalates into a confrontation, prompting the intervention of the head of the police station. However, the situation takes an unexpected turn when the police chief closes the case upon learning the identities of Abdel Aziz's relatives. In retrospect, Hani reflects on this eventful episode:

> They didn't argue long, and so far Abdel Aziz hadn't been formally detained. No police report had been written and no grounds for detention had been cited. They didn't need any fuss or headaches over detaining someone from such a family, and their scheme was still in its early stages.
>
> (Abdelnabi 2018: 28)

This passage reveals the ongoing pattern of oppression experienced by Egyptians at the hands of the police. It is a commonly acknowledged reality in Egypt that even the most severe crimes can be unjustly attributed to an unknown individual if the true culprit holds wealth or connections to powerful figures in the country. This scenario unfolds with Hani when he remains detained and his alleged lover is set free: 'Some of us managed to do likewise, but others, like me, didn't know anyone they could contact' (27).

Abdelnabi's novel brings into focus the corruption of Egyptian police, who are believed to forbid behaviour they perceive as being immoral. In reality, punishment is meted out based on an individual's identity and background, rather than solely focusing on the crimes they have actually committed. Hani highlights this issue when he expresses that 'all the non-Egyptians – Arabs and non-Arabs – were released' (29). In this regard, one can posit that political power in Egypt experiences a decrease in its authority when faced with another power with greater dominance. Termed *fasad* (فساد), signifying 'corruption' in English, this form of immorality was a spark for the Egyptian upsurge during the Arab Spring in 2011 in the wake of the Tunisian Jasmin Revolution.

Hani, whom the police accuse of propagating moral *fasad*, experiences severe torment and degradation when faced with their abuse. The authorities unanimously label Hani as a 'certified queer' (خول رسمي) (28), identifying him as a homosexual man known for engaging in multiple same-sex relationships. From the moment he sets foot in the police station's cell, he undergoes all forms of anguish:

> While they were taking us into the holding cell at Azbakiya police station, one of the informers or policemen came up to me, pulled a strand of hair that was hanging down at the back of my neck, and gave it a violent tug, jerking my neck back until I was looking at the horrible ceiling. 'It's the first time I've seen this whore, though she looks like she's been around', he said, addressing his colleagues half seriously and half in jest.
>
> (49)

The Egyptian penal institution can be identified as an institution with a strong association with masculinity considering how bodies are perceived and language is utilized.[4] Symbolic authority is strongly linked to masculinity in this context. Ergo, highly masculine prisoners are granted a privileged status among both male and female inmates, affording them the ability to hold sway over other prisoners. This is made clear by Hani: 'Then the orgy of beatings began, at the hands of other prisoners who had been ordered to attack us' (145).

Within the confines of Egyptian prisons, derogatory language is used to demean and attack the masculinity of homosexual men. These expressions include *hagg* (حاج), a typically Egyptian pronunciation of the Arabic *hajj* (حاج), which usually denotes an elderly man as a sign of respect, or someone who has gone on pilgrimage to Mecca. However, in prison, it is intended to denigrate the male prisoner by insinuating that he is sexually impotent, like an elderly man. *'Agala* (عجلة), which translates as 'bicycle', has recently begun to be used to refer to a homosexual man to emphasize the similarity between him and the bicycle, since both are ridden by someone. The saddle of a bicycle is also believed to resemble a homosexual man's 'ass'. *Byetba'* (بيتباع) suggests that a man can be 'sold', euphemistically used to imply that he can be penetrated. *Gada' meery* (جدع ميري), humorously inverting the true meaning of 'authority guy', derogatorily alludes to the individual as an inferior homosexual man.[5] Hani is no exception and is humiliated. This is evident in his tone when reporting the speech of a kind officer who tells him that he has to brace himself for whatever is about to happen (52). In women's prisons, the prisoner with lesbian tendencies is beleaguered with disgraceful expressions, the most famous of which are *markuba* (مركوبة), meaning 'ridden' and is used in the same context as *'agala*; *hayga* (هايجة), a word used to describe a woman who is hypersexual, randy and promiscuous; and *sharmuta* (شرموطة), the street word to describe a 'whore' (Wynn 2018: 133).

Hani's oppression in prison is witnessed when he is labelled a 'whore', which is a way of denigrating him first by drawing attention to his perceived moral transgression due to his identity as a homosexual man, and second by using a derogatory label relegating him to a position associated with female subjectivity. Hani confirms this act of denigration:

> In the morning the guards took us out and ordered us to strip down to our underwear. They stopped in front of one man who looked unusually effeminate and ordered him to take off all his clothes, possibly to make sure they didn't have a real female as a guest in their cells.
>
> (Abdelnabi 2018: 144)

The case of the man imprisoned with Hani illustrates the Arab attitude towards men who do not exhibit masculine traits. These traits are both behavioural and physical. As a rule, if a man exhibits masculine behaviour but has long nails, long and styled hair, trimmed and shaped eyebrows, and fully shaved beard and legs, he is likened to a woman. Similarly, if he has a beard, medium-length hair, hair on his body, yet wears tight clothes, speaks and laughs in a feminine voice, walks sensually and behaves softly, he is considered effeminate and is also likened to a woman. Hani describes how Egyptian society associates even underwear colours with a man's level of masculinity:

> I knew that if they found anyone in colored underwear they beat them and humiliated them especially brutally, on the grounds that this was irrefutable evidence that they were effeminate. They laughed throughout the process and their tone of voice was surprisingly triumphalist. With each new pervert that stood in front of them for them to play with, their sense of their own virility seemed to rise, until it reached stratospheric levels.
>
> (51)

Arab standards of effeminacy diverge considerably from those observed in the West. For Arab men, choosing the appropriate style and colour of underwear holds a firm value. In the past, men used to refrain from wearing underwear due to the belief that it could exert pressure on their groin, potentially leading to sterility or reduced virility. When they started wearing it, it had to be large and white, considering that these conditions would inevitably preserve their *rujula* when they were with other men and their *fuhula* when they were with their wives.

In Egyptian culture, an effeminate man is commonly described as *menaswen* (منسون), a term derived from the Arabic *nisa'* (نساء), 'women', which is the plural form of *imra'a* (امرأة). In formal Arab settings, the standard Arabic term used to describe an effeminate man is *mukhannath* (مخنث), originating from the verb *khannatha* (خنث), signifying 'to bend'. This term designates a man who imitates women in behaviour and speech, and who chooses to have a feminine clothing style. In his *Encyclopedia of Gay Histories and Cultures* (2000), George Haggerty conceptualizes the term:

> The common meaning is thus explained by the effeminate's 'pliability' and 'languidness' *(takassur),* for suppleness and lack of firmness both in gestures and moral standards are seen as feminine.
>
> (Haggerty 2000: 950)

This definition was preceded by Gary David Comstock and Susan E. Henking in *Que(e)rying Religion* (1997), in which they confirm that the term *mukhannath* refers to an effeminate man regardless of whether he was voluntarily so, and was, nonetheless, not synonymous with a transvestite (Comstock and Henking 1997: 63). There have been other discussions of the term *mukhannath*, but all with the same definition.[6]

It is vital to establish a precise definition of the term *mukhannath* due to the possibility of confusion with *khuntha* (خنثى). Although both terms originate from the same verb, *khuntha* is the Arabic equivalent of the term 'intersex', alluding to an individual born with both male and female genitals, lacking either of them or with ambiguous ones. This distinction is essential in avoiding misinterpretations that may arise from the use of these closely related but distinct terms.

In Egypt, prisoners endure torture from the onset of their detention, commencing with degrading measures that strip male and female inmates of their clothes. Moreover, they are deprived of bathing facilities and access to hot water, even during winter. Further restrictions include bans on exercise, sunlight and family visits. As detailed earlier, instances of torture frequently involve the insertion of hard objects into prisoners' anuses. This entire process is cynically referred to as *tashrifa* (تشريفة), a term that means 'honorific' but has ironically become synonymous with the ceremony of receiving new prisoners. Cases of men being discovered engaged in homosexual intercourse have been documented. Once authorities confirm this, the two individuals are subjected to a punishment party. During this event, they endure physical beatings in front of their fellow inmates. Following this, they are confined to *ta'dib* (تأديب) (disciplinary) cells, usually measuring two square metres, where they remain isolated for several days. Subsequently, they are transferred to other, mostly more intimidating prisons. This procedure is known as *taghrib* (تغريب), signifying alienation as they are further isolated from society and subjected to intensified conditions of solitary confinement.

Hani endures many a torturous experience, akin to what Michel Foucault describes as 'supplice' (Foucault 1995: 33).[7] While Hani may have managed to evade some of the consequences for his sexual orientation, his time in prison severely curtails his sexual freedom and results in considerable mental and physical distress. The anguish he undergoes epitomizes the gravity of the torment that any homosexual man in Egypt confronts:

During the sessions of the trial, the security presence was absurd, as if we were indeed terrorists and as if someone were going to try to set us free. A permanent wall of policemen separated us from everyone else—the lawyers, the journalists, and the families. Even the relatives were subjected to the vilest forms of abuse. When some poor-looking women asked the police about their sons, the police said, 'Are you the mothers of the faggots?'

(Abdelnabi 2018: 173)

The typical response of the state towards homosexual individuals involves accusing them of spreading depravity and violating what is known as *al-haya' al-'amm* (الحياء العام; public decency). Ironically, Hani draws a comparison between the horrific torture endured by individuals accused of terrorism in Egyptian prisons and the treatment of homosexual men, who see that their actions bear no resemblance to what Egyptian authorities consider terrorism. Nevertheless, both crimes of *khadsh al-haya' al-'amm* (خدش الحياء العام; violation of public decency)[8] through homosexual acts and *tahdid al-amn al-qawmy* (تهديد الأمن القومي; threat to national security)[9] through terrorist attacks are treated with equal severity by Egyptian authorities.

In the above quote, one can observe the stigma that haunts the mothers of homosexual men. 'Are you the mothers of the faggots?' is not a common question that Egyptian women may hear from the police; rather, it is a way of looking down on them for not succeeding in educating their sons properly. The word 'faggot' is used by Jonathan Wright in his translation of the novel, but in Abdelnabi's original Arabic version, the word used is *khawal* (خول),[10] a condescending Egyptian street word for 'gay'. It is used in front of the mothers in a most humiliating tone, and is also used by Hani's mother when he recalls her suspicion that he may be in love with a man named Prince:

She used the derogatory term without thinking, and at that moment something changed in the whole world, something very small but fundamental and permanent, as if the world had dimmed slightly, in a way that no one could tell unless they noticed that little lamp in the sky go out.

(Abdelnabi 2018: 72)

In the Egyptian Arabic dialect, *khawal* describes the passive male partner in sexual relations with men. *Khawal* derives from *khawalat* (خولات), which used to refer to men who performed belly dancing. It ranges from the famous transvestite *khawalat* dancers, introduced when Muhammad Ali, the founding Pasha of Egypt, banned women from performing in weddings. The female performers who were replaced by *khawalat* dancers were known as *ghawazi* (غوازي), as they had faced a prohibition on engaging in sensual public dance as of 1834. This restrictive measure was addressed by Frédéric Lagrange, and its rationale rested on the belief that undermining the *khawalat* dancers' masculinity posed a lesser threat to social harmony and entailed a comparably lower risk of instigating *fitna* (فتنة; social disorder) (Lagrange 2000: 190).

In contemporary Egyptian society, a linguistic phenomenon unfolds when discussions around homosexuality are met with sarcasm. Amidst the colloquial exchanges, where a certain individual would typically be referred to as *khawal*, the Egyptians, with a clever linguistic twist, replaced the term with *khawaga* (خواجة).[11] This word traditionally designates a foreigner, especially a westerner. Egyptians use the term *khawaga* to refer to a homosexual man, an artful wordplay that allows them to avoid the negative tone that the term *khawal* carries. They also creatively match the plural form of *khawal*, which is *khawalat*, with the plural form of *khawaga*, which is *khawagat* (خواجات).

Hani makes multiple references to the term *khawal*, consistently adopting a tone of contempt. It becomes evident to Hani that this term is invariably used by the guards as they subject the homosexual prisoners to brutal beatings, leaving him unable to overlook the cruel context in which the word is used. The phrase '[h]i faggots, hi devil worshippers, hi perverts, you sons of whores' (Abdelnabi 2018: 172–3) almost becomes a song that the guards sing while beating them with sticks and fists. Labelling the women as 'the mothers of the faggots' and the homosexual men as 'sons of whores' is a pretext to besmirch the homosexual man's family and stigmatize his mother, regarded as the most important element of the family, with the accusations levelled against her son.

As a consequence of enduring a series of harrowing mistreatments throughout his months of incarceration, Hani becomes unable to speak. Upon his release, he seeks the assistance of Dr Sameeh, a psychotherapist who provides tenacious support and aids him in reclaiming his ability to communicate verbally. Dr Sameeh, in his professional approach, refuses to perceive homosexuality as an illness and adopts an enlightened perspective that concurs with David M. Halperin's assertion, which denounces the discriminatory and derogatory attitudes historically directed towards homosexuals for well over a century (Halperin 2007: 1). Instead, Dr Sameeh acknowledges the societal pressures and challenges confronting Egyptian homosexuals (Abdelnabi 2018: 104). Only in writing, which Dr Sameeh encourages him to continue, can Hani find sanctuary. Spending all of his post-release time in a hotel room, Hani affirms:

> That's when my relationship with writing things out began; writing became a substitute for my tongue. I was suffering from a form of transformational hysteria, as I later understood from Dr. Sameeh. When I could no longer take any more pressures and conflicts, my mind transformed them into a physical symptom to reduce their impact.

> (175)

Hani's acceptance of his homosexual identity is closely tied to his desire to survive. Despite leaving prison profoundly scarred and voiceless, he continues with unwavering determination. The oppressive forces he has confronted are challenged by his sheer survival, and they will continue to be resisted by the power of his pen, which serves as a balm to mend his physical and psychological wounds. Michel Foucault posits that if power is action, resistance is reaction. Resistance, Foucault argues, does not stem from a limited set of diverse principles, nor are they mere enticements or assurances bound to be ultimately betrayed. Instead, they exist as a peculiar element within power dynamics, firmly inscribed within them as an irreducible opposite (Foucault 1990: 96). If prisons are indeed spaces where power is largely concentrated through organized regulation and other uncodified patterns, resistance to these policies and practices becomes transparent. Resistance varies from one imprisoned person to another according to several factors, the most important ones being their social background and the reasons that led to their imprisonment.

As the narrative progresses, Hani's innumerable homosexual relationships prior to his imprisonment come to light. Surprisingly, the novel reveals that he was married to a woman named Shireen. Nevertheless, this marriage was nothing more than a façade, ingeniously used to evade the societal constraints that arise when an Arab man reaches the age at which marriage is typically expected. Hani considers marriage a game: 'And even if I got married, the option of divorce was always available' (Abdelnabi 2018: 99). This situation, which may seem paradoxical at first, allows him to maintain a peaceful homosexual life while sidestepping the social stigma associated with a man who declines to wed. When the pressures to marry weigh heavily on Hani, Prince offers advice, urging him to undertake this socially obligatory path. In Prince's view, such a decision would open doors to more sexual freedom:

> In the end I took Prince's advice and, like a radar antenna, I started looking around for a victim or maybe a partner in the farce in which I meant to play the lead role.
>
> (100)

For Prince, marrying a woman, either due to family pressure, to avoid suspicion or purely for the sake of having children, is a circumstance not uncommon among homosexual men, and Hani would not be the first or last to do so. Hani agrees to the idea, but he lacks a quality that some men possess: 'I reconfirmed what he already knew – that I had no sexual desire for women in any way, unlike some men who are bisexual' (102).

Through getting glimpses of Hani's psychological recesses, the reader uncovers the presence of his beloved daughter, Badriya. However, following his arrest, Shireen finds herself compelled to initiate divorce proceedings due to what Hani himself refers to as a 'scandalous' affair. Divorce, in this case, is not only driven by the scandal but also by the unfortunate perception that the husband is no longer regarded as a true 'man'. To Shireen, Hani reiterates:

> 'I'll never forgive myself for anything that happened to you two because of me.' I looked at the piece of paper for a moment before I handed it to her. My handwriting looked shaky, like that of a child who has only just started learning to write. I shuddered as I saw Shireen struggling for words.
>
> (109)

If an Arab man's masculinity comes under suspicion or scrutiny, there is little chance of winning his wife back, as society collectively devalues him and perceives him as being sexually impotent, effeminate and *fasid*. These labels are ascribed to the man once his homosexuality is confirmed. Hani grapples with recurrent self-blame for the stigmatization his wife and daughter have endured because of his sexual orientation. He is well aware that Shireen will start being referred to as 'the homosexual man's wife'.

Writing becomes important for Hani, as it helps him heal and restore his voice. When he reunites with Abdel Aziz, he ardently seeks to assert his homosexuality as a bold act of defiance against the overriding social, cultural and hegemonic forces that once oppressed him:

> I kept imagining the extraordinary white coat spattered with blood, and it wasn't a pleasant sight. Yet I insisted on going all the way with Abdel Aziz, whether as murderer or as victim, it didn't matter.
>
> (125)

Abdelnabi portrays Hani as a militant or warrior who had to fight alone against a multitude of entities despite torture in prison, his mother's suspicions, his divorce, *kalam il-nas* (كلام الناس; people's words)[12] and the pressures that he will always be confronted with. Deciding to start his homosexual journey with dozens of male partners, Hani agrees to meet Abdel Aziz on the same square where the nightmare began, but this time, with his face uncovered in broad daylight and without his glasses, he holds Abdel Aziz's hand and proudly admits: 'And at that moment, everything seemed possible' (196).

Final Considerations

Muhammad Abdelnabi effectively shows the ways in which Egyptian social and cultural constructs are intertwined, both directly and indirectly, by addressing the issue of queer sexuality. *In the Spider's Room* explores themes historically associated with (homo)sexuality and the Arab world. The exertion of pressure upon those deviating from the heteropatriarchal code of behaviour operates across varied strata of society. Abdelnabi portrays it as a tool wielded by political power, which Hani perceives as submerged in *fasad*, to repress and suppress homosexuality, a phenomenon also considered by this political power as a form of moral *fasad*. It becomes manifest that for Egyptians who object to political oppression and queer sexuality, one *fasad* will have to survive. In light of this, the struggle against societal resistance has no apparent resolution in sight.

Hani's drive to assert his homosexual identity finds roots in the lexicon employed to demean Egyptian homosexuals. The range of derogatory terms explored in this chapter serves as a compelling impetus for him to defy the social stigma linked to such labels. For Hani, it is not just about being called *khawal* or not; it is about showing that the label *khawal*, designed to render individuals invisible, must be challenged. In this regard, language becomes a source of power for non-heterosexual subjects, wrestling it from the heteropatriarchal powers that have first used it to humiliate and stigmatize them. Hani regards queer sexuality as the norm and heterosexuality as the exception. For him, queerness is action, while heteronormativity becomes a reaction to this. When he openly reveals his sexual orientation, society responds with stigmatization, exclusion and erasure, challenging the notion that heterosexuality inherently precedes queerness. In this sense, Hani's resistance to this stigma becomes a reaction to the reaction. This process aims to legitimize marginality. Through the novel, the exploration of queer sexuality transitions from the periphery to the forefront of discourses unfolding within the literary sphere. As Abdelnabi grafts queer experiences onto his novel, he becomes liberated from the constraints imposed by conservative Arab society and enables Hani to unmute himself.

Notes

1   In Egypt, people have their full names, including their fathers', grandfathers' and great-grandfathers' names, on their national identity cards. This means that there could be thousands of Egyptian men named Muhammed Abdelnabi, and to differentiate between them, they are referred to through their full names.

2   *Izdira' al-adyan* refers to any act or behaviour that offends religion and religious beliefs, and aims to defame religious symbols, values and sanctities of individuals or groups. The penalty for *izdira' al-adyan* in Egypt is found in Chapter 98 of the Egyptian Penal Code.

3   In their book *Gay Shame* (2009), David Halperin and Valerie Traub argue that shame has historically been used as a tool of oppression against queer individuals, both by society at large and within the queer community itself. They suggest that shame can be reimagined and reclaimed as a form of resistance and empowerment. They propose that embracing one's own shame and rejecting societal expectations can be a radical act of self-affirmation and defiance against oppressive systems.

4   The information about Egyptian prisons and the diverse types of torture that Egyptian prisoners endure have been compiled from an interview that I conducted with Egyptian-Palestinian political activist Ramy Shaath in Paris, France on 20 May 2022.

5   In Egyptian culture, the colloquial word *meery* is a borrowed word from the French word *mairie*, which refers to the building where the municipal affairs of a town or city are managed. *Meery* is used by Egyptians to describe someone working with the police or the military. Sometimes, it is used to refer to the uniform of policemen or soldiers.

6   See Meisami and Starkey (1998: 548), Geissinger (2015: 34), Jahangir and Abdullatif (2016: 73), Dagyeli, Ghrawi and Freitag (2021: 221), and Rosenberg, D'Urso and Winget (2021: 290).

7   Michel Foucault's book *Discipline and Punish* (1995) was originally written in French under the title *Surveiller et punir* (Paris: Gallimard, 1975).

8   Article 178 of the Egyptian Penal Code No. 58 of 1937.

9   In Egypt, *tahdid al-amn al-qawmy* mostly refers to terrorist crimes. Egyptian Anti-Terrorism Law includes several chapters in Law No. 94 of 2015 regarding combating terrorism and criminalizing its financing. This law is found in Chapters 12 to 23.

10   The term *khawal* has a disparaging connotation and is used as a means of attacking a man's homosexual orientation. Moreover, in Egyptian culture, there is no specific term to refer to the active homosexual male, as the notion of Egyptian masculinity is predominantly associated with a diminished status only when the male assumes a passive role in sexual encounters.

11   The Egyptian Arabic word *khawaga* is a colloquial term that originated from the Arabic word *khawaja*, which historically referred to foreign, particularly European merchants. In modern Egyptian slang, *khawaga* can be used both neutrally and playfully, depending on the context and tone of the conversation.

12   In most Arab countries, *kalam il-nas* refers to gossip or conversations about people's private matters and personal affairs.

References

Abdelnabi, Muhammad. 2018. *In the Spider's Room*. Giza: Hoopoe.

Christensen, Tina Dransfeldt. 2021. *Writing Queer Identities in Morocco: Abdellah Taïa and Moroccan Committed Literature*. London: I.B. Tauris.

Comstock, Gary David and Susan E. Henking. 1997. *Que(e)rying Religion: A Critical Anthology*. London: Bloomsbury.

Dagyeli, Jeanine Elif, Claudia Ghrawi and Ulrike Freitag. 2021. *Claiming and Making Muslim Worlds: Religion and Society in the Context of the Global*. Berlin: De Gruyter.

Foucault, Michel. 1977. 'Entretien de M. Foucault avec B.- H. Lévy'. *Le Nouvel Observateur* 12 (644): 92–130.

Foucault, Michel. 1990. *The History of Sexuality*, Vol 1. New York: Vintage.

Foucault, Michel. 1995. *Discipline and Punish: The Birth of the Prison*. New York: Vintage.

Geissinger, Aisha. 2015. *Gender and Muslim Constructions of Exegetical Authority: A Rereading of the Classical Genre of Qur'an Commentary*. Leiden: Brill.

Ghaziani, Amin and Matt Brim. 2019. *Imagining Queer Methods*. New York: New York University Press.

Golia, Maria. 2004. *Cairo: City of Sand*. London: Reaktion Books.

Haggerty, George. 2000. *Encyclopedia of Gay Histories and Cultures*. London: Routledge.

Halperin, David M. 2007. *What Do Gay Men Want?: An Essay on Sex, Risk, and Subjectivity*. Ann ArborAnn: University of Michigan Press.

Halperin, David M. 2012. *How To Be Gay*. Cambridge, MA: Harvard University Press.

Halperin, David M. and Valerie Traub, eds. 2009. *Gay Shame*. Chicago: University of Chicago Press.

Jahangir, Junaid and Hussein Abdullatif. 2016. *Islamic Law and Muslim Same-Sex Unions*. Lanham, MD: Lexington Books.

Kafaji, Talib. 2011. *The Psychology of The Arab: The Influences That Shape an Arab Life*. Bloomington, IN: AuthorHouse Publishing.

Khalaf, Samir and John Gagnon. 2014. *Sexuality in the Arab World*. London: Saqi Books.

Lagrange, Frédéric. 2000. 'Male Homosexuality in Modern Arabic Literature', in M. Ghoussoub and E. Sinclair-Webb (eds), *Imagined Masculinities: Male Identity and Culture in the Modern Middle East*, 169–98. London: Saqi Books.

Long, Scott and Human Rights Watch. 2004. *In a Time of Torture: The Assault on Justice in Egypt's Crackdown on Homosexual Conduct*. New York: Human Rights Watch.

Massad, Joseph. 2007. *Desiring Arabs*. Chicago: University of Chicago Press.

Meisami, Julie Scott and Paul Starkey. 1998. *Encyclopedia of Arabic Literature*, Vol. 2. London: Routledge.

Pickett, Brent L. 2022. *Historical Dictionary of Homosexuality*. Washington, D.C.: Rowman & Littlefield Publishers.

Rosenberg, Tina, Sandra D'Urso and Anna Renée Winget. 2021. *The Palgrave Handbook of Queer and Trans Feminisms in Contemporary Performance*. London: Palgrave Macmillan.

Sion, Avi. 2008. *Logical and Spiritual Reflections*. Geneva: Avi Sion.

Wynn, L. L. 2018. *Love, Sex, and Desire in Modern Egypt: Navigating the Margins of Respectability*. Texas: University of Texas Press.

Chapter 2

VISUALIZING TRANSGENDER MOROCCO: DAOUD AOULAD-SYAD'S *BYE-BYE SOUIRTY (ADIEU FORAIN)*

Todd W. Reeser

When considering links between language and transgender in a Moroccan cultural context, it may be difficult to ignore the French colonial and postcolonial contexts in which Casablanca became closely associated with 'transsexualité'. Casablanca was a major capital of gender-confirmation surgery because of the fame of French gynecologist Georges Burou (1910–89), who performed and perfected vaginoplasties at the famous Clinique du parc beginning in the mid-1950s.[1] French singer, actress and cabaret megastar Coccinelle famously went to Casablanca for gender-confirmation surgery in 1958, and her story became widely known in France through the press as well as her autobiography *Coccinelle* (1987) and an earlier biography by Mario A. Costa, *Coccinelle est lui* (1963).[2] Jan Morris' popular English-language *Conundrum* (1974), translated as *L'Enigme* (1974), includes a chapter titled 'Casablanca'. In addition to Coccinelle's biographies, numerous narratives circulated about trans women who went to Burou, including Bambi as well as English trans women April Ashley and Roberta Cowell. *Roberta Cowell's Story* (1954) was quickly published in French in 1955 as *Comment je suis devenu(e) femme*. Casablanca was for Jay Prosser 'a way for troping the transsexual transition, part of the autobiographical frame' in white transfeminine autobiographies (1999: 100).[3]

Along with life-writing, French medical discourse of the 1950s to 1980s is peppered with references to Casablanca, often without naming Burou. To take one emblematic example, a 1970 journal article on 'trans-sexualisme' by Dubois and Marcel notes that 'in North Africa, a very comprehensive approach has been adopted, and operations are performed as a matter of course in Casablanca' (1970: 980). In 1974, a high-profile article on Burou was published in the popular magazine *Paris Match*, documenting in text and image for a French-speaking public the medical care that had been taking place for about twenty years. Described as a 'pioneer of transsexual surgery' who 'changes sex', Burou is presented in the

I thank Omar Boukhatem, Yacine Chemssi, and Abdellah Taïa for help on this article.

opening paragraph as a gynaecologist in whose practice 'veiled Moroccan women' come to see him, as do those seeking gender-affirming medical care (Merlin 1974: 38).

More recently, Cerdan in a book on Islam and transgender calls Casablanca 'the hub of transsexuality' and describes Burou's office address as 'known all around the world' (2010: 111). A 2012 web article for African readers describes Casablanca as 'the mythic Mecca of transsexuals' (Hazan 2012). Leïla Slimani's 2020 memoir of her youth in Morocco of the 1950s, *The Country of Others* (*Le pays des autres*), includes a chapter referring to gender-confirming surgery, suggesting that at least some Moroccans knew about Burou's office at the time (though the doctor is not himself mentioned by name). With this 'mythic' status, Casablanca (or Morocco more broadly) and western articulations of 'sex change' were difficult to disassociate in the popular imaginary – at least in French discursive contexts.

What about transgender *outside* western discursive contexts however? Is there a Moroccan transgender? For better or for worse, the western identity category of 'transgender' often passes under the radar – or is not legible as such – in Morocco today (Dialmy 2019: 256–7). Yet, indigenous notions of gender movement or fluidity are certainly not absent in cultural contexts, even as they lack the linguistic or discursive fixity conveyed in French and may not even look to fall under the western 'transgender' umbrella. Most famously, the Moroccan artist-actor Bouchaib El-Bidaoui (1928–65) – who dressed as a woman and sang popular songs (*ayta*) at events and on television, including the comedy show *Laugh with Me* – did not provoke homophobic or transphobic backlash, nor were his/her identity/ies defined linguistically (as 'homosexual' or 'transvestite', for instance).[4] And veiled performers dressed as women but assigned male at birth dance publicly in areas of Marrakech (such as Jāmm'a al-Fnā).[5] Medieval Sufi notions of gender mixture – for instance those in Abdelkebir Khatibi's Francophone novel *Le livre du sang* (1979) – could be taken as akin to the concepts transgender or transsexual (Zaganiaris 2012b: 75). The main character Tarik in Hicham Lasri's film *The Sea is Behind* (2014) cross-dresses to dance for pre-wedding and engagement ceremonies as per the tradition of H'diyya. Western discourses of transsexuality linked with Morocco can be juxtaposed or counterposed with non-western representations and cultural practices that avoid constructing or employing linguistic categories in the first place. Even so, it may be difficult to simply dispel western discourses, meaning that the Moroccan context may be composed of complicated dialogues between western and non-western constructs, in which neither is fully absent nor dominant. In his novel *Au bonheur des limbes* (2006), Mohamed Leftah portrays Jeanne's new vagina in poetic and imagistic terms that for Chantal Zabus refer to images of Burou's vaginoplasties (2019: 80). Western constructs of transgender might haunt Moroccan texts as references, such that the very relation between those constructs and Moroccan texts or contexts forms part of the textual content itself.

From this perspective, I will take up a case study in how a western/non-western dialogue around non-medical and non-identitarian transgender formulations constitutes narrative itself: Daoud Aoulad-Syad's *Bye-Bye Souirty*, or *Adieu Forain* in French (1998). The Arabic-language film performs indifference to western discourses of gender and highlights indigenous traditions. One of the three main characters, named Rabii, dresses in feminine clothing and accessories – without passing as a woman – and performs dance numbers with a travelling lottery stand (the *forain* of the French title), evoking the spectre of Bouchaib El Bidaoui. Rabii appears to have a lover who has left him, but although male pronouns are used in reference to this person (and to Rabii), it is not clear what orientation he might have or to what extent he or his lover could be called 'transgender'. Rabii uses phrases gesturing towards western categories, subsequently avoiding any categories and thus resisting the idea of categories themselves. 'I always wanted to be someone else', he notes at one point, but the viewer never learns who that other person is. Does he mean he wants to be 'gay'? Or a woman? Or 'transgender'? Or something else? Manuel Billi suggests that 'he does not say himself, but also he does not seem to recognize himself' (2017: 131). I would say that he does not say or recognize legible categories of gender, for *Adieu Forain* is decidedly *not* about any kind of stable category of gender or sexuality, or about the need to know, to define or to become a gendered self. Stable identities are not part of Rabii's gender. Rather, as I will argue, something resembling the broad category of transgender is constructed through visual language, skirting the problem of language, discourse and gender tags entirely. Such avoidance of language, I suggest, takes place by virtue of a rejection of physical movement to or towards the West, and by extension towards western discourses of gender. While it is certainly possible to call this character 'queer', I take him as transgender since gender movement is the most pronounced element of his gender presentation and since questions of gender are more prevalent in the film than questions of desire or sexuality (though they are not absent).

Western constructs of transsexuality are not fully expunged in this case, remaining just one of many elements in the film's construct of transgender. My approach resembles that of Zaganiaris, who considers gender identity in Moroccan novels of French expression as 'creating as much as describing ... individuals' ways of becoming a subject by trying to free themselves from normative identities' (2012b: 78). Rabii's gender movements are as much about freeing himself from western notions of gender as about becoming a subject. At the same time, they free his self from the necessity to be defined by Moroccan epistemologies of gender. He cannot simply be a reincarnation of Bouchaib El-Bidaoui, on the one hand, or 'transgender' or 'transsexual', on the other. In the end, *Adieu Forain* constructs transgender as an assemblage of multiple definitional elements, corresponding to the call by Zaganiaris to consider queer as constituted by 'pluralities', 'hybridities', 'mixtures' and 'identitarian ambivalences' in Arab texts (2013: 10).[6]

The plurality of gender gestures towards the future. Mohammed Bakrim notes that 'the good-bye of the title is a nod to the end of an era' – or, perhaps, the end of a decade and a century (2004: 184).[7] Similarly, Amadou Gaye's review of the film in *Ecrans d'Afrique* considers the film as about 'bygone days, bygone customs' and a 'new generation' (1998: 61, 62). In this new era, transgender is not necessarily defined through 'bygone' western or colonial epistemologies, or in traditional

Moroccan terms. For Bakrim, the film signals 'the end of an era and announces another' (2004: 185). It is a new twenty-first-century form of transgender on the horizon – one whose contours remain not fully defined as of yet (at least as the film closes), putting into question more than answering the question of what Moroccan transgender ambivalences might mean at the dawn of a new century.

Lies of Migration, Lies of Gender

Central to the film's avoidance of western categories is the rejection of the need for a Maghrebi trans person to migrate to the tolerant West to be liberated from supposedly unavoidable transphobia or homophobia. There is decidedly no liberation to be had in Paris, Brussels, London or New York. The film mirrors approaches in migration studies that critique simplistic assumptions that LGBTQ African refugees migrating to the West are necessarily liberated (e.g. Chossière 2022; Murray 2014). Moreover, Rabii will not fully realize gendered subjecthood by leaving Morocco and becoming 'transgender', 'transsexual' or even 'queer'. In broader terms, the character of Rabii serves to reject traditional constructs of transgender as analogical with migration from one country to another. As Prosser discusses this metaphor: 'an appropriate analogical frame for the transsexual's writing of transition as a journey may be that of immigration: the subject conceives of transsexuality as a move to a new life in a new land, allowing the making of home' (1999: 92). But what happens when metaphoric immigration is not that of a wealthy, white, trans person from one wealthy country to another (e.g. from the United Kingdom to the United States)? And what happens when a stable idea of 'home' is not the telos in the first place? Bhanji critiques Prosser's discussion because of its 'lack of engagement with the dynamics of race and class' (2012: 165). Like Bhanji, Aizura sees the transsexual homecoming metaphor and the normality it assumes as a fantasy, 'racially and culturally marked as Anglocentric, heteronormative and capitalist' (2006: 290). Aizura takes issue with Prosser's 'assumption that "home" in a gendered or geographical sense has a universal or self-evident meaning' since, in particular, trans narratives based on travel and homecoming may be colonialist and imperialist in nature, referring back to the history of racist travel writing for a broad reading public (Aizura 2018: 61). In the case of *Adieu Forain*, there is no telos of home at all as Rabii lacks any home: in the opening scene he is seen living like a migrant in a rural hotel in need of money. This opening corresponds to Bhanji's reconsideration of Prosser's idea of telos: 'Akin to the transitory space of an airport terminal, the in-between space of gender transition figures as a site of *future* homely possibility …, where the subject has an itinerary, a destination and a future but has not yet arrived' (2012: 165). For Rabii, that future itinerary is not necessarily western in orientation. *Adieu Forain* evokes the idea of transgender as a journey from the Global South to the Global North – or, towards liberation and identitarian ways of being a gendered subject – but then rejects that trajectory – and thus the narrative model outlined by Prosser – in favour of a non-linear form of movement not defined in western terms but not necessarily non-western either.

In *Adieu Forain*, no Maghrebi subject actually goes to France or to Western Europe as the entire film takes place in Morocco. Larbi and Rabii travel through southern Morocco co-hosting a travelling lottery stand along with Larbi's ill father Kacem, the *forain* (stall keeper) of the French title. Kacem is ill and dies late in the film, ending the travelling lottery show altogether and effectively breaking up the threesome. Though the film has buddy and road-movie elements, the two main characters are an unlikely pair and are disconnected much more than they are connected. While Rabii dances dressed as a woman to attract locals to come play the lottery, Larbi is unlikeable, choleric, macho and at times homo/transphobic.

The disjuncture between the two characters, however, pertains not just to masculinity but also to migration. At first, Larbi embodies the concept of migration away from the Maghreb to the West as he interacts with Rabii, who is not invested or interested in leaving Morocco. Larbi explains that he has recently spent three years living in Belgium, where he worked as a mechanic, boxed on the side and found a blonde Belgian woman whose photograph he carries with him and shows to Rabii. He had to marry her, presumably for reasons related to visa or working papers. Larbi wants to return to Belgium again to be with his wife, and he tries to convince Rabii to come as well, despite not wanting to be friends with him. 'I came home when I wanted, I went out when I wanted', he says.[8] Larbi's story of freedom in Western Europe transposes easily onto the possibility that Rabii could be free to express his gender as he desires. Considering the invitation and then reflecting on it, Rabii in a later scene tells Larbi's father that he feels stuck, that his life is not leading anywhere and that he would like to leave. Since Larbi knows people abroad, Rabii believes, they will be able to manage somehow. 'At least abroad …, ' he lets slip seemingly accidentally, conveying that his relation to gender would be a different matter abroad. Kacem asks him where he will go specifically, and he can only say 'abroad' since what is really at stake is migration to the West, the specific cultural context lacking importance. He later tells Larbi that his 'dream is to save money and leave'. The viewer learns too that he had a friend or a lover that an American man brought back to the United States, presumably as a lover, suggesting that Rabii could follow in his friend's footsteps and be taken in by a (presumably older) white man. On one level, then, the film would seem to be focussed on how a trans character can be easily convinced to migrate as a non-normative Maghrebi subject to the West, where he will finally find a tolerant LGBTQ community and the rights that he is deprived of in Morocco. Though Rabii's lack of erotic desire for women is clear and his desire to become someone different from his male-presenting self is also clear, he may well want to migrate to be able to live as a trans woman or transsexual. The West looks to be a space of potentiality where Rabii imagines himself to come into being. By implication, his imagined journey to the West parallels Prosser's metaphor of realizing trans subjectivity as a journey from point A to point B, reversing the direction of the narrative journey of European trans women to Casablanca.

Despite this imagined potential, it turns out that Larbi has been lying about Belgium, that the photograph of his Belgian wife is fake and that he has only ever been in Morocco. In fact, he has been incarcerated, his father tells Rabii, not abroad. 'You have lying in your blood', Rabii tells him when confronting him.

For me, the point is not so much that Larbi is lying about migration, for it is the necessity for trans subjects to migrate to the West in the first place that is the big lie. The necessity is revealed to be a discursive construct, imagined to be true but not based in reality. It is a made-up narrative that a Maghrebi trans subject should or must leave for the West to find freedom.

That narrative is not a natural or universal one applicable to all trans subjects but is instead randomly generated – much like the travelling lottery which is based on a random selection of numbers. The three main characters travel through Morocco to convince locals to buy numbered tickets that match randomly generated numbers from three wheels that Larbi spins for the local public in each village that they visit. One person in the audience may well win, but it is just one person in the large crowd. The narrative of transgender migration is a result of a postcolonial spin. There is something randomly generated, too, about the characters' relations: they came together accidentally as Kacem quickly needed a dancer for the show and happened to find Rabii at a hotel where he was staying at the opening of the film. Nothing is natural or inevitable about the connection between Rabii and Larbi: they stay together for the show only, and the metaphor of migration represented by the latter has no natural link to Rabii's gender. Links between migration and trans are themselves arbitrary, existing for no reason in the first place. It is no accident that after Rabii dances in a long take, a young man comes up to the side of the lottery stand to flirt with him and light his cigarette. Rabii is not simply in an intolerant cultural space that must be left behind, but in spaces defined by constant negotiation that do not have to be the starting point – or the place to be left behind – for a journey to the liberated West. 'Home' is not necessarily abroad.

In a long-take dance scene, Rabii is filmed from the perspective of the crowd, calling attention to the concept of looking itself. The locals are revealed to be looking subjects as much as Rabii's gender is staged for the public. The camera in turn pans the interested faces of the onlookers, dispelling any idea that Moroccan rural spaces are simply intolerant or transphobic. A slow look at the locals reveals their physical diversity, affording the viewer the time to wonder who they might be, what their clothing says about them and more broadly what their identities might be underneath the visible. Rabii is simply one among many Moroccans whose identities are interrogated visually. They may be transgender, queer or some such as well. The scene invites questions such as: How are the locals performing their gender? How is Rabii's gender presentation like or unlike what looks to be the locals' cisgender presentation? The slow pan of the audience suggests the perspective of Rabii up on the lottery stand, as he looks at their gender performance as much as they look at his. The angle shifts again, showing Rabii from behind and the audience in front. Some abstract, incorporeal watching subject is now present, conveying that the trans body deserves to be watched as much as the cisgender bodies of the public. The entire sex/gender system is the object of the gaze as much as Rabii's own gender is. The public might be 'lucky' because their gender is not put into question in the same way that Rabii's is, but that does not mean that it is not a randomly gendered gender subjectivity that can be watched and examined as well. The lottery wheels have been spun and the public's gender has been culturally determined, as has the cisnormativity that surrounds Rabii.

On the Road Again

Once the lie of Larbi's migration is revealed, Rabii's relation to trans migration becomes complicated and ambiguous, resulting in the ambiguity of the film's final scene. The two characters split up after Larbi's father dies and the lottery truck is sold (the 'Adieu' of the French title). If Rabii has the option to be taken away – like his friend whom we never meet – by a wealthy American to the United States, it is not clear that he takes the option. He picks up his bag and heads off, directionless into the dark night as cars pass by quickly on the nearby road. His movement is not like that of those fast-moving cars which function as foils. The lie of migration on Larbi's part – or the trip that existed only in his mind – is transferred into an indeterminacy on Rabii's part. If the necessity for migration is a lie, then what is a trans subject to do? Before leaving, Larbi tells Rabii that he does not like Americans or Hollywood, but that nonetheless 'with a bit of luck, we will be together over there'. But where is 'over there'? If over there is an imagined place, then where will they be together? Over there somewhere in Morocco? Or somewhere else that is a fantasy on his part or their part? Over the rainbow? Is over there somewhere western? The trip itself ends up as rhizomatic, without an identifiable endpoint as 'over there' comes to signify a place where there is no identifiable or discursive notion of gender or sexuality. Over there is a new space to be determined, a new form of movement yet to be defined, opened up to new ways to be a gendered subject. The road movie has no telos, does not end 'at home'.

While talking about the death of his father to Rabii in one of the last scenes of the film, Larbi realizes that both of them are orphans. They are both parentless as much as they are directionless, freed from the constraints of the past and now able to establish their own new subjectivities. Rabii had told his woman friend Nezha that he 'had always dreamed of being someone else' and that he lived as a projected image of someone else. As the ending of the film suggests, he will in fact become 'someone else' as he moves on from the narrative into the night and into new geographical spaces and undertakes new journeys. He is in a sense in Bhanji's 'airport terminal', with a future to be determined, but his gendered becoming may or may not be predicated on a relation to the West. It is no accident that the lottery truck moves south over the course of the film (from Tahannaout to Tamesluht): the movement of the characters is away from Europe since the direction of Rabii's migration or travel does not have to be towards the Global North. Rabii ends the film in an indeterminate space of his own, incarnating what Olivier Barlet (2011) calls in reference to Daoud's oeuvre broadly 'a human metaphysics in the reduced space of a village' ('Entretien'). He embodies a broad, directionless transgender way to be while remaining in the localized spaces of Moroccan villages. Rabii does not opt for gender in this non-teleological movie, or as Denise Brahimi says about the character: 'by its very definition, the road movie … allows … for deep incertitude, or the choice to not choose' (2009: 194).

Transing Language

Adieu Forain is in Arabic, and French plays almost no role. There is one minor exception early on however as Rabii the character is introduced. He lives in a hotel room in the town centre and as he prepares to depart the hotel and the town, the camera focusses on a wall with signs to hotels nearby, before following Rabii from behind with his travel bag. The signs are bilingual, but the most visible sign is the 'HOTEL Du SUD' (The Hotel of the South). It is not fully clear whether Rabii has been living in this particular hotel, but it is clear that his character will have a relation to heading south, in two language modes. The idea of Rabii's transgender directionality as a character is defined in part in French colonial terms, unable to be fully uncoupled from the past. Already ensconced in the 'HOTEL Du SUD' before his departure, Rabii is decidedly not living like an LGBTQ global northerner – defined by linguistic tags such as *transgenre, homosexuel* or even queer. To head south is to reject the French name on the sign, or in larger terms, of any western signifying label, in favour of other signs. After the narrative concludes, in whatever direction he may be moving, linguistic signifiers will be left behind in favour of localized ones. The *Adieu forain* in the French title refers to Larbi's father's death, but it also refers to the original sense of *'forain'* as 'foreigner', as per the English sense.[9] The film is saying goodbye to the American foreigner who came to take Rabii's friend to the United States and to the idea that foreign terms and constructs of gender define Rabii. Not only does he head south instead of north – unlike transgender characters in Franco-Maghrebi films such as Merzak Allouache's *Chouchou* (2003) or Nadir Moknèche's *Lola Pater* (2017) – but he redefines the whole system of trans travel itself, rejecting directionality and remaining an errant subject.[10] Where he ends up will be determined more like the travelling lottery – a game of chance. The Arabic title *Bye-Bye Souirty* suggests a goodbye to the luck that one might have while playing a game like the lottery (a literal English translation might be something like 'Good Bye, Game of Luck' or 'Good Bye, Lucky Lottery Winner').[11] In other words, Rabii leaves behind the luck of the draw of the colonial narrative, which won in a random game without a predetermined outcome and gained control of gender discourses and gender language. The winner can henceforth be anyone. The point is not that Rabii will necessarily win out in this gendered game of definition, but that he can participate freely with the same chances as anyone else.

Rabii's friend Nezha, a teacher living and working in one of the towns he visits, longs to leave the backwards, sexist town where the locals want a male teacher. Luckily, she says, vacation is coming soon, and she will head to Casablanca. In a trans Moroccan film, Casablanca cannot be unrelated to its status as Dr Burou's mecca. The teacher's friend, family member or partner died and bears a resemblance of some kind to Rabii, as she notes when he spots a photograph of the deceased man on a shelf in her home. This man was 'taken by the sea', the teacher notes, not in any definitive or concrete manner, but rather 'as one says' since she did not actually see him die or see his body. She adds that it is a 'long story that haunts [her]'. The image of a former friend or lover of hers also establishes that Rabii's current gender presentation may, too, be lost at sea one day – as one might say – were he to transform into another self physically and leave a former self behind. If to be trans is to be lost at sea, trans is not a journey, but a journey that includes a shipwreck in which one may or may not die – an in-between image not unlike Bhanji's airport terminal. Rabii may himself want to head to Casablanca too: it is in fact a distinct possibility in the final scene that Rabii is heading to Casablanca. But this city would not be the trans capital of the past: Rabii would be heading to an image of a former trans capital, a place with a trans aura but that is no more trans than any other city where surgery or medical care is possible. Casablanca then might resemble – but not be – the trans capital that it was decades earlier, as the image of Casablanca – like the photograph – does and does not resemble the past image, 'taken by the sea' but not definitively dead. Rabii's potential movement north to Casablanca reinscribes the traditional movement from France or Europe to Casablanca for health care, reimagining the directionality of a former orientalist travel narrative. Were this homeless orphan to head to Casablanca, it would not be to find a gender and national home or to complete a teleology. Instead, Rabii delineates a space that transes the trans in its Moroccan reconfiguration of movement itself.

Transing Media

If Rabii does not rely on western discourses of transgender for self-definition, it is in part because visuality offers better representational possibilities. Overall, the film is characterized by beautiful and often lingering shots of people, emphasizing that subjectivity is defined visually at least as much as discursively. I have cited two scenes in which photography plays a central role in representing transgender, but broader questions of media and gender subtend the film. Rabii shares to Nezha that he has always been 'the reflection of someone' when she notes that the photograph in her home looks like him. Though she notes that she did not mean that, Rabii responds that it is fine since that was what he 'always wanted' and that he 'always dreamed of being someone else'. For me, it is not so much that Rabii does or does not look like some other specific person as much as that he does not feel like the physical person that others see, or that his gender does not match the gender that others ascribe to him based on looks and perception. He always dreamed of *looking like* someone else to others. His body, taken by others as cisgender male, might be metaphorically lost at sea and unable to be found as it is phenomenologically dead. But that lost body cannot be found by others since it has not actually died and is still seen by others. In terms of the photographic medium, still images of Rabii do not and cannot represent his gender and are a false image – in much the same way that Larbi's photograph of his supposed wife is a fake. Photographs lie when they pretend to convey someone's portrait or claim to be mimetic, and, above all, photographs of Rabii are representationally incorrect. For this reason, then, the scene between Rabii and Nezha may seem to be arguing that film (including the one that we are watching) better represents Rabii's experience of gender and that photography – as a still medium – cannot represent transgender successfully. Film presents the character in a complicated location between genders and between western and Moroccan representations of transgender, whereas a simple photograph cannot convey in-betweenness. If Rabii's movement in the final scene embodies his version of gender, it has to be conveyed via the moving image.

More broadly, transgender photographic representation may be problematic because it cannot faithfully or fully represent gender change or transition. In Sébastien Lifshitz's *Wild Side* (2004), to take one example from French film, the main character Stéphanie goes through stacks of old photographs from her childhood after the death of her mother. The scene suggests, as I have argued (Reeser 2022: 222–3), that film represents the movement-centredness of transgender in a way that still or traditional home photography simply cannot do on its own. In this case, Stéphanie looks to others to be a cisgender boy in the photographs, whereas in cinematic flashbacks, a boy already in gender movement can be presented. The unquestioned normative gaze does not complicate gender in photographs, seeing only cisgender bodies. Prosser studies how 'photographs of transsexuals are situated on a tension between revealing and concealing transsexuality' (1998: 209). A trans person who passes will be seen as cisgender, and a trans person who does not pass will be seen as only trans. Consequently, Prosser discusses that photographic representation has to function in other modes, in particular by including two different gendered moments that together represent another representational modality or by 'bring[ing] into relief the reader's gaze' (223). While the relation between photography and transgender may often be fraught, I want to suggest here that *Adieu Forain* questions the relation between transgender and photography from another angle that takes the Moroccan context into account.

It Is no accident that photography figures in the film, for Aoulad-Syad is as accomplished a photographer as a director, with four major books of his photographs (1989, 1996, 2000, 2015) and a number of shows in Europe, the United States and Morocco. For him, photography is not simply a static medium. As he has himself noted in a documentary on Moroccan photography, there is a long history of photography creating clichés of Moroccans in an orientalizing, colonial frame (*Les chemins du visible ou le Maroc inventé par la photographie* 1999).[12] He does not take portraits of people who ask him to do so for this very reason, so as to avoid replicating fixing Moroccans in static clichés lacking complexity. Aoulad-Syad acknowledges the influence of Swiss-born American photographer Robert Frank, whose photographs incorporate movements of various kinds in their framing and ask implicit questions by virtue of that movement. It may not be fully clear what someone is doing in the frame, what their motivation is or where they are going. Similarly, Aoulad-Syad's photographs invite viewers to ask what someone is doing or why they are doing what they are doing. His oeuvre functions as a medium of visual interrogation, pushing back against the tradition of colonial photography and avoiding the hegemony of the western gaze. The photographic act for him is like an 'act of love', he notes (*Les chemins du visible ou le Maroc inventé par la photographie* 1999): leaving a trace of reality while respecting those who are different from the photographer in some way. 'I don't want to convey reality', he states in the documentary, since something must be happening in his images. In one photograph in the collection *Daoud Aoulad-Syad* (2015), an effeminate-looking man in a caftan dances on the left side of the frame, in front of a wall painted with frescoes of women, while a man on the right side looks to be possibly selling tickets and collecting money, but for what reason or for whom remains an open question to be answered only by the viewer. Visual happening-ness is also highlighted in his short films *Mémoire ocre* (1991), *Entre l'absence et l'oubli* (1993) and *Al-Oued* (1995), in which the dividing line between photograph and moving image is fluid, to the point that at some instances it is not easy to determine whether the image on the screen is still or moving. Photographic representation is defined as potentially cinematic, as inherently based on the concept of movement. *Adieu Forain*, too, positions photography as a medium asking a series of questions, not as mimetic portraits. The photographs ask questions of those who view them. Do they represent properly? What is the subject doing and why? What kind of movement is taking place? What movement is *not* shown? How is a photograph transmitting a feeling or an idea more than the subject represented? The two photograph scenes discussed above both ask questions about gender, and they do not represent people per se, instead revealing the limits of representation. In fact, the viewer does not even really see the portraits because they are largely irrelevant to the narrative.

Questions about gender are asked in a third photographic moment, during the scene when Rabii dances for the crowd. A random man watching snaps a photograph of him from afar. Rabii seems uncomfortable at first, but then realizes something about the image that changes his mind. Whatever photograph is produced will not create a cliché of Rabii but will open up questions about gender. The photograph will be of a person dancing, in movement on stage, but also part of a lottery travelling show, also in movement. Like Aoulad-Syad's photographs, this photograph will raise questions: What is this person doing? Why? Rabii will be on stage next to three lottery wheels, which could lead to questions about links between chance and gender. The photograph, taken from afar, will likely include members of the crowd watching Rabii with interest, opening up questions about Moroccans looking and their relation to gender. Prosser's 'reader's gaze' will be brought 'into relief'. In the scene, the person photographing is shown to be a looker, and like the others in the crowd, stands as a gendered subject too, subject to questioning. What does it mean that Rabii sees someone photographing him? What does that gaze, turned back on the photographer, suggest about the gazer? Is the photographer replicating the colonized gaze? Does Rabii turning the gaze back on the photographer parallel a Moroccan photographer turning the gaze back on the colonial gaze? Or is the photographer an embodiment of the Moroccan eye looking at Moroccans? Is the photographer an inscribed image of the Moroccan director-photographer himself? After all, Aoulad-Syad stated that as a child he admired and imitated the male dancer of the Amar Circus who one Sunday invited him to come up and dance with him (Aoulad-Syad 2000: [ii]). Is the photographer an image of a Moroccan who idealizes and wants to be like the dancer and will later recreate his gendered movement in some manner? Such questions are raised but not answered.

The idea of photographic subjects being lost at sea is not just a metaphor about representation, however, but the concrete subject of Aoulad-Syad's short film *Between Absence and Oblivion* (*Entre l'absence et l'oubli*). A potter buys a frame at a market with a photograph inside of a man and, fearful of having an image of someone that he does not know, decides that he should not remove it. He intends to put his family photographs in the frame but then changes his mind. Following the advice of his friend who tells him that it is bad luck to have photographs of strangers in his home, he sets off to find the man. In his search, he learns that he is a fisherman, and locals who know him think that he is out at sea fishing and will return at the end of the workday. Assiduously trying to locate him with the help of locals on the watch, the potter waits for the man on the shore but in the end is unable to. He leaves the framed photograph on shore and heads back home at the very end of the short film. The message of *Entre l'absence et l'oubli* seems to be that photographs do not resemble actual human beings, as subjects of photographs cannot physically be located. There is in fact no subject of the photograph to find in the first place, the very idea of locating him is a priori impossible. A local suggests that the sea has been rough, and perhaps that the man has been lost at sea or that he will not return for some other reason.

The short does not treat the concept of transgender directly, but it does suggest an epistemology of gender that pertains to *Adieu Forain*. The potter's photograph lacks a physical referent because photographs do not simply represent. The inability to find the fisherman – his being out to sea somewhere perhaps not to be found – allegorizes the split between photographic image and physical referent. The photograph without a referent in *Entre L'absence et l'oubli* directly evokes Nezha's photograph of a person 'taken by the sea', inviting a reading of *Adieu Forain* in light of Aoulad-Syad's short. In both cases, the photographic referents are lost and cannot be found. They may be alive or dead. What is being suggested is that gender presentation very broadly is defined by a gap between image and referent, a gap that opens up a series of questions about the subject of the image. Does the person in the photograph resemble Rabii because both are trans? Or queer? Larbi's gender is not the way it looks either. His masculinity corresponds to a referent that does not simply exist as static and that asks questions about his male body. What is he doing gender-wise? And why is he doing it? Why is he so isolated from Rabii? And why is he so phobic about non-normativity? This take on photography necessarily informs the dancing scene in *Adieu Forain*: the photograph of Rabii taken by the photographer in the audience will convey not simply a portrait but absence as well. It will suggest that he cannot be located, that he – or his gender – cannot be found, no matter how long anyone waits for him. His gender whereabouts cannot actually be located. Is his true gender out at sea, unable to be located? Perhaps across the Mediterranean or the Atlantic in Europe or the United States? Or is his gender missing precisely because it is inflected with western notions of gender and is not Moroccan? Will it remain outside such discursive contours? In any case, Rabii's gender is not simply present, and the film more broadly does not depict his gender as it 'is' in the present but as an image with a missing referent.

In the end, then, *Adieu Forain* rejects discourse and language in favour of visual language so as to reveal the gap between image and referent. Visuality itself, I would contend, skirts the issues discussed in my introduction around language, offering another epistemology or quasi-epistemology – a way to know and not know what trans in a Moroccan framework is or might be. Aoulad-Syad does not want to convey reality, as he says. In this case, he does not convey a Moroccan trans subject who accepts or rejects western modes of being a trans subject. He does not fix the image of transgender as a cliché. Instead, he conveys a movement-centred, referent-destabilizing mode by which to be a trans subject and to question subjectivity. Rabii dances his way out of colonial discourse and visual fixed representational forms in favour of another mode located 'somewhere else'.

Notes

1　For an overview on Burou, see Hage, Karim and Laub 2007. The year 1956 may be the date when Burou began his surgeries (Merlin 1975: 38).

2　All translations from French are my own. Foerster describes Coccinelle as emblematic of 'the transsexual condition' in the 1950s and 1960s (Foerster 2018: 77).

3　On Casablanca as an orientalizing space in trans narrative, see Aizura 2018: 70–80.

4　See, for instance, Zaganiaris 2012a. The extent to which this figure is queer or trans is an open question, however.

5　See, for instance, Bailleul n.d.; Fortier 2017, 2020. Tahar Ben Jelloun's *L'enfant de sable* (1985) and *La nuit sacrée* (1987) might also potentially be considered in relation to these local traditions.

6　An open question is the extent to which Aoulad-Syad's training at *La Fémis* film school in Paris influenced the content of the film.

7　Since the 'lead years' under King Hassan II ended in 1999, the film could – unknowingly perhaps – announce a new political era as well.

8　My citations are based on the French subtitles in the online version of the film.

9　*Forain* comes from *foire*, meaning normally a 'fair', which refers to the travelling lottery stand in its standard sense here.

10　The errancy of the final scene might be connected as well to Sufism, which might render meaningless the borders of nations (along with other types of borders). My reading here resembles Carbajal's reading (2019) of queer Sufi errancy in Abdellah Taïa's *Salvation Army*.

11　The film's title is often translated as 'Farewell Traveling Player'.

12　See, for instance, Abdelghani 2018; Bate 1992; Goldsworthy 2010.

References

Abdelghani, Fennane. 2018. *La photographie au Maghreb: Enjeux symboliques et créations artistiques*. Marrakech: Éditions Aimance Sud.

Aizura, Aren Z. 2006. 'Of Borders and Homes: The Imaginary Community of (Trans)sexual Citizenship', *Inter-Asia Cultural Studies* 7 (2): 289–309.

Aizura, Aren Z. 2018. *Mobile Subjects: Transnational Imaginaries of Gender Reassignment.* Durham, NC: Duke University Press.

Aoulad-Syad, Daoud. 1989. *Marocains.* Paris: Contrejour/Belvisi.

Aoulad-Syad, Daoud. 1996. *Boujaâd, Espace et mémoire.* Data Press.

Aoulad-Syad, Daoud. 2000. *Territoires de l'instant.* [Casablanca]: La Croisée des chemins.

Aoulad-Syad, Daoud. 2015. *Daoud Aoulad-Syad.* Paris: Filigranes; Maison européenne de la photographie.

Bailleul, Adeline. n.d. 'Saïd, homme danseuse de la place Jemaa el-Fna', *Huffington Post, Maroc.*

Bakrim, Mohammed. 2004. '*Adieu forain* de Daoud Aoulad Syad, un film beckettien', in Michel Serceau (ed.), *Cinémas du Maghreb*, 184–6. Paris: Télérama.

Barlet, Olivier. 2011. 'Entretien avec Daoud Aoulad-Syad.' BUALA. https://www.buala.org/fr/afroscreen/entretien-avec-daoud-aoulad-syad-a-propos-de-la-mosquee-a-jamaa (accessed 18 July 2023).

Bate, David. 1992. 'The Occidental Tourist: Photography and Colonizing Vision', *Afterimage* 20 (1): 11–13.

Bhanji, Nael. 2012. 'TRANS/SCRIPTIONS: Homing Desires, (Trans)sexual Citizenship and Racialized Bodies', in Trystan T. Cotton (ed.), *Transgender Migrations*, 160–78. New York and London: Routledge.

Billi, Manuel. 2017. 'La double altérité cinématographique de l'autre maghrébin-homosexuel, entre exotisme, identification et décorporisation', in Michael Gebhard and Claudia Gronemann (eds), *Masculinités maghrébines: Nouvelles perspectives sur la culture, la littérature et le cinéma*, 122–34. Leiden: Brill.

Brahimi, Denise. 2009. *50 ans de cinéma maghrébin.* Paris: Minerve.

Bye-Bye Souirty. 1998. Directed by Daoud Aoulad-Syad, Les Films du Sud. Available online: https://www.youtube.com/watch?v=MlIHktWKghg (accessed 29 July 2023).

Carbajal, Alberto Fernández. 2019. *Queer Muslim Diasporas in Contemporary Literature and Film.* Manchester: Manchester University Press.

Cerdan, Alexandra. 2010. *Transsexuelle et convertie à l'Islam.* Monaco: Alphée.

Les chemins du visible ou le Maroc inventé par la photographie. 1999. Directed by Sylvain Roumette. Tanguera Films.

Chossière, Florent. 2022. 'Debunking the Liberation Narrative: Rethinking Queer Migration and Asylum to France', in B. Camminga and John Marnell (eds), *Queer and Trans African Mobilities: Migration, Asylum and Diaspora*, 221–37. London: Zed Books.

Dialmy, Abdessamad. 2019. 'Transitional LGBT in Morocco: LGBT between Islam and Human Rights', in Hamza Tayebi and Jochen Lobah (eds), *Dynamics of Inclusion and Exclusion in the MENA Region: Minorities, Subalternity, and Resistance*, 249–72. Rabat: Hanns Seidel Foundation.

Dubois, J-C. and J-E. Marcel. 1970. 'Le transsexualisme', *Bordeaux médical* 4: 963–84.

Foerster, Maxime. 2018. *Elle ou lui?: Une histoire des transsexuels en France.* Paris: La Musardine.

Fortier, Corinne. 2017. 'Derrière le "voile islamique," de multiples visages. Voile, harem, chevelure: identité, genre et colonialisme', in Anne Castaing and Élodie Gaden (eds), *Écrire et penser le genre en contextes postcoloniaux*, 233–58. Bern: Peter Lang.

Fortier, Corinne. 2020. 'Troisième genre et transsexualité en pays d'islam', *Droit et cultures* 80. https://doi.org/10.4000/droitcultures.6763.

Gaye, Amadou. 1998. 'Bygone Days, Bygone Customs: An Era is Disappearing', *Ecrans d'Afrique* 23: 61–3.

Goldsworthy, Patricia. 2010. 'Images, Ideologies, and Commodities: The French Colonial Postcard Industry in Morocco', *Early Popular Visual Culture* 8 (2): 147–67.

Hage, J. Joris, Refaat B. Karim and Donald R. Laub Sr. 2007. 'On the Origin of Pedicled Skin Inversion Vaginoplasty: Life and Work of Dr Georges Burou of Casablanca', *Annals of Plastic Surgery* 59 (6): 723–9.

Hazan, Aurélie. 2012. 'Casablanca, la Mecque mythique des transsexuels', *Slate Afrique*, 3 October. Available online: https://archive.wikiwix.com/cache/index2. php?url=http%3A%2F%2Fwww.slateafrique.com%2F95531%2Fsociete-maroc-casablanca-la-mecque-des-transsexuels#federation=archive.wikiwix.com/ (accessed 29 August 2024).

Merlin, Virginie. 1974. 'L'Homme qui change le sexe', *Paris Match*, 1300.

Murray, David A.B. 2014. 'The (not so) Straight Story: Queering Migration Narratives of Sexual Orientation and Gendered Identity Refugee Claimants', *Sexualities* 17 (4): 451–71.

Prosser, Jay. 1998. *Second Skins: The Body Narratives of Transsexuality*. New York: Columbia University Press.

Prosser, Jay. 1999. 'Exceptional Locations: Transsexual Travelogues', in Kate More and Stephen Whittle (eds), *Reclaiming Genders: Transsexual Grammars at the Fin de Siècle*, 83–114. London: Bloomsbury Academic.

Reeser, Todd W. 2022. *Queer Cinema in Contemporary France*. Manchester: Manchester University Press.

Zabus, Chantal. 2019. 'Transing the Algerian Nation-State: Textual Transgender and Intersex from Pre-Independence to the Black Decade', *Acta neophilologica* 52 (1–2): 69–96.

Zaganiaris, Jean. 2012a. 'Sexualité et gouvernabilité des corps au Maroc: la question des transidentités au sein des productions artistiques marocaines', *Observatoire des Transidentités*, 16 March. https://www.observatoire-des-transidentites.com/tag/sexualite/ (accessed 29 August 2024).

Zaganiaris, Jean. 2012b. 'Transgenre et transsexualité dans la littérature marocaine de langue française', *Savoir/Agir* 2: 71–8.

Zaganiaris, Jean. 2013. *Queer Maroc: sexualités, genres et (trans)identités dans la littérature marocaine*. Paris: Des ailes sur un tracteur.

Chapter 3

DIASPORIC TRANS/FORMING IN DIRIYE OSMAN'S *THE BUTTERFLY JUNGLE*, AFDHERE JAMA'S *BEING QUEER AND SOMALI*, TOFIK DIBI'S *DJINN* AND LAMYA H'S *HIJAB BUTCH BLUES*

John C. Hawley

Queer East African writers instantiate Christopher Ian Foster's assertion that 'neoliberal globalization and the management of movement – immigration – cannot be disentangled from heteronationalist discourses' (2019: 123). These discourses offer a platform for these and similar writers to reflect on their identities in less fraught, imagined spaces that present difficulties of their own. Diriye Osman, for example, writes: 'Even as a child I knew I was going to be the teller of my own story in a world that repeatedly told me I had no right to do so' (2022: 33). Tofik Dibi similarly writes: 'It's ironic, really: however good I am with words, the thing I really want to speak about is stuck in my mouth' (2015: 116). Muslim writer and politician, Tofik Dibi, born in the Netherlands to Moroccan parents, embodies the broader implications of that entanglement, which demonstrably includes questions of religion shaping an individual's cultural identification(s), questions of binarism, of race and of political engagement. This is very much the case, as well, for the lives of Somali writer Afdhere Jama and Pakistani (apparently, though the home nation is never directly mentioned) 'Lamya H' in the United States and Canada: Islam is kept alive in their lives and plays a significant role in the pace of their coming out to themselves and others. The criticism that one read years ago, and still reads and sees play out in legislation in Africa and elsewhere – that the gay and lesbian 'lifestyle' is a western imposition on African identities, that those Africans who espouse such identities for themselves are inherently un-African or even anti-African – is now ensconced in many African nations as well as many Islamic nations and in the debates in all sorts of governments throughout the world, making it dangerous to remain in one's native land if one publicly expresses a sexuality that is non-normative or nonbinary. The former is sometimes tolerated if the gender roles reinscribe the traditional roles of male and female; the latter, though, is seen (in Africa and elsewhere) as outlandish and more destabilizing (cf. Törnkvist 2013).

Destabilization is actually central to the evolving notions of queer on the African continent and in, no doubt, an ongoing and mutually informing conversation between those in Africa and those in the diaspora. This chapter will discuss representative migrants who have gone abroad to escape (arguably un-African or un-Islamic) procrustean categories of gender and who understand their sexuality as one facet of their free personal expression of gender identity – identities that are experienced by many as shifting and open to further evolution, and who thereby join the challenging conversations on these topics in their adopted homes. But do the liberatory empowerments of neoliberal western nations themselves become procrustean inhibitions, too easily setting in stone expectations of conformity to comfortably outdated notions of binarism (a pink picket fence de-queering gays and lesbians, for example, and domesticating their formerly transgressive sexuality) – and do such straightjackets implicitly forbid members of the diaspora from challenging as queers the 'welcoming' gay and lesbian communities in which they have found a new home; that is, how much must such migrants compromise with local standards of gay and lesbian in order to express their sexuality, and how likely are they to serve as prophets (even missionaries) who queer those western notions? Meanwhile, from the other flank, some more conservative commentators argue that an inappropriately high number of individuals, especially in the younger generations, feel unnecessarily troubled by the whole notion of gender fluidity from queer activists who, so it is argued, push the young to fixate on themselves as questionably atypical in their 'male' or 'female' affect.

As Jama writes, '[n]o matter where we are[,] queer Somalis are fighting for our rights; even against western police who are not valuing our lives, or faith leaders who don't recognize ours' (2022: 166) – or, one might add, western thought police and cancel culture that recognize and accept the challenges of gay and lesbian lives, but only up to a point, and only if those lives are indisputably queer. Much the same sort of criticisms inevitably can be brought against the varying levels and kinds of normalizations of non-normative sexuality, even from within subcommunities that intend to be supportive. The tenuous nature of conditional acceptance necessarily takes a toll on minorities of various stripes who seek assimilation or integration, prompting some, out of exhaustion or defiance, to settle into migrant queer households and social networks.[1]

What role does citizenship and 'nation' play in this context, as a queer African migrant? In his perceptive analysis of *Fairytales for Lost Children* (2013), Christopher Ian Foster writes that one of Osman's characters 'tactically owns his "Somaliness", as a way to reassemble his other selves, shattered in and through the system of immigration and institutional and epistemic responses to desiring otherwise, back together'. He notes that 'this is not nationalist, given that he is exiled in part from Somali national culture due to his sexuality' (as are the other characters in *Fairytales*, whether in Kenya or London). In fact 'the Somaliness he utilizes is rather a queer "DIY process [do-it-yourself]", a temporal and spatial making a home of himself as a *practice* – rather than an achievement – of freedom' (Foster 2019: 136).[2] As Osman's protagonist proclaims, 'the Somali community [in London] is all about tradition and that sense of tradition comes with an air of secretiveness, suppression and Puritanism. I had no desire to live in secrecy anymore. I had experienced what it was like to lead an open, healthy, guilt-free life and I liked it' (Osman 2013: 110). For that character, setting up shop in a 'little Mogadishu' somewhere in London is not as attractive as something more individually curated by himself and by each queer migrant in his social circle.

Osman began *Fairytales* with a quote from Audre Lorde – 'When I dare to be powerful – to use my strength in the service of my vision – it becomes less and less important whether I am afraid'. If that conflict with one's inner fears suggests the motivation for the panoply of characters in *Fairytales* (scattershot throughout the book's tales as clouded expressions of various components of his own experiences in life and steps in self-knowledge), in *The Butterfly Jungle* (2022) that interior battle has taken several steps forward into uncharted territory, resulting in deeply personal howls of pain and a pushing through to celebration and defiance. The voice of this more recent novel is *more* queer, more confident, more self-revelatory, more playful – and yet, it is also more integrated and 'claimed' as one single spokesperson for the ongoing stories of characters who enter and exit his life. Diriye Osman begins the slim volume with an entry to which he signs his own name, describing himself as 'a map of new dreams; a cartography of a smooth-and-swift-with-the-scalpel imagination', and he thanks the reader for 'bearing witness to each bowel-deep-howl and hallelujah that follows' (2022: 1). 'Butterfly Jungle' is the nickname his protagonist, Migil, gives to the mental hospital to which he is assigned early in the story (59), a story that begins with the revelation that he is taking daily medication to help manage his schizoaffective disorder (because 'sometimes storytelling wasn't enough to stem the bowel-to-core sadness ... the struggle to connect to others stung one's consciousness in ways that were startling and hallucinatory').[3] Sometimes he feels imaginary ants crawling all over his skin; sometimes he sees an elephant wearing glass butterfly wings walking peacefully down the street. As he tells his boyfriend, 'people wax poetic about mental illness but it's not poetic. It's about finding a reprieve. A way to exist inside a body in revolt' (91). Migil is an individual creation, one might say, and not typical enough to be a spokesperson for any whole class of people – gays, queers, Somali in exile, those with similar psychological problems. He is complicated enough to force a reader to actually see him and hear him, and imagine seeing and imagine hearing no one else.

It would be an understatement to describe Migil's home as an ongoing confection: for example, explaining why he had not gone into central London in over six months, he notes that '[m]y family was black and queer [his mother is lesbian, his father is gay, they live with their partners and Migil], my doctor was black and queer, my psychiatrist was black and queer, my bosses were black and queer, my friends were black and queer' (74). Late in the book Migil interprets how this came about: 'I thought about how [my mother] and [my father] made a pact at the age of eighteen, which was, when they got married, about how they would build a queer family of their own: a small, self-designed universe predicated on kindness, joy and tenderness' (104). Since they apparently succeeded, they offer Migil hope that he, too, can expand this little group, and aid in its passive defiance of the 'heteronationalist' norms of London society. Nonetheless, as his father's husband tells him, 'I don't know anyone from our community who isn't caught up in the quagmire of psychic damage. We dress it up, perfume that *mierda*, say our prayers, medicalise religion' (74–5).

How one defines 'our community' in this context is debatable. Migil lives in a part of London where 'hipsters, halal housewives and hobos wandered up the high street, speaking in Somali, pidgin, patois and Polish'.[4] Many might feel uncomfortable in such a mish-mash of cultural expectations, but in describing it Migil is 'momentarily stunned by [his] tremendous good fortune' (57). He works as an assistant editor for an online magazine (*The Afrosphere*, the name, coincidentally, of Osman's own blog) and an assistant manager of a clothes shop (Neon Gumbo), and he hosts a club night of 500 people in Peckham that he calls Anima Kingdom. That night is one of freedom, described a bit like a scene drawn from *Paris is Burning*, but more pointedly postcolonial:

> This was an opportunity for performativity and potent blackety-black blackness. The club night became a haven for men both young and old who were coming into their own, flexing their femininity while paying homage to their respective cultures. So the Somali brothers wore dirac—sheer dresses embroidered with mermaids and honeysuckle—their hands adorned with henna filigrees, lips painted the colour of coral stones. The Nigerian bredrin came draped in gold and lace wedding gowns, and my Jamaican brothers rocked quadrille skirts accented with platform boots and bomb beads. It was pure cultural pluralism and everybody served it up straight, no chaser.

(66)

One of his friends is Kayd, a bit older than Migil's parents but eventually someone who becomes Migil's lover. Kayd 'engineered his [own] life so that he could sit quietly and marvel at the minarets, museums and ruins located in his memory, which was rooted in ravishing Mogadishu, Somalia, even though his body was based in Peckham, South London'. Given Migil's glocal imaginary and countercultural twang, it is perhaps surprising to hear Migil describe Kayd as 'too much like [him]: too gay, too Somali, too Muslim' (61). Admitting that he 'initially couldn't see the value of this man', he goes on to conclude that 'he was my mirror and I refused to acknowledge my reflection'. Reflecting on this 'mirror' image, he recalls his father's description of the Somali Civil War and the effect it had had on all the people, pushing them into 'a decades-long psychosis that shows no sign of abating'. The effects are clear in his life and in all those he knows: 'we circle the globe, settling in Minnesota and Mumbai and Mombasa, attempting to shake off our stigmatized shadows, failing to realise that a shadow cannot be shed' (62). It would seem that this describes not just queer Somalis, but all migrant Somalis, and by implication, most of the others, from whatever culture, who populate Migil's daily life. The traditional notion of 'nation' faces significant challenges in many contemporary countries, regardless of their apparent economic stability. Which members of any of these societies actually define the nation? *How* non-normative will those nations continue allowing the non-normatives' lives to be?

But *Butterfly Jungle* arises from a particular subcommunity, and is housed in a very specific and unusual individual. Indeed, all of the books under discussion in this chapter embody an insight that Osman's Migil offers readers: 'for my people, storytelling was a portal to something primal and sacred: it was how we got closer to the softest, most holy parts of our humanity' (98). Osman's work operates in the naturalistic tradition of Hubert Selby, Jr.'s *Last Exit to Brooklyn* (1964), William S. Burrough's *Naked Lunch* (1959) and Malcolm Lowry's *Under the Volcano* (1947), with their embodiment of altered consciousness, but Osman writes with a lightness and sense of optimism that those earlier works do not exhibit. Migil's world may be small and a fragile creation, which he knows better than anyone, but in the book's closing words he thanks God for his life. One senses that it is through writing stories such as *Fairytales for Lost Children* and *The Butterfly Jungle* that Osman himself is clearing a space for agency, defiance and occasional leaps of infectious imagination, inviting his readers to step outside their own trained monotony and conformism, and to step more bravely into the jungles in which they are living.

He did this in a different way in *We Once Belonged to the Sea* (2018), the novel he published between *Fairytales* and *Butterfly*. He said he wrote this to portray 'a queer black female artist in her prime who couldn't care less about anyone's approval, naysayers be damned' (Osman 2017). She is countered in the novel by her protégé, whom Osman describes as 'a talented teenaged hijabi punk who finds herself grappling with her morality as she edges towards her creative goals'. For her, there is a tension between 'her desire to become a great artist and the Islamic faith which has sustained her during moments of self-doubt and trauma'. Curiously, he says he set the context as a challenge to himself as a writer, relishing, he says, 'the thrill of literary androgyny', and asserting that this is a book that is 'not anchored in autobiographical details'. One might quibble over how to define an anchor, but it seems clear that the novel is dealing with issues very similar to those in *Butterfly Jungle*. He did, after all, write that it is a book about 'the intersection between art, faith, trauma and ambition'. The fact that the central character is queer seems to have slipped his mind in this summation, unless he files that under 'trauma'. One can imagine, without much difficulty, that Osman struggle(s/d) with the tension, as he perceived it, between Islam (and its consolations) and his own artistic ambitions, just as his artist/protagonist's protégé does in *We Once Belonged to the Sea*.

In writing a novel without a male voice, Osman is signalling a desire to represent for his readers a broader cross-section of the migrant queer community. Afdhere Jama's book is less imaginative because it is an accounting of the lives of actual queer Somalis whom he has met in his travels, a demonstration of the affirmation of his book's dedication 'to all the young people who grow up thinking they are alone'. His first chapter is entitled 'Queer', his second 'Somali' and his third 'Muslim', clearly setting the terms for what follows. For him, there are various ways of being queer, being Somali, being Muslim and shifting contexts determine which of the three terms dominates the other two. As he acknowledges,

> My life in the United States as a Muslim is a very different life than my life would have been in Somalia. It would also be different if I was an Iranian immigrant, and I came from a country where the death penalty currently applies to people like myself. But it would also be very different if I were a Turkish immigrant, as Turkey hasn't had any anti-homosexuality laws since the mid-1800s.
>
> (Jama 2022: 39)

Osman and Jama write as Somalis, but Jama notes that 'tribalism has hurt me more than homophobia. It hurts women more than sexism' (34). In many ways mirroring the daily life of Osman's characters in London, Jama writes that 'the influences of African, Arab, Indian, and European were part of our lives. They were part of what made us Somali because we consumed them regularly' (29). He interviews queer Somali Muslims in Mogadishu, Baidoa, Bardera, Brava, Kismayu, Hargeisa, Shalaamboot, Nairobi, Cape Town, Jeddah, Dubai, Mumbai, Oslo, Paris, London, Geneva, Toronto, Seattle, Minneapolis, Washington, D.C. and Atlanta, concluding that 'no matter where we are[,] queer Somalis are fighting for our rights; even against western police who are not valuing our lives, or faith leaders who don't recognize ours. … The future is here' (166).

That future is more obvious in *Djinn* and *Hijab Butch Blues*. Serendipitously, the authors of both autobiographies use 'djinn' in the same way, as this sometimes-seen-sometimes-hidden powerful essence that they only gradually acknowledge as part of themselves – their queerness. In Dibi's accounting, it is the thing that cannot be named, let alone embraced, but also cannot be denied. As he writes, '[h]ere in Morocco … [djinns] can be good or bad. … It's said that people who talk to themselves out loud, who curse for no apparent reason, who are always sad, or who are plagued by strange thoughts are possessed by a djinn', concluding ominously, 'I think strange things. I think that there's a bad one inside of me. It's just like that girl from *The Exorcist*. That's how it feels: like a bad spirit that makes me think forbidden, dirty things and wants to act those things out' (Dibi [2015] 2021: 33). And when Lamya H., pseudonymous author of *Hijab Butch Blues*, is in seventh grade, and some girls in her class ask the teacher why the teacher wears the hijab when the class is made up of girls, the teacher responds: 'It's not women that I cover my hair from, it's jinn' (H. 2003: 36). Listening to the teacher tell a story about a girl their age who had been possessed by a jinn when she was naked in the shower, Lamya grows quiet, tries to tune out her teacher's voice and starts to feel like she is 'floating above the classroom, flying like a jinn and listening to this story from a distance, terrified and numb' (37). The light-skinned popular Arab girls in her class shun her because she is from the 'curry people' (35) and she asks herself: 'Do I look scary? Am I a jinn?' (46). Is she invisible because she wears the hijab, because she is brown or because she is a jinn, or is there some other reason? By the time she is in graduate school in New York, she reports that her family in the United States have floated the idea that 'gay people might be possessed by jinn'

(250), but she has learned on her own that 'they're just like us, jinn … not creatures we need to fear' because 'difference should not mean scary; difference should not mean less than' (59), and much like Tofik Dibi she concludes that 'I need to stop hating jinn. And then I can stop hating myself?' (60). Dibi and Lamya tell stories of how they came to the recognition reached by those in any minority in any society when they grow tired of accepting their lesser status; difference, for them, becomes something to celebrate, to proclaim; derogatory terms are reclaimed and shouted from the rooftops.

Lamya reports that her first coherent memory is of her father leaving, and her second coherent memory is of the rest of the family (her, her brother and mom) leaving to join their father – 'we leave everything and everyone we know to join him' (219). Her sense of abandonment is strong, prompting her to identify with the Qur'an's story of Yusuf (Joseph), abandoned by his brothers. Her raw sadness defines her social life ('I've spent decades living on the brink of this loss – of my family, of my friends, my Muslim community'), and explains why she flirts for a long time only with straight girls – 'their leaving was inevitable, so I never had to let them in' (227). Abandoned, yes, but importantly, in the Qur'an Yusuf is eventually triumphant and able to extend an olive branch to his brothers, and that is the vector of Lamya's own coming out process. She regrets that, for some of her family and other acquaintances, 'it's completely outside the realm of their imagination that it feels natural for me to love both God and this woman I'm bringing to meet them' (250) – but, the point of her memoir is that in fact she does find it natural now. In a move that some readers may find outrageous, throughout the memoir Lamya implicitly compares herself to important figures in the Qur'an (and Bible) – Maryam (Mary), Musa (Moses), Muhammad, Nuh (Noah), Yusuf, Yunus (Jonah), Hajar (Hagar) – finally identifying most clearly with Hajar, and asking Allah: 'will You raise a village, a community around me like You did for Hajar? An ummah of my loves, this family that I am building with this woman, with this chosen family of Billy, of Manal, of Zu, of my queer Muslim friends?' (260). By book's end she still claims to be 'a walking target and visibly different – a jinn, seen but unseen, a receptable for the world's violence, ignorance, fear and harm' (271). Now identifying with Yunus, she sees her pseudonym as *her* whale, her protection that keeps her in the fight, writing to fend off 'racists, sexists, homophobes, transphobes, Islamophobes' (277).[5] 'This', she concludes, 'is the world fourteen-year-old me couldn't even begin to imagine. I'm already here' (281). A further implication in this comparison is with the purpose of the whale – the Lord will not allow Yunus to evade his role as prophet; the whale is provided as the magic carpet to an unwanted responsibility in society.

At twenty-three she had mused: 'If Allah isn't a man or a woman, maybe Allah is trans' (71), and had made the choice to step away from conversations where that concept was ignored – God as genderqueer, as nonbinary, as trans. She allows herself to ponder the implications of this transgressive way of thinking, and does so against the background of Adam and Eve, noting that 'among the legacy of their punishments to all of their descendants, is the consciousness, the rigidity of gender' (73). This is a rigidity that 'follows [her] like a punishment everywhere, across oceans and continents' (77), a transcultural straightjacket. She finally finds herself rebelling against any further pigeonholing by others. When a male friend tells her she would 'make a beautiful trans man' she bristles with the acknowledgement that she (that is her chosen pronoun) definitely does not want that, but she also feels 'so politically aligned with womanhood and yet hate[s] inhabiting it' (81). She finds herself in uncharted waters, 'as if the only way to be trans is to transition to a binary gender, as if I can't exist as I have been, in some space in between or beyond, using she or they pronouns and seething when people call me a woman and laughing when people tell me I should transition' (82). Instead, she returns to her religious roots for her answer in response to recurrent protean calls for some clearly legible gender stability:[6]

> This God, who teaches us that we can be both and neither and all and beyond and capable of multiplicities and expansiveness. Nonbinary, genderqueer, They, this God that is the God, my God, my Allah. Who created the world and created language and created the first person, Adam, this first person who was man and woman and neither and both and not a mistake, never a mistake. Like me.
>
> (83)

Lamya's story finds many echoes in Tofik Dibi's personal account. During his time as a member of the Dutch parliament (2006–12), Tofik Dibi was anything but invisible, but he was living in the closet, haunted by his djinn, admitting that 'defending a freedom that I don't allow myself is a way to clear my conscience, for not having the strength to be a mirror for people like myself' (Dibi 2015: 96). For a long time in his life, especially as he took on the public life of a politician, he saw this 'djinn' inside him as an underdog, an unlikely challenger to his Moroccan heritage (also, one might argue, one of his 'djinns'):

> *They* [society] would take away my roots and my religion and only see *it* [my homosexuality]. Where does that leave me? *It* has been nothing more than wandering, tipsy, high and numb, from empty encounter to empty encounter, looking for Allah knows what. *It* is bruises and bloody lips. *It* is the eternal confessional box. *It* has only caused confusion and sadness. I'd rather hold on to the sound of a teapot held high in the air, from which a stream of tea lands in the middle of colorful glasses; I prefer to hold on to the serene peace that comes over me when my mother puts on a DVD of Koran recitations on Friday. *It* can't compete with the moment when I enter the house that my father was born in— ochre-yellow loam with a straw roof, in the Sahara—and his sisters pour out a bottle of perfume on my brothers and me as a sign of happiness and hospitality. *It* can't coexist. I have to choose.
>
> (77)

Looking back on his subsequent evolution to more complete self-revelation, Dibi asserts that this came through his reading of the Koran and (in another example of individual contexts as determinative) through his love of action comics, among other unlikely sources. Among the multiple homophobic voices that he hears as he matures are his favourite rappers, whose use of 'faggot' clearly sends the message that he always hears when that word is spoken: 'I just need to pray, then *it* [the djinn, homosexuality] will stay away. … I don't want them to think that I'm not a real Muslim. I am' (41).

Some Muslims might dispute Dibi's confident assertion of his credentials as a true Muslim, but it certainly echoes Diriye Osman's understanding of his own place within the religion, and the place held by characters in the eyes of Islam – even if it seems somewhat Sufi in its (heretical?) elevation of spiritualism and even ecstasy, over doctrine. Speaking of Migil's family, Osman writes that

> this is a family that is decidedly Afrofabulist in their approach to their spiritual practice as Muslims. Migil's parents delight in the thrill and vigour and whimsy of their faith, which is anchored by a sense of cheekiness and lived-pleasure. They do not see Islam as a spiritual practice that has excluded any of them. They see Islam as an expansive, vibrant lushness that can accommodate all their quirks and fears and joy. This is a group of characters for whom Islam is as malleable as melted gold. It is a universe shorn of the judgement of overly pious Pollyannas or petty-minded cynicism.
>
> (Osman 2023)

Tofik Dibi's Islam is not quite that latitudinarian, perhaps, but he is open to a broader interpretation of scripture: 'Say what you will about Mohammed', he writes, 'at least he isn't afraid to ask questions' (Dibi 2015: 41). Dibi worries that to do otherwise would be to become someone unengaged with *true* faith. For Dibi, to ask questions fearlessly is an act of putting faith in Allah's providence and wisdom. 'Most of our understanding of Islam', he writes, 'comes from religious scholars, who have studied the Arabic in which the Koran is written. Who knows if they got it right? If I blindly follow a scholar's explanation, simply because everyone else does, without doing any research myself, who am I really worshiping?' (42). Underscoring his skepticism over such authorities' honest interpretation of scripture, he scoffs that 'one of the signs of the end of our existence, according to one of them, is "men in dresses". He means drag queens' (42). Questioning 'authoritative' interpretations suggests an embrace of individual interpretation, which is traditionally seen as risky, illegal and/or sinful. But it seems clear that the unspoken djinn is here asserting a strong voice, seeking an avenue of escape from the assaults on the young boy's burgeoning recognition of this *verboten* something, looking desperately for a way out of the lamp.

As a boy, Dibi finds clearer guidance from the X-Men than from religious authorities because 'underneath all of the adventure is a story of how to deal with being feared and hated when you are different. … I learn a lot from the way the X-Men deal with being seen as "the other"' (43). That mishmash of otherness had become increasingly *de rigueur* in Holland after 1980, the year of his birth. Born in Holland to Moroccan parents, his playground chatter was in Dutch and Moroccan, with a little Surinamese and Turkish and American slang thrown in. Finding himself in this cosmopolitan stew is a daily adventure. Sounding a bit like Osman's Migil, Dibi writes that '[i]t's crowded inside me: the Netherlands, Morocco, Islam, *it* [queerness], and *them* [society's censoring over-voice]. They're elbowing each other, stepping on each other's feet, pointing the finger at each other. It's hard to keep them away from each other or to bring them together' (44). At this point in his life he identifies most, when playing Super Nintendo, with a female character, but always plays as a male character, worrying that 'if there is a hierarchy of what's haram [forbidden or unlawful], I'd be on top' (46). Much like the family that Osman's Migil has found himself in, in Peckham, Dibi yearns for a world similar to the one Migil describes when recalling *Paris in Burning* – new families forged by outsiders. Dibi sees it happening among his generation, the children of guest workers where cultural and religious differences carve out the possibility of other transgressive moves – 'a headscarf on stilettos. Freckles with frizzy hair. Not just double, but triple citizenship' (92). Dibi draws his inspiration from individuals such as Irshad Manji, a lesbian Muslim with whom he is on a panel while still closeted ('I've been looking for so long since that glimpse in *My Beautiful Laundrette*, and finally someone who's truly free is sitting in front of me. ... She seems happy. How is that possible?' [101]). It does take time, but he recognizes through his secret life that 'monsters are created when people don't allow themselves to have a face and a voice' (130). Time passes, and by book's end he is finally asserting that even if there were some magic way to become heterosexual, he 'wouldn't do it. To dispel *it* would mean to dispel Allah' (129). He seems to have forged an identity that is Dutch, Moroccan, Islamic and queer, though, of course, many Muslims have condemned him, and had done so even before he made that amalgam (cf. May 2012).But Dibi pushed back, issuing a fatwa of his own on the eve of the tenth anniversary of the 9/11 attack in New York City.[7]

I have argued elsewhere that 'unlike odyssey, sojourn and travel, that provide amusement, relaxation, and even an objectification of the foreign destination, a different and ironic agency is offered by migration, diaspora, and exile. One gains a voice while losing a rooted identity. In the process, the best of such writers move from lyric self-expression to communal prophecy' (Hawley 2011: 154). Nuruddin Farah writes, from exile, that 'one of the pleasures of living away from home is that you become the master of your destiny, you avoid the constraints and limitations of your past and, if need be, create an alternative life for yourself' (quoted in Glad 1990: viii). V. J. Vassanji, on the other hand, writes that, '[a]lthough there is no denying the gains brought about by emigration, with each move – from India to Africa, within Africa, from Africa to North America – we fragmented our stories, lost parts of our history, and carried the broken-up remains like a peddler's items in a sack' (2002: 26). With those remains, though they are broken-up, queer African migrants in Europe and America are, ironically, moving from lyric self-expression to communal prophecy and 'writing back' to their African homelands, serving as prophets of wholeness and drawing silent inspiration from Ernest Renan's ironic but prescient observation that 'getting its history wrong is part of being a nation' ([1882] 1992: 12). If those lies push Africans away from their homelands, from new perches those exiles challenge their places of birth to see a more complete and honest picture of themselves, and what they can become.

As this brief survey suggests, the amount of queer writing coming from African writers is growing (see Fekurumoh 2023; Hawley 2017; Obi-Young 2017), and much of it comes from Muslims. Some of these authors interpret 'queer' via a prior pre-diasporic cultural lens, for example the djinn. It remains to be seen how this will develop, and how prophetic these writers are. Organizations, such as Maruf (http://www.maruf.eu) providing a platform for queer Muslims in the Netherlands, will monitor the progress. As Osman suggests, 'if my first book, *Fairytales for Lost Children*, explored the desire to attain freedom from the tyranny of doublethink and oppression, *The Butterfly Jungle* simply asks, "What now? What does one do with all this newfound freedom"?' (Osman 2023). It would be encouraging to learn that the problem of too much freedom was the problem in most African nations, but that is certainly not the case. This chapter focussed on the migrant experience for that reason, underscoring the felt need among queer Africans to step outside their continent, if they are to find a supportive community for non-normative sexual expression that does not rely on the binary system. Other chapters in this volume provide the wider context on the continent, and some no doubt suggest fresh ways of conceiving of sexual expression, and more joyful communities of liberation within, in many cases, an entrenched larger social system of reactionary denials of the need for such communities.

Kit Heyam concludes her account of trans people in history with this clarion cry:

> A trans gaze is what allows us to accept and take seriously the fact that a person's gender can be a spiritual or sexual experience, in a way we can't empathise with – or, indeed, that what looks like gender sometimes isn't at all. ... The simple precept of *knowing people on their own terms* can transform more than history; it also has the power to liberate us in the present.
>
> (Heyam 2022: 226)

In his travels, Afdhere Jama meets a Somali imam who is now the first openly gay Imam in Australia, Nur Warsame (see BBC News 2018). Once he came out, he was forbidden from entering any mosques. He lives in hope. Jama argues, with his book of interviews, that gay history matters, that gay Somalis matter, regardless of where they are now living. 'Who knew', he writes, that there were 'gay religious leaders in our faiths like Caliph Al-Amin, or lesbian queens in our national histories like Queen Arawelo, or openly gay people in our cities like those described by Hamdi Suldan, Ali Abdulle, or Hadiyo Him'ale?' (Jama 2022: 43). The future seems better for such people, going forward, in the west and eventually, in Somalia and the rest of Africa. 'Now we have these histories', writes Jama, 'and now no one can deny them. No one can deny us any longer' (43).

Notes

1　James Penney writes that 'there's no such thing as (a particular) "transgressive sexuality". As a result, the injunction to (be) queer tends to have perversely normalizing effects. This is the case, for example, with the various queer vanguardisms that wish to normalize promiscuity, inveigh against same-sex marriage, or impose regimes or aesthetically-conceived forms of alternative social being' (Penney 2014: 6). Penney's position, of course, is that 'the identification of class antagonism places the queer on the side of what we used to call the bourgeoisie' (4). I have suggested (Hawley 2014: 148) that there is no one 'correct' way to be genderqueer.

2   Much as I have argued in 'In Transition' (Hawley 2017).

3   Defining schizoaffective disorder, see Icahn School of Medicine, Mount Sinai Hospital 2023; and Royal College of Psychiatrists 2023; and on the intersection of 'gender dysphoria' and schizophrenia, see Myers 2022.

4   Other languages represented in the novel include Bengali, Chinese, French, Kiswahili, Portuguese, Spanish, Sheng, Turkish and Yoruba.

5   See the work of the Somali-Norwegian, lesbian activist writer who writes under the pseudonym Amal Aden and was the recipient of the Amnesty Prize of Amnesty International for Norway in 2012. See Wikipedia 2024.

6   Kit Heyam makes a compelling argument against what they (Heyam's chosen pronoun) describe as a narrow understanding of trans: this 'begins in childhood, with the trans person articulating their early, stable sense that they were "in the wrong body", and conforming to stereotypes "opposite" to those of the gender they were assigned at birth. After a long and traumatic struggle with themselves, they come out, medically transition to male or female, and live a conventional, gender-conforming and heterosexual life' (2022: 11). But these stories, while appropriate for many, prefer to leave out 'fluidity, non-binary identities, play, external motivations, ambiguity. … [F]or one thing, not everyone … understands themselves as *having* a core, stable internal self that remains the same at all times' (25). 'Being "really" a man, a woman, a non-binary person or any other gender isn't incompatible with fluidity, situationality, ambiguity or creativity' (26). In their historical accounts, Heyam wishes to show 'the *moveability* of gender' (28). Also cf. Bowers (2023).

7   'Dibi's "Final Fatwa", launched 10 years after the attacks on the World Trade Center in New York City, calls on Muslims to reject all fatwas issued by extremists and to reclaim their religion' (Cowan 2011).

References

BBC News. 2018. 'How Australia's first gay imam is "saving lives"'. YouTube. Available online: https://www.youtube.com/watch?v=U6bLwRmF8EE (accessed 30 August 2024).

Bowers, Marci L. 2023. 'What decades of providing trans health care have taught me', *New York Times*, 1 April. Available online: https://www.nytimes.com/2023/04/01/opinion/trans-healthcare-law.html (accessed 1 July 2023).

Cowan, Roberta. 2011. 'Dutch MP issues fatwa to free Muslims from extremism', Reuters, 10 September 2011. Available online: https://www.reuters.com/article/us-dutch-fatwa/dutch-mp-issues-fatwa-to-free-muslims-from-extremism-idUSTRE7891VH20110910 (accessed 31 July 2023).

Dibi, Tofik. (2015) 2021. *Djinn*. Translated by Nicolaas P. Barr. Albany: State University of New York Press.

Fekurumoh, Sybil. 2023. '25 Queer Books from African and African Diasporan Writers', Afrocritik, May 2023. Available online: https://www.afrocritik.com/25-queer-books-from-african-and-african-diasporan-writers/ (accessed 29 July 2023).

Foster, Christopher Ian. 2019. *Conscripts of Migration: Neoliberal Globalization, Nationalism, and the Literature of New African Diasporas*. Jackson: University of Mississippi Press.

Glad, J. 1990. *Literature in Exile*. Durham, NC: Duke University Press.

Gorayshi, Azeen. 2023. 'Landmark study shows higher suicide risk for transgender people', *New York Times*, 27 June 2023. Available online: https://brittlepaper.com/2017/12/dear-paper-queer-literature-trend-africa/ (accessed 1 July 2023).

H, Lamya. 2023. *Hijab Butch Blues: A Memoir*. New York: Dial Press.

Hawley, John C. 2011. 'The Bittersweet Taste of Exile as Muse', in Marianne David and Javier Muñoz-Basols (eds), *Defining and Re-Defining Diaspora*, 145–57. Freeland, UK: Inter-Disciplinary Press.

Hawley, John C. 2014. 'Trans Autobiographies as Performative Utterances', in Chantal Zabus and David Coad (eds), *Transgender Experience: Place, Ethnicity, and Visibility*, 137–52. New York and London: Routledge.

Hawley, John C. 2017. 'In Transition: Self-Expression in Recent African LGBTIQ Narratives', *JALA: Journal of the African Literature Association* 11 (1): 120–34.

Heyam, Kit. 2022. *Before We Were Trans: A New History of Gender*. New York: Hachette Book Group.

Icahn School of Medicine, Mount Sinai Hospital. 2023. 'Schizoaffective Disorder'. Available online: https://www.mountsinai.org/health-library/diseases-conditions/schizoaffective-disorder (accessed 26 July 2023).

Jama, Afdhere. 2022. *Being Queer and Somali*. Self-published. Las Vegas, Nevada.

Manji, Irshad. 2011. *Allah, Liberty and Love: The Courage to Reconcile Faith and Freedom*. New York: Atria Books.

May, Clifford D. 2012. 'Muslims Attacked!', *National Review*, 12 January. Available online: https://www.nationalreview.com/2012/01/muslims-attacked-clifford-d-may/ (accessed 31 July 2023).

Myers, Sarah A. 2022. 'When Gender Dysphoria and Schizophrenia Overlap', *Psychology Today*, 17 October 2022. Available online: https://www.psychologytoday.com/us/blog/living-outlier/202210/when-gender-dysphoria-and-schizophrenia-overlap (accessed 26 July 2023).

Obi-Young, Otosirieze. 2017. 'Dear Mr. Brittle: queer literature in Africa is not a trend, has always existed', Brittle Paper, 18 December. Available online: https://brittlepaper.com/2017/12/dear-paper-queer-literature-trend-africa/ (accessed 1 July 2023).

Osman, Diriye. 2013. *Fairytales for Lost Children*. London: Team Angelica Publishing.

Osman, Diriye. 2017. 'The Thrill of Literary Androgyny', The Afrosphere. Available online: https://www.diriyeosman.com/post/2017/09/02/the-thrill-of-literary-androgyny (accessed 31 July 2023).

Osman, Diriye. 2018. *We Once Belonged to the Sea*. London: Team Angelica Publishing.

Osman, Diriye. 2022. *The Butterfly Jungle*. London: Team Angelica Publishing.

Osman, Diriye. 2023. 'The Spiritual Lives of Queer Afrofabulists', The Afrosphere. Available online: https://www.diriyeosman.com/post/the-spiritual-lives-of-queer-afrofabulists (accessed 5 July 2023).

Penney, James. 2014. *After Queer Theory: The Limits of Sexual Politics*. London: Pluto Press.

Renan, Ernest. [1882] 1992. *Qu'est-ce qu'une nation?* Translated by Ethan Rundell. Paris: Presses-Pocket.

Royal College of Psychiatrists. 2023. 'Schizoaffective Disorder'. Available online: https://www.rcpsych.ac.uk/mental-health/problems-disorders/schizoaffective-disorder (accessed 26 July 2023).

Törnkvist, Ann. 2013. 'Death threats for lesbian Somali-Norwegian', *The Local*, 3 July. Available online: https://www.thelocal.no/20130703/death-threats-for-lesbian-somali-norwegian-activist-pride-lgbt-rainbow#:~:text=Somali%2DNorwegian%20author%20Amal%20Aden,of%20being%20Muslim%20and%20gay (accessed 1 July 2023).
Vassanji, V. J. 2002. 'Canada and Me: Finding Ourselves', in Westwood Creative Artists and the Dominion Institute, *Passages: Welcome Home to Canada*, 14–33. Toronto: Doubleday.
Wikipedia. 2024. s.v. 'Amal Aden'. Available online: https://en.wikipedia.org/wiki/Amal_Aden (accessed 29 July 2023).

WEST AFRICA

Chapter 4

'DARE SPEAK THEIR NAME': THE POETRY OF LOGAN FEBRUARY

Chris Dunton

Introduction

Between 2017 and 2019 the Nigerian poet Logan February published three chapbooks (small collections of poems) in the United States, namely *How to Cook a Ghost*, *Painted Blue with Saltwater* and *Mannequin in the Nude*. During this period another chapbook was announced as forthcoming, to be titled *The Bodies of Dead Boys*; in the event the poem so named appeared in *Painted Blue with Saltwater* and will be the key text for the final section of this chapter. In 2021 came the publication of *Fuckboys* (another challenging title), a bilingual edition, English and Spanish; this substantial collection contains forty-six poems, half of which are reprinted from the second and third of the US-published chapbooks, half of which appear in none of the latter. The very able and imaginative translations were carried out by the Argentinian poet and translator Ezequiel Zaidenwerg. *Fuckboys* has a Preface by Argentinian author Mariana Spada, which says little about February's subject-matter or thematic concerns, but which is alive to their very distinctive poetic voice. In 2024 February took up a one-year DAAD artists' residency in Berlin, and this was marked by the publication of *Mental Voodoo* (2024), a substantial bilingual (English/German) collection of around 200 poems, many of which had not appeared in the US-published chapbooks. The translator of most of the poems was Christian Filips and the volume also includes a substantial interview with February by Filips, which focusses especially on the poet's relationship with the Yoruba language and belief system (see Filips 2024).

The title of Spada's 'Prologo' ('Preface') to *Fuckboys* is 'A kind of mental voodoo'.[1] This might suggest that her approach is to exoticize February's work, but it stems rather from the fact that her starting-point was her reading the poem 'Stillbirth, Yemoja' (in February 2018: 41), Yemoja being a Yoruba goddess who also features in *voudoun*, and her being struck by February's mental agility and verbal dexterity. She goes on to speak of 'a voice that is rigorous (but not solemn), lucid (but not monotonous), and above all extraordinarily original', a voice that is poised between 'the visceral and the sardonic' (Spada 2021: 7–8).

As detailed below, February self-identifies as nonbinary; hence the use of 'their' as possessive in the title of this chapter. Before proceeding, a note on that title, with apologies for drawing upon a poem by the execrable Lord Alfred Douglas for the title of my chapter.[2] It used to be the case that LGBTQ+ relationships and same-sex sexual practices were greeted by African writers with a sustained outburst of silence.[3] Nowadays, as Lindsey Green-Simms has remarked in an essay entitled 'The Emergent Queer', that silence 'is not only eroding but is turning into a polyphony' (2017: 141). From Nigeria alone over the last twenty years there have been LGBTQ+-themed novels by Jude Dibia, Unoma Azuah, Chinelo Okparanta, Elnathan John and Akwaeke Emezi, amongst others, as well as several volumes of edited testimonies. Notable among the latter is *Blessed Body: The Secret Lives of Lesbian, Gay, Bisexual and Transgender Nigerians* (2016), edited by Unoma Azuah. From this period, too, beginning in 2017, have come the four collections of poetry by Logan February cited above.

This is despite the fact that on 13 January 2014 a law was approved in Nigeria that burdened the country with some of the most homophobic legislation in Africa.[4] Though in some instances a publication appeared not 'despite the fact' but 'on account of the fact', as with *Blessed Body*, which was produced under the aegis of the Nigerian NGO Queer Alliance and was put together explicitly as a response to the legislation of 2014. Chinelo Okparanta's novel *Under the Udala Trees* also falls into this category, a novel that resonates with E. M. Forster's dream of 'a life to come' and one in which the Author's Note that concludes the novel begins:

> On January 7, 2014, Nigeria's president, Goodluck Jonathan, signed into law a bill criminalizing same-sex relationships and the support of these relationships, making these offenses punishable by up to fourteen years in prison. In the northern states, the punishment is death by stoning. The novel attempts to give Nigeria's marginalized LGBTQ citizens a more powerful voice, and a place in our nation's history.
>
> (Okparanta 2015: 325)

As things stand, LGBTQ+ authors – or authors who produce LGBTQ+-themed work – and who are based in Nigeria operate under severe constraints and at great risk to their well-being. In an interview with fellow novelist Elnathan John, Jude Dibia[5] records:

> I left Nigeria in 2014 when our country came up with the law that supposedly was created to forbid same-sex marriages. However, what it really was is an attack on the LGBTI community as a whole. And what worried me was that this law encouraged mob actions against LGBTI people … when I am out of the country I can take a deep breath and look from outside into Nigeria more objectively. So it is easier for me to write from outside but I left the country on my own accord, which makes it a self-imposed exile.
>
> (Dibia 2021)

Also relevant in this context is *Here Again Now*, a novel by the Nigerian British author Okechukwu Nzelu, the chief focus of which is on how to dare to speak, to express love. Two of the central characters are Achike and Eneke, Nigerian British and gay. At one point the latter comments to the former: "'What's Nigeria got to do with us? … You know what I mean. They hate us there'" (Nzelu 2022: 24). A little later, after mention of a homophobic lynching, Eneke confirms: "'Sometimes I don't want to be a Nigerian'" and Achike replies "'I *am* Nigerian … I just wish they didn't make it so hard'" (73).

On the question of self-identification, in the interview with John cited above, Dibia comments: 'I frown at the term "gay writer" or "gay author" in describing me. You won't go to a doctor or business manager and introduce them as "a gay doctor" or "gay business manager" would you?' (Dibia 2021).

Dibia's strategy contrasts with that of Logan February, whose candour is total. Whilst February was Nigeria-based when their early poetry appeared, they are now based in the United States, where they are currently a graduate student and instructor in creative writing at Purdue University. In an interview with the present author, February has commented on this and on the thorny issue of Afropolitanism as follows: 'Being a queer person, I often question the value and cost of identifying with and caring for Nigeria. It does feel particularly true and comforting to think of myself as an "African of the world", so perhaps I am more Afropolitan in spirit than I had known' (personal communications, February with Dunton, 18 February 2022 to 7 August 2022).

Acknowledging that February's experience straddles two very different cultural *milieus* – Nigeria and the United States – and with reference to their publishing history, one recognizes the importance to them of being outside the cultural mainstream, until, that is, incorporation occurs (if it does occur – for example, through the production of an academic essay on their work). In approaching February's poetry, one should bear in mind the influence of tantra; the importance of performance;[6] the significance of the poet's Yoruba heritage; the broad context of modernism within which the poetry can be located and the possibility of specific influences; and what Daniel Kane refers to as the 'confessional impulse' of a poet such as Sylvia Plath.[7] Thus, as with any poet whose work is as rich and complex as that of February, a number of avenues are open along which to interpret the corpus and ideally one should navigate these avenues simultaneously; the present chapter is not so bold, hence the focus of each of its sections on a specific approach to February's work.

Afropolitanism

Two quotations from Helon Habila provide an ideal starting point for this section. In 'Elegy for Pius', he observes: 'Because we did not feel at home at home / We travelled the world' (Habila 2020: 131). And one of the epigraphs to his novel *Travellers*, taken from Theodore Adorno's *Minima Moralia: Reflections from a*

Damaged Life, reads: 'It is part of morality not to be at home in one's home' (Habila 2019: [iii]). The purpose of this section is to establish how relevant to February's work is the concept/experience of Afropolitanism, and more particularly to establish the extent to which its relevance is surpassed by February's own highly distinctive take on displacement. This is not the forum to embark on a discussion of the Afropolitanism debate, which, since the coining of the term by Taiye Selasi in 2005, has often remarked the dangers of fetishizing or claiming too much centrality for the Afropolitan experience.[8] Suffice to note that (1) a key principle stated in Selasi's 2005 essay 'Bye-Bye Babar (What is Afropolitanism?)' is the 'refusal to over-simplify' and (2) that a provocative contribution to the Afropolitanism debate, which, as it happens, resonates with the work of February, is to be found in Olanike Lawore's 2021 article 'A Critique of Afropolitanism: Toward the Formation of a New Reading Model – Nigeriopolitanism'. Perhaps the most relevant of Lawore's recognitions to the present chapter is that 'the primary objective of Afropolitanism is to dismantle the views of African identity as simple, uniform, firm, and static' (2021: 141); certainly none of these adjectives could be applied in the slightest to the work of February.

Over the last twenty years or so, Afropolitanism has become a major field of exploration for Nigerian literature. Among the best-known works from that country to explore Afropolitan experience are the novels *Open City* by Teju Cole and *Americanah* by Chimamanda Ngozi Adichie. A remarkably wide-ranging and formally experimental exploration of the subject is to be found in Maik Nwosu's novel *A Gecko's Farewell* (2016). This interweaves the life stories of three main characters, two female, one male, from Nigeria, Egypt and South Africa, respectively, with the plot spanning a dozen or so other countries as diverse as Tanzania, France and Belize.[9]

Turning to poetry, in 2021 Nduka Otiono published his *DisPlace: The Poetry of Nduka Otiono*, a collection of his poems (new and selected) edited and with an Introduction by the Namibian-born Canadian poet Peter Midgley. The punning title of the volume synthesizes the verb 'displace' with the Nigerian Pidgin for 'this place'. Like February, Otiono is based in North America, in his case in Ottawa, Canada, and has written in his poetry on his interactions with poets from North America and Europe, creative interchange being a major benefit of the Afropolitan experience. Writing of that experience in his Introduction to the book Midgley makes a comment that applies poignantly also to the work of February: 'Where the centre cannot hold, or no longer holds, the tongue pushes back and owns the space the centre has vacated' (Midgley 2021: xv).

The poem of February's whose title most obviously suggests a reference to Afropolitanism is 'Self-Portrait with Foreign Tongue' (February 2018: 18). In the same chapbook comes 'Self-Portrait as a Study in Asphyxia' in which February acknowledges: 'A new place that is not home' and goes on to recognize: 'The Wizard of Oz teaches/ that air can take / you elsewhere / if you are already lost' (24). That phrase 'already lost' leads into the recognition that for February the idea of place (whether homeland or place of expatriation) is bound up with multiple recognitions: these range from the experience of homophobia as a spur to rejecting their birth country to the contesting components of the self. The idea of 'homeland' as an unrealizable sense of self is explicit in 'Deadly Sin: Envy', in which February asks: '*hiraeth* do you understand me / I mean my body is / another homeland that rejects me' (February 2019: 20).[10]

To return to the simple sense of homeland, to homophobic Nigeria, February's take on the place can be bitterly sardonic, as in the final lines of 'Portrait of My Country as a Cheap Restaurant': 'I'm leaving and I'm not paying / for the wine / and your décor is horrible by the way / what's the idea anyway is there a theme / it's just dreadful if you didn't already know' (February 2017: 20–1). The strain of displacement can register, as in 'A Night of No New Things': 'I have gone swimming with sea monsters, / I have gone swimming in sand buckets, / teaching myself to breathe Neptune air / with Nigerian lungs' (February 2018: 16). But when all is said and done, the emphasis, finally, is on autonomy, on a wilful independence, so that although there is a sense of home and there is grief at the loss of this or inability to attain this, it hardly enters into the equation. Hence the closing lines of 'Prayer of the Slut': 'I'm wilding / with boys, going out / for drinks and never coming back home' (February 2019: 37). And in a powerful paradox February recognizes 'Home to me, / is the distance from home' ('Deadly Sin: Sloth', February 2019: 43).

Locating the Self

In her 2019 interview with February, Lagos *Guardian* staff writer Melissa Mordi begins by commenting: 'Logan February's every bit as quirky and beautiful as their name.' 'Beautiful' will seem an understatement to anyone who has seen the photograph of February used as the cover image for *Fuckboys* and also reproduced for the *Guardian* interview (book cover); the adjective 'quirky' may be taken as teasing rather than pejorative; applied to the poetry it would no doubt reference February's use of modernist techniques, a subject that will be discussed in the final sections of this chapter. Mordi is a gifted and experienced journalist, and her interview contains some engaging material; the interview makes, however, no reference either to February's expatriation or to their sexuality. As indicated above, the latter subject is central to February's poetic output.

February's autobiographical note in their first poetry chapbook, *How to Cook a Ghost*, tells us they are 'a happy-ish Nigerian owl who likes pizza and typewriters' – a rare instance of February in light-hearted mode. By the time of their second chapbook, *Painted Blue with Saltwater*, that had been reworded to read 'a queer and happy-ish Nigerian owl'. Whilst from their poetry and other (online) publications it is clear that February identifies as nonbinary, it is only more recently that they have started using the 'they' pronoun. In the interview with the present author cited above, in a surprising (and perhaps tongue-in-cheek?) comment, February states: 'my main basis for this choice is really my native Yoruba, in which the third-person pronouns and their plural forms are gender-neutral and apply to individuals in certain contexts [see February in this volume]. I like to think I am challenging the English language towards a similar possibility'.

A number of February's poems address the subject of homophobia. One of these, 'Rhythm O' (February 2021: 86, 88, 90),[11] can be read with a wider application, as it imagines/recounts February's harassment by a police officer, the Nigerian police force being notorious for their violence and their bribe-taking. The excerpts that follow comprise two sections from a long poem on the creative artist:

In Lagos, the officer stops the taxi, knocking / On my window. He wears plain clothes

but his rifle is real. / He represents the people as a whole

when he interrupts my living. Cracks / the cerebral shell like a sheet of white chocolate.

He does not like my tattoo, my leather boots. / Breathes fury into my face mask. My punctured thumb

Throbs, deviant pulse, from getting tested / For the other, older virus. I am a suspect of

Nothing, yet an object of interest. / ….

With both of his palms locked around / my thigh, he tugs at me like prey, cornered

Amongst his colleagues, I will be taken,

I will be cuffed, made to beg / without aggression. I will submit my pride.

I will disappear and my poems will remain unfinished.

Other poems that expose homophobia in Nigeria include 'Boy Lolita' and 'Three Witch Haibun'. The first contains the following lines, in which, typically, references to death run in tandem with references to desire:

Boy
Lolita knows hiding and fear too well. A country will burn the
Taboo out of him, hates him for what he is known as. For
Instance, homoerotic. For instance, a boy who eats glass.
(February 2019: 48)

The second is equally explicit on the subject of homophobia, though here death is meted out rather than internalized:

the black witch, *aje dudu*. She curses and haunts
and follows. Like the eyes in my country, when I am

touching the boys I love. These people terrify me.
They would kill me if they could … the black
lights a match, seething against everything queer.

(February 2019: 15)

A further poem from the same collection (February 2019: 47), 'Deadly Sin: Wrath', focuses on multiple aspects of February's self-identification and the hostile reception of these; unlike the two poems quoted before it also demonstrates February's trademark use of space, a matter to be explored in a later section of this paper:

<pre>
                                         maybe that is
why you   are the way you are all that   white people
shit did you say   Buddhist did you say gay   did you
say psychotic   bipolar I don't believe you
</pre>

'Un-Masking Difference'

Having noted February's thematic preoccupations as revolving around their self-identification as nonbinary and bipolar, and having detailed the frequent highlighting of homophobia as subject matter for their poetry, in this section I discuss their essay 'A Good Person', published in the multi-author anthology *Un-Masking Difference*, an essay February has described as 'a short essay in theatrical and social performance of gender, reading Brecht's *Der Gute Mensch von Setzuan* (*The Good Person of Setzuan*) through a queer and psychoanalytic lens' (personal communication, February to Dunton, 31 October 2022).

Brecht's parable-like play has its central character, the kind and generous female shopkeeper Shen Te, disguise herself as the cold-hearted and tight-fisted male Shui Ta in order to avert financial ruin.[12] February's essay opens with an epigraph from Akwaeke Emezi, whose fiction (see Zabus in this volume) has frequently explored multiple identity: '"You wear the mask, you are the thing."'[13] February's opening remarks have to do with their chosen life strategy, living under a condemnatory heterosexual gaze: 'In an age of infirmity and violence and heat, it is preferable to frolic in private, away from the judgement of spectators. Courting agoraphobia,[14] I immerse myself in fictional life. This is how I discover Bertolt Brecht's play *The Good Person of Setzuan*' (February 2020b: [1]). February continues: 'Brecht's drama is concerned with dualities: cruelty / kindness, idealism / realism, communism / capitalism, masculinity / femininity – antithetical divisions within one character' ([1]), the notion of duality here resonating with February's self-identification as nonbinary.

February proceeds by discussing the relevance to his essay of Carl Jung's theory of *anima* and *animus*, and then inquires: 'If my body is a mask, what piece am I performing? When I walk the streets, I am seen as a "man" – do I do justice to that role? Do I fail to perform my real self? Or perhaps that is my performance. Failure, the ache of it pressing a line into the meat of my mind – a real knife' ([4]), the reference to the knife hinting at February's history of self-harm, a topic explored in his early poetry, but more crucially referring back to a quotation earlier in the essay from Marina Abramovic. The conclusion of the essay must constitute one of the most poignant passages February has written:

> You have this dream where the gods really do come down in search of a good soul [as at the outset of Brecht's play]. You spend a long time looking. You spread sun-cream over your mask. Dabs of cologne. You go out because you can. To smell fake roses. To play in the world you are given each day, uneasy as it may be. You melt as you walk through town. People think you look good in pink. And you do. You look so good.
>
> ([6])

The anthology *Un-Masking Difference* also includes '"Bodies of Experience": tales across the spectrum', a substantial (22-page) mixed genre work co-authored by February and Olumide Popoola, the title taken from a collection of photographs by gay Nigerian photographer Rotimi Fani-Kayode. The dual stimulus for this piece are Nigerian events – the suppression of the EndSARS movement and the Lekki massacre in which peaceful protesters were gunned down by the military[15] – incidents that speak volumes to the authors' alienation from their homeland. As February puts it to Popoola in the epistolary opening pages of this work: 'Many lives were lost. And for those of us left alive, there is a sense of something in us having died, too' (February and Popoola 2020: [4]).[16] February goes on to ask: 'Are there safe places in this world for a body both Black and queer?' ([6]).[17]

The influence of Tantra

In the poem 'Still Life with the Evangelist',[18] February writes:

> __i would say   I'm a Buddhist
> Because   breathing   is something
> People like me have to learn
> And   living is such a difficult task
> Almost like   swimming.[19]

A number of poems in February's 2019 collection *Mannequin in the Nude* reference Buddhism: for example, 'The Mannequin's *samsara*' (February 2019: 9: the collection's glossary refers to *samsara* as a Buddhist term for the cycle of death and rebirth to which life in the material world is bound); the poem 'Deadly Sin: Wrath' (47), already quoted, which explores multiple identity (Buddhist, gay, psychotic, bipolar) and in which February imagines a hostile voice challenging them: 'Buddhist did you say gay'; and 'Deadly Sin: Sloth' (43), which includes the following lines: 'I can never / get this Buddhist thing right, / this requisite stillness. The / first time I said *samsara* it felt / like native tongue'.

In an interview with the present author, February commented at length on their attraction to Buddhism, as follows:

> Regarding Buddhism – I think from quite a young age I had felt an inclination towards Buddhist ideas without being fully aware of it. I started to think more consciously of myself as a Buddhist perhaps around when I was 17. Buddhism offer some hope, peace and relationship to the universe and my own life, in a way I would never have imagined in my upbringing as a Christian. My interest in mindfulness is also supported by my background in psychology – I think about the unconscious mind, about understanding and compassion, about desires, fantasy, longing, and how they relate to human suffering. I would say that being a Buddhist has lessened my suffering, and brings me closer to accepting and understanding what remains of it. That is, at least, my hope, and a lifelong journey, too. I also love that, so far, Buddhism does not contradict my curious identifications with astrology, the Ifa and Orisha traditions, and other avenues of spiritual inquiry.
>
> (personal communications, February with Dunton,
> 18 February 2022 to 7 August 2022)

The present writer's first reading of February's poetry coincided with a chance reading of a review by Jonathan Jones of an exhibition of Tantric art at the British Museum, London (Jones 2020). This led to the hypothesis that Tantra, Tantric sexuality and Tantric art might form a repertoire of thought and practice informing February's poetry, a hypothesis encouraged by February's comment in an interview with the present author:

> I haven't had the luck of experiencing much of this, except through a bit of reading. I've spent recent months researching Marina Abramovic's work in performance art,[20] and how much of it is influenced by her interest in tantric practices and her studies with Tibetan lamas. It adds a lot of meaning to her use of the body as an art medium, and explains some of her key themes: endurance of pain, time, and other natural conditions; tests of mental and physical limitations; transformation and exchange of energy; etcetera. I have also been thinking about the power of tantric sexuality since I read the introduction to Andrew Harvey's 1997 anthology *The Essential Gay Mystics.*
>
> (personal communications, February with Dunton,
> 18 February 2022 to 7 August 2022)

Tantra can be briefly described as a radical belief system that emerged around 500 CE in India, with its origins in Hinduism but which soon impacted on Buddhism also; the key texts are tantras, religious dialogues written in Sanskrit. The movement challenged political, sexual and gender norms, with a central emphasis on female sexual energy. Taboo-breaking, sexually explicit and anti-authoritarian, it advocated the overcoming of disgust as a path to truth (Tantric art foregrounds body parts, especially skulls, which appear often as drinking-vessels; a review by Hettie Judah of the British Museum exhibition reproduces an image of a stone carving of a goddess dancing on a corpse; Judah 2020). All of this seems germane to February's poetry, taboo-breaking as it is, and with its fearless immersion in the realities of death and the dead body.

In a review of the work mentioned by February in interview, Andrew Harvey's *The Essential Gay Mystics*, Malcolm Body cites 'the tantric vision of reality, which rejects the old separations between heaven and earth, body and spirit, heart and mind in favour of an erotic, sensual appreciation of human existence' (Body n.d.). The final phrase of that comment and February's reference in interview to 'the power of tantric sexuality' lead one to the latter principle: a slow, meditative form of sex, often exercised in a ritualized or yogic context, in which the end goal is not orgasm but the enjoyment of the sexual journey and sensations of the body.

At the risk of multiplying analogies, I should like to draw a parallel between the principle of journey/process in Tantric sexuality and a similar principle in Work Without Edges, a term that has been applied to both painting and poetry and one that resonates with the willingness of February's poetry to embrace discontinuities. Edgeless Work does not attempt a definite and therefore paraphrase-able meaning, but aims to linger over, to draw out, experience, in the way Tantric sexuality privileges each moment as it occurs.

The principle of embracing discontinuities is central to Edgeless art and indeed to modernism in general and in February's poetry this emerges most clearly in the use of space: spaces between words and phrases and between lines, as in the excerpt given above from 'Deadly Sin: Wrath' or in the short poem 'The Exhumation (prelude)' (February 2019: 19), in which the sensual and the absence of revulsion at a corpse have a strong Tantric weighting:

> the mist   within
> this body is named
>
>   my lifeline
>
> crumpled boy
>   hangs open
>
>   the best baptism
> is with teeth

Context and Influence

That February's use of space can be extremely elaborate in its configuration is evident from the following excerpt from 'Almond Blossom, Vincent van Gogh, February 1890' (February 2021: 48), a poem inspired by the work of a modernist artist famous also for self-mutilation:

> Against a blue sky
>   there can be no thrashing

> no wailing, no flailing
> of the painter's instrument
> —the hands. Broken,
> all of it: the dream of hot stars
> filling a bedroom, being trapped
> inside, the sleep itself,
> a waste of common things.

February has commented to me: 'The use of space in this poem is largely an ekphrastic choice to represent the dispersion of blossoms, and the blank / blue spaces in the van Gogh painting' (personal communication, February to Dunton, 17 December 2022). More generally speaking, when first encountering February's use of space the present author was reminded of this technique as used by the first and second generation New York School of poets and artists,[21] and, most strongly, of its use in the work of Lewis Warsh. In my interview with February, I opened up the matter and they responded as follows:

> The general idea of space interests me; on the page and between words, it allows me to visualize the distance I sense between the thought and the language, between one language and another, and between images and ideas. I like to think as some texts performing themselves on the page, or being installed there. My uses of visual caesura have been influenced by contemporary poets whose work features the same, notably Kaveh Akbar and Safia Elhillo … Some poets of the New York School I've been drawn to are Frank O'Hara, Alice Notley and John Ashbery.

As noted above, a first encounter with February's poetry strongly recalled the work of the first and second generation New York School of poets and especially that of Lewis Warsh, whose focus on the quotidian, on intimacy, and whose use of devices such as spacing suggest a strong kinship with February's poetic technique. I am struck, too, by February's reference in their interview with me to their sense of kinship with the earlier New York School poet Frank O'Hara, a gay man who took his inspiration from jazz, surrealism and abstract expressionism. In her book *Frank O'Hara, Poet Among Painters* (1997) Marjorie Perloff refers to the influence on O'Hara of the work of William Carlos Williams, another poet relevant to the broad context of modernism within which February's work appears. Perloff goes on to speak of the production of 'simple statements split at irregular intervals' (Wikipedia 2024), a hallmark of February's work.

A full and systematic account of the context in which February's work appears would have to take into account the work of early modernists such as Stephane Mallarmé, Arthur Rimbaud and Vladimir Mayakovsky; in the work of the latter, especially, as in February, the layout of spaced phrases is painterly, pointing towards an art movement such as abstract expressionism. There is also the work of Pierre Reverdy, one of whose maxims resonates strongly with February's procedures: 'The image cannot spring from any comparison but from the bringing together of two more or less remote realities' (quoted by Kane 2003: 93).

Daniel Kane's meticulously researched *All Poets Welcome: The Lower East Side Poetry Scene in the 1960s* contains one observation or insight after another that suggests the kinship of February's work with the corpus the book describes and the relevance to both of the modernist heritage. For example, Kane's take on the notion of the 'alternative': 'writing that is indebted to innovative laws of prosody … that beatifies scandalous or licentious behaviour; that threatens generic distinctions between prose, poetry, performance, and visual art; and so on' (Kane 2003: 3). There is the emphasis on earlier modernist poets, especially Ezra Pound and William Carlos Williams, including Kane's quotation from founding New York School poet Ted Berrigan's 'Sonnet LVIII', which ends with a dictum from Williams:

> A glass of chocolate milk, head of lettuce, dark-
> ness of clouds at one o'clock.   No truth except
> in things.

And there is the recognition of the possibilities that opened up for the New York poets from the late 1950s of revisiting Ezra Pound's Imagism 'for a way around the verse orthodoxy inspired by New Criticism back to the roots of Modernist experiment' (Kane 2003: 91), the idea of the deep image newly imbued with an absorption in psychology (one notes that February's early academic training was in that discipline).

Conclusion

On first examination I was inclined to relate February's use of space to the embrace of discontinuities, to a disinclination to build a master narrative that irons out disjunctions.

It seems to me now that the technique has more to do with the Tantric emphasis on connectedness, and on the lingering over and drawing out of experience. Whilst certainly enabling discord, the shock of disjunction, each space acts to cast a spotlight on the words or phrases on either side of it, enhancing concentration and denying a facile syntactical run-on.[22] This is evident especially in the poem 'The Bodies of Dead Boys' (February 2018: 42), as in the following lines:

> my boyfriend   is a mortician...
> I strip myself   he thinks it is
> About sex and preservation
> I call myself   a half-dead thing
> this romance   my embalmment
> he claims to be able to make me trickle
> I tell him I love him   in a wounded way

A key line here is the fifth line ('this romance my embalmment') in which space focusses attention on each of the two phrases, the one articulating love and sex, the other death, while the consonance of the *m* sound draws the two terms together, opening up a Tantric recognition.

In this final section I focus on two poems of February that, taken together, demonstrate the range of the poet's concerns and practices. The first of these, 'Left' (February 2021: 84), does not employ the technique of spacing discussed above, being laid out in six two-line sections – somewhat reminiscent of the classic couplet form – each of which has strong, run-on coherence. The first three of these sections confront love and death and the loss of the means of self-identification (located here in Yoruba ancestry and the conventions of naming):

> Love does not want this mouth, / toothless maw, hanging open.
> My father died and I became no one. / In Yoruba, your father is your name.
> Love does not want this body / that belongs to nobody's son.

Following this, comes a section that refers to self-harming (part of February's experience of mental illness):

> My left hand knows how to open itself / when I need to find my blood

The last two sections draw the preoccupations of the poem together, with reference to the principle – shared by numerous belief systems – that contact through the left hand is forbidden:

> One must never offer gifts with the left hand. / I hold the boy I want to love, in my left hand.
> Love is my left hand closing into a fist. / Love is the hand that belongs to nobody.

In the end the poet is an outcast, the wish to love being unfulfilled, with only the threat of violence remaining.[23]

Finally, I turn back to 'The Bodies of Dead Boys', one of February's most striking achievements to date. When it first appeared, in the April 2017 issue of the online *Glass: A Journal of Poetry*, it was accompanied by a note that does not appear in the print version (in the chapbook *Painted Blue with Saltwater*), perhaps because it does not fully do justice to the poem's polysemy: 'This poem is an examination of what it is to be the mentally ill partner in a relationship; the unspoken frustration that blooms when a partner is thoroughly convinced of their ability to heal a mind that has already collapsed inward' (*Glass: A Journal of Poetry* 2017).

From its opening line the poem proceeds to explore the relationship between the dead body and the unknowable one, representing February's struggles with self-identification, with the notion of the stable self, leading to their questioning whether they are a river (that is, never for two consecutive moments the same thing):

>   my boyfriend   is a mortician
>   the kind that sits next to   crows
>   enjoying the odor of departure
>   the coming   and the going
>   I am unfamiliar but he claims
>   to know me   I sell my body to him
>   for information   tell me
>   what you know of me   am I truly
>   a river   or is that a hallucination too

Although the poem is laid out as a single 27-line block, what is in effect a second section or movement begins with a reference to 'shovels' – the gravedigger's tool, but here surely with a penile connotation (the phrase 'be gentle' suggests the cliched plea 'be gentle with me'). There follows a lightening of tone, with a reference to lovers' small talk, and then the subject's attempt to establish their hold on reality by engaging with semantics, the terms all being death-related: murder, shovel and crow, a carrion bird.[24]

>   is it normal to talk to shovels
>   and ask them   to be gentle
>   I'm sorry   how did we meet again
>   something about bicycles   wasn't it
>   about going round   about brakes
>   he claims I am not an ending
>   I try to prove myself   a group
>   of crows is a murder   a group
>   of shovels is a pile   a pile
>   of bodies is the pilgrimage where scorpio hands
>   touch me   to open my bones
>   and reveal insects and marrow

The final six lines of the poem have already been quoted at the start of this concluding section: here every sexual act represents a little dying, the final phrase, 'in a wounded way', connoting both February's tone of voice and a further step towards death on the part of a persona who has allowed themselves to be loved.

If one could extrapolate a scenario for 'The Bodies of Dead Boys' then, as with February's encounter with the police officer in 'Rhythm O', its action would only take a few seconds. In recognizing February's undermining of linearity, one doesn't feel that a horizontal or narrative progression has been sacrificed or was ever even desirable. There is little spatial reach in 'The Bodies of Dead Boys', but, as in Tantric recognitions, its vertical reach is immense, plumbing consciousness and the voicing of consciousness, through love to death.

Acknowledgements

I am indebted first and foremost to Logan February for the friendly and considerate way in which he has corresponded with me about his work, and for the time he took in providing me with some of the primary texts and in answering my interview questions, answers that are quoted at length in this chapter. Thanks also for their critical comments on the initial drafts on this chapter and on its sprawling structure, to James Gibbs, Nduka Otiono, Alison Love and Nathan Suhr-Sytsma. And, of course, to Chantal Zabus for inviting me to the Paris conference at which, so to speak, I fired the first shot at the chapter.

Notes

1   The Preface appears in the original Spanish only. English translations here by Chris Dunton.

2   Douglas was despicable on account of his disloyalty, greed, vengefulness and rabid anti-Semitism. But the line 'the love that dares not speak its name' has become common property, virtually a standard idiom.

3   On the few occasions when same-sex experience was foregrounded, it tended – as in Soyinka's *The Interpreters* – to be deployed in the service of some other thematic concern.

4   For an account of the furore that attended the passing of this bill and the unintended consequences of the protests of political leaders in the Global North and of human rights activists, see Dunton and Hoad 2014: 478.

5   Dibia is the author of the first LGBTQ+-themed novel to come from Nigeria, *Walking with Shadows* (2005; second, expanded edition 2007). Following its publication, the Nigerian press had a field-day with the question whether Dibia was himself gay.

6   Regarding performance, in his study of the poets of New York's Lower East Side, Daniel Kane has observed that poetry is 'inherently public' (Kane 2003: 12). One fundamental aspect of February's work that is not addressed in this chapter is their role as performer (several films of February in performance are accessible on the internet). Orality must be, however, a major consideration in understanding February's work, encompassing elements such as February's reflections on their Yoruba heritage, and the still vibrant production of African oral poetry, with the written corpus frequently influenced by oral production and its techniques (or the other way round: towards the end of his life Nigerian poet and scholar Harry Garuba was researching the influence of written poetry on oral poems produced in his L1, Edo). Watching February perform their poems is to experience, in Kane's words, 'a poem actualized in its aural / oral form as ... performed and received in communal territory' (30).

7   One of February's poems, 'Hope is a Box of Bees' (February 2018: 35) is tagged 'after Sylvia Plath'. The poem 'Boy Lolita' contains the following lines: 'Boy Lolita read a poem by Plath – now he eats men like air, unless they're paying for his food' (February 2019: 48).

8   The Afropolitan debate still holds central ground, as witnessed by the fact that the theme of the 2023 conference of the African Literature Association was 'Crossings: Africans Moving In / Across Space and Time'.

9   For a detailed account of this remarkable novel, see Dunton 2020: 9–11. Both Nwosu
     and Akin Adesokan have more recently completed novels that may mark the most
     complex and searching explorations of Afropolitanism to date, but as these works are
     as yet unpublished they cannot be discussed here.

10   The glossary to the volume notes of the Welsh word *hiraeth* that this denotes 'a
     homesickness for a home to which you cannot return, a home which maybe never
     was; the nostalgia, the yearning, the grief for the lost places of your past' (February
     2019: 82).

11   The pagination here reflects the fact that the poem is to be found in the bilingual
     collection *Fuckboys*, with the English original followed, page by page, by the
     Spanish translation. The poem is tagged as being 'after Marina Abramovic', the
     Serbian conceptual artist and performer, referenced in February's interview
     with the present author, and noted for focussing on the body and its limits and
     endurance.

12   An important starting-point for February's essay is Eric Bentley's decision in his
     English translation of the play to use the word 'Woman' rather than the more usual
     'Person' to translate *Mensch*.

13   Although not so glossed by February, the line appears in *Dear Senthuran: A Black
     Spirit Memoir* (Emezi 2021: 38–9). For both February and Emezi the notion of
     masking is a potent one, deriving from Yoruba and Igbo masquerade performance,
     and having a meaning that goes beyond (though also encapsulates) the idea
     of concealing the self, of the mask as a disguise worn to avoid risk in a hostile
     environment (as noted above, the poem 'Boy Lolita' is on an individual who 'knows
     hiding and fear too well').

14   The word 'agoraphobia' denotes not simply a fear of open spaces, as is often assumed,
     but a fear of being in situations where escape might be difficult (for example, when
     surrounded by a hostile crowd) or where help would not be available if needed.

15   The EndSARS movement (SARS being the acronym of the Nigerian police force's
     Special Anti-Robbery Squad) had, amongst other demands, the release of arrested
     protesters and compensation for families of those murdered by the police. In
     the Lekki massacre, though the number is disputed, up to seventy-five peaceful
     protesters were gunned down. This is not to deny that the EndSARS protesters finally
     committed acts of extreme violence themselves (see Soyinka 2020).

16   The word 'agoraphobia' comes to mind again.

17   The bulk of 'Bodies of Experience' comprises a play inspired by the Gelede
     masquerade, which raises issues too complex to discuss here, and a photo-essay.

18   This does not appear in any of February's three published collections to date, but is
     available on the internet, and is listed as such in the References (February 2020a).

19   The opening phrase, 'I would say', needs to be read as Nigerian English idiom, in
     which the verb form 'would' does not have the same conditional force as in British
     English.

20   In 'A Good Person' February quotes Abramovic with approval: "'To be a performance
     artist, you have to hate theatre. Theatre is fake … Performance is just the opposite: the
     knife is red, the blood is red and the emotions are real'" (February 2020b: [1]).

21   In the present context, the use of the word 'generation' in the nomenclature of the
     Schools is ironic, given the debate that has developed over the use of the terms first,
     second and third generations to describe Nigerian authors writing in English. Harry
     Garuba has usefully questioned the instability of the term, as he poses the question
     'when is a generation?' (Garuba 2005: 52).

22   This is not always the case, as in the following lines from 'Chef' (February 2017: 24) in which there is a space between the lines, but much more run-on or syntactical continuity than often obtains: 'I come home before dark, smelling like / The cadaver of a man who made me call him lover.'
23   The reference to the fist is, admittedly, open to several interpretations.
24   One recalls Ted Hughes' use of the bird in his scandal-provoking poem of 1970.

References

Azuah, Unoma, ed. 2016. *Blessed Body: The Secret Lives of Lesbian, Gay, Bisexual and Transgender Nigerians*. Jackson, TN: Cooking Pot Publishing.

Body, Malcolm. n.d. 'Review of Andrew Harvey, *The Essential Gay Mystics*', The Free Library. Available online: https://www.thefreelibrary.com/The±Essential±Gay±Mystics -a020164897 (accessed 20 February 2022).

Dibia, Jude. 2021. 'Jude Dibia interviewed by Elnathan John', The African Courier. Available online: https://www.theafricancourier.de/culture/nigerian-authors-in-berlin-talk-about-homosexuality-in-Africa (accessed 6 January 2022).

Dunton, Chris. 2020. '"Wherever the Bus is Headed": Recent Developments in the African Novel', *Research in African Literatures* 50 (4): 1–20.

Dunton, Chris and Neville Hoad. 2014. 'African Literatures', in E. L. McCallum and Mikko Tuhkanen (eds), *The Cambridge History of Gay and Lesbian Literature*, 477–97. Cambridge: Cambridge University Press.

Emezi, Akwaeke. 2021. *Dear Senthuran: A Black Spirit Memoir*. London: Faber and Faber.

February, Logan. 2017. *How to Cook a Ghost*. Glass Poetry Press.

February, Logan. 2018. *Painted Blue with Saltwater*. Brooklyn, NY: Indolent Books.

February, Logan. 2019. *Mannequin in the Nude*. [PANK] Books.

February, Logan. 2020a. 'Still Life with the Evangelist', Agbowo. Available online: https://www.agbowo.org/still-life-with-the-evangelist-Logan-February (accessed 19 November 2020).

February, Logan. 2020b. 'A Good Person', in Natasha A. Kelly (ed.), *Un-Masking Difference: Literary Voices from Behind the Mask*. Berlin: Mikrotext.

February, Logan. 2021. *Fuckboys*. Bilingual edition, English/Spanish. Preface by Marina Spada. Barcelona: Kriller71 Ediciones.

February, Logan. 2024. *Mental Voodoo*. Bilingual edition, English/German. Schupfart, Switzerland: Engeler Verlage.

February, Logan and Olumide Popoola. 2020. '"Bodies of Experience": Tales across the spectrum', in Natasha A. Kelly (ed.), *Un-Masking Difference: Literary Voices from Behind the Mask*. Berlin: Mikrotext.

Filips, Christian. 2024. 'The Inherent Queerness of Traditions: Logan February Talking with Christian Filips', in Logan February, *Fuckboys*, 206–19. Barcelona: Kriller71 Ediciones.

Garuba, Harry. 2005. 'The Unbearable Lightness of Being: Re-Figuring Trends in Recent Nigerian Poetry', *English in Africa* 32 (1): 51–72.

Glass: A Journal of Poetry. 2017. 'Logan February: The Bodies of Dead Boys'. Available online: https://www.glass-poetry.com/journal/2017/april/february-bodies.html (accessed 24 September 2022).

Green-Simms, Lindsey. 2017. 'The Emergent Queer: Homosexuality and Nigerian Fiction in the 21st Century', *Research in African Literatures* 47 (2): 139–61.

Habila, Helon. 2019. *Travellers*. London: Hamish Hamilton.

Habila, Helon. 2020. 'Elegy for Pius', in Nduka Otiono and Uchechukwu Umezurike (eds), *Wreaths for a Wayfarer: An Anthology of Poems in Honour of Pius Adesanmi*, 131. Ottawa: Daraja Press.

Jones, Jonathan. 2020. 'Review of exhibition of Tantra, British Museum, London', *The Guardian* (London), 22 September: 21.

Judah, Hettie. 2020. 'Honest to goddess' (review of exhibition of Tantra, British Museum, London), *i* (London), 21 February: 38–9.

Kane, Daniel. 2003. *All Poets Welcome: The Lower East Side Poetry Scene in the 1960s*. Berkeley, Los Angeles and London: University of California Press.

Lawore, Olanike. 2021. 'A Critique of Afropolitanism: Toward the Formation of a New Reading Model—Nigeriopolitanism', *Research in African Literatures* 52 (1): 139–55.

Midgley, Peter. 2021. 'Absent Allusions and the Politics of Dislocation in the Work of Nduka Otiono', in Nduka Otiono, *DisPlace: The Poetry of Nduka Otiono*, xiii–xxii. Waterloo, ONT: Wilfred Laurier Press.

Mordi, Melissa. 2019. 'Logan February: Poet in Glorious Bloom', *The Guardian*, 13 May. Available online: https://www.guardian.ng/life/logan-February-poet-in-glorious-bloom (accessed 10 June 2022).

Nzelu, Okechukwu. 2022. *Here Again Now*. London: Dialogue Books.

Okparanta, Chinelo. 2015. *Under the Udala Trees*. London: Granta.

Otiono, Nduka. 2021. *DisPlace: The Poetry of Nduka Otiono*. Waterloo, ONT: Wilfred Laurier Press.

Perloff, Marjorie. 1997. *Frank O'Hara: Poet Among Painters*. Chicago: University of Chicago Press.

Selasi, Taiye. 2005. 'Bye-Bye Babar', LIP Magazine, 3 March. Available online: https://thelip.robertsharp.co.uk/2005/03/03/bye-bye-babar (accessed 10 October 2018).

Soyinka, Wole. 2020. 'For me it is humanity first', The News Nigeria, 29 December. Available online: thenewsnigeria.com.ng/2020/12/29/for-me-it-is-humanity-first-a-conversation-with-wole-soyinka (accessed 21 November 2022).

Spada, Mariana. 'Prologo: una especie de vudu mental', in Logan February, *Fuckboys*, 7–11. Barcelona: Kriller71 Ediciones.

Wikipedia. 2024. s.v. 'Frank O'Hara'. Available online: https://en.wikipedia.org/wiki/Frank_O%27Hara (accessed 1 October 2022).

Chapter 5

'DELIVER US FROM EVIL': PENTECOSTAL CHRISTIANITY, QUEER SEXUALITIES AND THE LANGUAGE OF DELIVERANCE IN NIGERIAN LITERATURE

Adriaan van Klinken and Belinda Qaqamba Makinana

Introduction

Deliverance prominently features as a central theme in the emerging body of queer Nigerian literary writing. For instance, Jude Dibia's *Walking with Shadows*, which has been hailed as the first Nigerian gay novel,[1] includes a dramatic scene where the protagonist undergoes a physically violent deliverance ritual by a Pentecostal pastor, where he is beaten with a whip on his bare back until he loses consciousness, while the pastor shouts at him: 'Banish the devil from your heart … and accept God in your life' (Dibia 2011: 175). In another acclaimed novel, *Speak No Evil*, by Uzodinma Iweala, the young gay protagonist who grows up in the diaspora in the United States is taken by his father back to Nigeria in order to be delivered by a Pentecostal preacher. The latter's diagnosis is that 'this demon of homosexuality has become so entrenched in America that you can't really fight it there. … You are right to bring him here, this is a place where the faith is strong and hasn't been infiltrated by the devil' (Iweala 2018: 72). Other texts centring around what has been described as 'the emergent queer' in Nigerian fiction (Green-Simms 2016) include similar scenes which, as discussed below, can be conceptualized as postqueer.

As we will argue in this chapter, deliverance is a critical and productive theme in contemporary queer Nigerian literature as a thriving subsection of queer African writing. It is critical, because through narratives about deliverance, Nigerian queer literary texts critique the dominant religious culture that is opposed to, and indeed demonizes, queer subjects. It is also productive, because through these narratives, literary texts stimulate a creative social and religious imagination, with the implicit suggestion being that perhaps it is not the queer body that needs to be delivered from the 'evil' of its nonconforming desires, but that it is society that needs to be delivered from religious views and practices that demonize and dehumanize a segment of the population, and that such views and practices need to be transformed for religion to affirm the dignity and worth of all human beings. However, before we develop this argument with reference to three recent Nigerian queer-themed texts – Elnathan John and Àlàbá Ònájìn's *On Ajayi Crowther Street*, Buki Papillon's *An Ordinary Wonder* and Chinelo Okparanta's *Under the Udala Trees* – let us first introduce the notion of deliverance, the religious culture of Pentecostal Christianity in which it is embedded, and the way in which it is linked to queer sexuality in contemporary Nigeria. Following that, we will briefly outline the methodology that guides our reading of the selected novels. The selection of the novels itself was informed by three considerations: (1) they feature the key themes at the heart of our discussion: queer sexuality, deliverance and Pentecostal Christianity; (2) they provide literary insight into different forms of queerness: male homosexuality, female homosexuality and intersexuality; and (3) they present different narrative strategies – of exposing religious hypocrisy, reclaiming indigenous religion and reinterpreting Christianity – that can be seen as offering alternative modalities of Nigerian queer, and in some respect postqueer, religious world-making. These points will be explored in the main body of this chapter, through a detailed reading of the three novels.

Deliverance, Pentecostalism and Queer Sexuality

In the Christian tradition, as those familiar with the Lord's Prayer[2] will already have remembered, the notion of deliverance is closely associated with the notion of evil. Yet, Christianity comes in different versions, and the meaning of these words – 'deliverance' as well as 'evil' – varies across denominations and translates into different religious practices. The type of Christianity that has become enormously popular across sub-Saharan Africa in the late twentieth and early twenty-first centuries is known by the shorthand 'Pentecostalism'. Nigeria in particular is considered as an epicentre of African and global Pentecostalism (Wariboko 2014), and the Nigerian state has even been described as a 'Pentecostal republic' given the close connections between religious and political actors (Obadare 2018). One typical feature of Pentecostal Christianity, and perhaps specifically Nigerian Pentecostalism (Adelakun 2021), is its prominent practice of deliverance which reflects a particular understanding of, and concern with, evil. The writer Elnathan John, in his satirical commentary titled *Be(com)ing Nigerian*, has a chapter about 'how to worship the Nigerian God', which reads:

> The Nigerian God performs signs and wonders. … As a worshipper you must let him deliver you because every case of sickness is caused by evil demons and not infections. Every case of infertility for example is caused by witches and demons and not things like endometriosis or low sperm motility. So instead of hospital, visit agents of the Nigerian God.
>
> PS. The Nigerian God does not cure corruption. Do not attempt to mock him.

(John 2019: 12)

As much as satire tends to involve exaggeration, it is intended to reveal a truth about society. In this case, John satirically exposes and critiques popular religious practice in Nigeria for its preoccupation with evil, its obsession with demons, and its relentless belief in the 'agents of the Nigerian God' and their power to protect one against, and deliver one from, any negative spiritual forces affecting one's life. Among these divine agents are, most notably, charismatic Christian pastors and prophets, but also Islamic sheikhs and marabouts, and indigenous *babaaláwos* or diviners – after all, Nigeria is known as a competitive religious marketplace where various religious entrepreneurs try their luck, and where religious consumers or shoppers, when they believe to be in need of deliverance, 'cannot afford to be picky' (Janson 2021: 5). In the same breath, John also draws critical attention to the corrupt economy that dominates not only Nigerian politics but also its thriving religious sector.

The phrase of 'signs and wonders' that John uses is particularly reminiscent of Nigerian Pentecostal Christian culture, where self-declared men (and sometimes, women) of God boast about their God-given spiritual powers to miraculously perform healing and deliverance, advertising their services on billboards along highways, via social media and in several cases via their own TV channels. These signs and wonders centre around the 'spell of the invisible' which, according to Nimi Wariboko (2014), is at the heart of the religious culture and economy of Nigerian Pentecostalism. Although in continuity with indigenous world-views where spiritual forces are believed to hold real power in the material world and to affect human bodies, in Pentecostalism these forces and the spell of their power are understood in a dualistic Christian framework of God versus the devil (Anderson 2018). Thus, Pentecostal deliverance practices are ritual performances of power, where 'anointed' pastors or prophets invoke the name of Jesus Christ, the Holy Spirit and/or God, in order to exorcize and cast out evil spirits, often in rather forceful and violent ways. As Wariboko comments:

> In some Pentecostal circles in Nigeria, deliverance involves ministers (exorcists) flagellating the bodies of those supposedly possessed by evil spirits. The punishment of the physical body is believed to drive out the nonphysical spirit lodged inside the person. The punishment of the visible cleanses the invisible, settles the debts (sins) that gave Satan permission to enter into the body.
>
> (Wariboko 2014: 120–1)

Spirits, in this religious culture, are often sexualized, and vice versa, sex and sexuality are spiritualized (Van Klinken 2023). Forms of sexuality considered to be immoral – such as homosexuality – are not just seen as sinful but are widely linked to evil spirits (Homewood 2020) and associated with a Satanic plan to bring about the end of the world (Ukah 2018; Van Klinken 2013). This is reflected in an increasingly popular discourse, in Nigeria and beyond, about 'the spirit of homosexuality' or 'the demon of gayism and lesbianism', and in subsequent deliverance practices that aim to drive out such spirits from the bodies believed to be possessed by them (Richman 2021). As Pastor Matthew, in the earlier cited novel *Walking with Shadows*, advises the gay protagonist, Adrian: 'Sometimes we let the devil come into our lives and rule our hearts. … It is the devil that tempts you my brother' (Dibia 2011: 174). Thus, the intense politicization of homosexuality in Nigeria and other parts of Africa in recent decades is partly driven by a 'spiritual panic' (Ukah 2016: 25) which has generated a Pentecostal culture, if not an industry, specifically concerned with deliverance of the queer body from the 'demon of homosexuality', which of course doubles as a deliverance of society from the 'evil of queerness'. Thus, in a sense, Nigerian Pentecostalism presents a postqueer conceptualization of sexual embodiment, as it goes beyond and against 'Eurocentric understandings of sexual and gender difference' (Jackson 2001: 7), which, after all, are fundamentally secular and based on a liberal concept of human rights, and which do not allow for spiritually enchanted perceptions of the body, sex and sexuality. Yet, obviously, such a postqueer conceptualization of sexuality is not necessarily a liberatory one.

A slowly emerging body of Nigerian LGBTQ+ life stories offers autobiographical insight into the traumatizing effects of this religious culture on queer people: first, queer individuals are made to believe that their sexuality and/or gender identity is caused by an evil spirit and links them to the devil; and, second, they are (often repeatedly) subjected to aggressive deliverance rituals which can be harmful both physically, psychologically and spiritually. Such stories can be found in the volume *Blessed Body* that was edited by Unoma Azuah. For instance, the following autobiographical account of Kehinde Bademosi about his first same-sex experience reflects an internalized demonization: 'I silently prayed that a higher spiritual power would win the battle that raged within and keep me from going any further. I prayed that I would stop enjoying the intimacy. I prayed that my penis would soften, and that my nipples would behave themselves' (Bademosi 2016: 191). Azuah herself narrates an experience of being whipped at boarding school after her homosexuality was discovered, with one of her born-again classmates afterwards offering to start prayers of deliverance for her, because 'the spirit of lesbianism is stubborn' (Azuah 2016: 197). Another collection of Nigerian queer life stories, *She Called Me Woman*, also includes autobiographical stories about deliverance, such as by a lesbian-identifying woman who is made to believe that she is possessed by an evil spirit, and who is taken for deliverance sessions that last days: 'They would wash me. They would anoint me with oil. They would pray and pray and pray and bind and cast out every demon. … I believed I was possessed. I felt less than human. I felt I was better off dead' (BM 2018: 218). These stories demonstrate that as much as the literary texts discussed in the next sections are fiction, they reflect and engage with lived experiences that are real for many Nigerian LGBTQ+ folks. As Chris Dunton (2023) points out with reference to the autobiographical stories in *Blessed Body* and their engagement with themes relating to religion and faith, '[t]he relevant narratives form an important non-fictional base from which to read creative texts' (Dunton 2023: 7).

Reading *for* Deliverance

The previous sentences are not to suggest that we simply consider the literary texts under discussion as factual mirrors of social reality. Instead, with Ato Quayson (2003) we consider them as calibrations of the social, which acknowledges the critical, creative and imaginative representation of, and engagements with, social reality. Quayson proposes his concept of postcolonial literature as calibration to advocate a method of 'reading *for* the social', which embraces 'the ideological notion of using the literary as a means towards social enlightenment' (Quayson 2003: 4). Tweaking this, we propose a method of 'reading *for* deliverance'. Deliverance is not only a topic centrally featured in the selected queer Nigerian literary texts ('reading *about* deliverance'), but the texts themselves can be read as seeking to bring about a deliverance – not a deliverance of the 'demon of homosexuality', but a queer deliverance of what Kenyan writer Binyavanga Wainaina once described as 'Pentecostal demon hunters' (KTN Kenya 2014) who in their obsession with fighting the 'demon of homosexuality' make life for queer persons in many parts of Africa unbearable. Deliverance is a term that, in the words of Biko Mandela Gray (2020: 321), 'invokes freedom, capacity, renewal, and possibility', and the texts under discussion enact a queer deliverance in a twofold way: they simultaneously critique the oppression and harm that Pentecostal deliverance practices do to queer bodies, and open up alternative imaginations of how queer life is, or can become, liveable within and beyond the constraints of a homophobic and heteronormative world.[3] Importantly, however, as much as these texts critique the Pentecostal demonization of the queer body, they do not necessarily have an issue with the spiritualization of sexual embodiment. They reimagine this spiritualization in a way that is affirming of the queer body, instead of reinscribing a Eurocentric and secular LGBT identities framework. As such, the deliverance enacted in these texts can be conceptualized as postqueer.

The three texts we are reading in this chapter are part of a rapidly emerging body of queer African writing, which itself has become subject of a steadily growing body of scholarship. Where Chris Dunton, in his 1989 overview of representations of homosexuality in African literature observed a 'sustained outburst of silence' around the topic of same-sex practices (Dunton 1989: 445), Lindsey Green-Simms in a more recent review argues that 'slowly this silence among African writers is not only eroding, but turning into a polyphony' (2016: 141). Green-Simms and other scholars (Courtois 2022; Manzo 2018; Munro 2016; Oloruntoba-Oju 2021) particularly highlight the role of a younger generation of Nigerian writers in tackling the hitherto taboo topic of queer sexuality in African literature. Indeed, this polyphony has further expanded the scope of queerness, as Nigerian writers over the past few years have not only engaged with male but also female same-sex desire, as well as with trans and intersex themes, such as in Chinelo Okparanta's *Under the Udala Trees* (2015), Akwaeke Emezi's *Freshwater* (2018) (see Zabus in this volume) and Buki Papillon's *An Ordinary Wonder* (2021), respectively. Our contribution to this body of scholarship on queer Nigerian and African literature is our specific focus on the theme of deliverance that, as we will argue, draws attention to the complex ways in which religion is engaged as 'central to ideological formations in Africa' (Dunton 2023: 11). There is a tendency, in queer studies at large, to mostly associate religion with conservativeness and anti-queerness, yet 'thinking queerness from Africa foregrounds religion – broadly defined – as a productive site and category' (Otu and Van Klinken 2023: 519). Indeed, in African queer social formations and cultural production, religion appears to be multifaceted – as much as it is subjected to critique, it also is creatively and constructively engaged to explore its potential for queer world-making (e.g. Ncube and Van Klinken 2023; Robertson 2021; Van Klinken and Chitando 2021). Even Pentecostal Christianity, often seen as particularly invested in anti-LGBTQ+ politics in Africa, might be open to queer-affirming interpretations and possibilities. The three novels discussed in the subsequent sections each have their own take on, and approach to, religion. We will demonstrate that, in their engagement with Pentecostalism, specifically the practice of deliverance, they respectively seek to expose religious hypocrisy, reclaim indigenous religion and reinterpret Christianity. Ethnographic studies have highlighted 'the particular role that language plays in the discourse of demon possession and deliverance within Pentecostal/evangelical/charismatic churches' (Rowan 2016: 248). We will take this into account in our reading of the selected literary texts, examining the linguistic and discursive registers that literary writers draw upon in their engagement with deliverance in relation to queer bodies.

Exposing Religious Hypocrisy in On Ajayi Crowther Street

Earlier in this chapter, we referred to Elnathan John's satirical take on worship of 'the Nigerian God'. He further elaborates on this religious satire in his 2019 book, *On Ajayi Crowther Street*, which as a graphic novel – illustrated by Àlàbá Ònájìn – makes a unique contribution to queer Nigerian literature. Notably, this is also the only text of the three under discussion that was actually published in Nigeria, by Cassava Republic, whose mission it is 'to change the way we all think about African writing' (Cassava Republic n.d.). The novel centres around the family of Reverend Akpoborie, who is the lead pastor of a Pentecostal church, called the Reformed End-Time Ministries. The setting is Lagos, a city which is 'generally regarded as the Pentecostal capital of the world on account of the strong presence of megachurches and the crowds they pull together each week' (Ukah 2020: 454). John and Ònájìn do not give a very sympathetic account of Reverend Akpoborie and his church. Instead, their novel is a literary version of the 'popular tales of pastors, luxury, frauds and corruption' that surround Nigerian Pentecostalism (Casciano 2021). The pastor, in this story, is a crook who runs his church as a money-making enterprise with scam miracles, and a moral hypocrite who preaches family values while forcing himself onto the housemaid and firing her when she protests against his advances.

One of the threads running through the novel is a 'miracle service' that Reverend Akpoborie is planning to hold in his church. Acknowledging his own inability to heal people and perform miracles, he plans to hire the services of a gang of 'scoundrels' to perform fake miracles, and even has some biblical justification of this scam (John and Ònájìn 2019: 22–3). His junior pastor is sent to negotiate with the gang about the price, which turns out to be a hard bargain because, as the gang leader claims: 'Good miracles cost money' (36). The agreed price doubles after Reverend Akpoborie comes up with the idea that the deliverance service should specifically focus on homosexuality, seeking to deliver 'these sick people' (106). His idea is inspired by the passing of an anti-gay law (the story here alludes to the Nigerian Same-Sex Marriage Prohibition Act, 2013). The novel suggests that the passing of the law has put the issue of same-sex sexuality into the public spotlight, recording a conversation between clients in a hair salon who refer to gay people as 'animals', instruments of the devil, sinners and carriers of disease (62). It further suggests that for Reverend Akpoborie, this moral panic is a business opportunity to market his church. In that sense, there is no difference between him and the gangsters he is hiring who are happy to stage any kind of miracle as long as they gain financially.

The miracle service is promoted via a billboard, referring to Reverend Akpoborie as 'the anointed man of God' and as 'the godly destroyer' (126). These words stand in shrill contrast to the earlier acknowledgement by the pastor himself that he actually 'can't really heal people' (23). The discrepancy is John and Ònájìn's way of suggesting that Pentecostal marketing is a swindle. The language of destroying is repeated as the billboard advertises the event as 'operation point and kill: night of divine demolition' where 'all enemies must die in Jesus' name' (126). Obviously, the enemies to be destroyed are demonic spirits. During the service, Reverend Akpoborie casts out spirits causing barrenness, illness, and other infections and inflictions, constantly invoking 'the mighty name of Jesus' (126–7). It culminates in the pastor introducing a young man – arranged by the criminals – as being possessed by the spirit of homosexuality. The graphics depict the drama that deliverance in a Pentecostal context is, with the pastor laying his hand on the young man and pushing him hard till he falls on the floor, while shouting at him, 'In da mighty name of Jesus, be loosed! … Be loosed! Be loosed! Loosed I say!' (131). The invocation of 'the mighty name of Jesus' is significant, as it illustrates how, for Pentecostals, Jesus Christ is a source of 'ultimate spiritual power' that can be mobilized to combat any perceived evil (Wariboko 2014: 63). The repetition of the phrase 'be loosed' is part of the speech act of deliverance, serving to add force to the instruction of the devil to leave. The young man's rolling over the floor is the sign that the evil spirit has left him, which the pastor verifies by asking whether he still likes men, to which the young man responds: 'Men? No o! God forbid! Why would I like men' (John and Ònájìn 2019: 132). The dramatic deliverance from the spirit of homosexuality has been successfully staged, and the congregation shouts in excitement, 'Praise da Lord!!!' (133).

In the meantime, there is a separate storyline in which Akpoborie's son, with the telling name Godstime, has become increasingly intimate with his friend, Onyeka. When his father finds out, he sees it as a threat to his reputation and ministry, telling his son: 'I will not allow the devil to use you to ruin me' (116). He then subjects Godstime and Onyeka to a private deliverance ritual, spraying them with 'anointing oil' while praying loudly: 'In the mighty name of Jesus, I command every demon of Sodom to get out of these children' (120). The phrase 'demon of Sodom' is striking here, as it illustrates how in 'the performative path of deliverance' the first step often is identifying the evil spirit (Rowan 2016: 249). The phrase itself refers to the biblical story of Sodom and Gomorrah, which, in popular Christian usage, is associated with homosexuality (Ukah 2020). Onyeka plays along during the deliverance, responding to the ritual by 'shaking and speaking in tongues' (John and Ònájìn 2019: 123); apparently, he has internalized the demonization of his sexuality. Following the deliverance session, Reverend Akpoborie instructs Godstime and Onyeka to stop seeing each other, and that Onyeka should stop coming to church, leaving Godstime broken-hearted. In a tragic turn of events, immediately after the successful miracle service where Akpoborie cast out the demon of homosexuality, the pastor receives a phone call from Onyeka's mother, who tells him that her son has committed suicide. Godstime blames his father for the tragedy, saying: 'It's all your fault! Jesus didn't drive people away!' (144). He further suggests that his parents, different from Jesus, only care about their reputation, not about other human beings. The truth of this is demonstrated later in the story, after online media break the news that Reverend Akpoborie's son is gay. The pastor tells his congregation the next Sunday that this false rumour proves that he is, in fact, an anointed man of God, as otherwise the devil would not be trying to break his ministry. Godstime is sent to Germany for studies but ends up in a severe depression; however, the Nigerian pastor – a friend of his father – who serves as his host, presents an accepting version of Christian faith fundamentally different from Reverend Akpoborie's, and helps Godstime to come to terms with his sexuality. According to Wariboko (2014: 77), 'anointing, holiness, and prosperity are the trinity of the Pentecostal experience and keys to understanding the Nigerian Pentecostal movement'. Yet, John and Ònájìn's satirical novel suggests that this trinity is at serious risk of becoming a false pretention. Reverend Akpoborie might claim to be anointed by God, but this is religious marketing language with no substance to it – it is a fake anointing. Likewise, his concern with holiness turns out to be a concern about his own reputation as a 'man of God', which he has carefully cultivated to hide his immoral character as a crook pastor, unfaithful husband and sexual harasser. He has built his wealth and prosperity on this reputation, but at the end of the novel he has lost all of it. Even though one of the characters in the novel says that 'God will not come down and give justice' (John and Ònájìn 2019: 197), the novel's ending suggests that justice is done as the crook pastor is served rightly. To conclude, *On Ajayi Crowther Street* offers a sharp critique of Pentecostalism as a hypocritical religious culture, and of deliverance practices as a scam exploiting people's fears and anxieties to enrich self-proclaimed 'men of God'. The main objective of the novel is to subject Pentecostalism, and specifically the Pentecostal preoccupation with homosexuality, to a satirical critique and to expose its moral and spiritual bankruptcy. This fits in with John's broader project of telling the story of Nigeria by 'telling the story of religion' and how it affects the country's social environment and political culture (Jackson and Suhr-Sytsma 2017: 93). Yet, in a subtle way, the novel can also be seen as engaging in constructive religious thought. First, the name Godstime for the central gay character is very well chosen, as it can be read as a suggestion that the time has come to accept all human persons, regardless of their sexuality, as created in the image of God. Indeed, it suggests that recognizing the dignity and rights of queer people is a divine imperative. Second, the way in which the character of Reverend Akpoborie is contrasted to that of Jesus is illuminating, as it invokes a model of religious ministry that instead of driving people away accepts them for who they are.

Reclaiming Indigenous Religion in An Ordinary Wonder

The novel *An Ordinary Wonder* by Buki Papillon (2021) is unique in Nigerian and possibly African queer literature for centring around an intersex protagonist. It presents the coming-of-age story of Otolorin (Oto), who grows up with his twin sister Wura. Upon birth, Oto's genitalia were found to be ambiguous; he is gendered as a boy, yet when growing up he becomes more attuned towards being a girl. Seeing the ambiguous genitals of the newly born baby, the midwife (who also was a prophetess) screams and prophesizes to Oto's mother that 'your true son from heaven was stolen from your womb by worshippers of Satan and replaced with an *emere* demon' (44).[4] The novel captures the stigma associated with Oto's condition immediately on the first page, which opens by saying, 'My name is Otolorin. I've been called "monster"', and which proceeds by making a comparison of Oto to Wura: 'Wura is everything to our mother, who will never have any other children because she is the woman who birthed the unspeakable, and my father has no desire to sire any other monsters' (5). In fact, as the story unfolds, it emerges that Oto's birth was the reason why his father left his wife – something Oto's mother never got over and which she blames her son for.

The stigma of being different results in Oto being bullied at school, such as by Bayo who forcibly strips Oto naked and then ridicules him: 'Hahaha … oh my God! *Hahahaha*! What is this tiny thing? How will you ever satisfy a woman? … You're really strange, Oto, do you know that? You look like an *iwin*. A mamiwater' (67). *Iwin* is the Yoruba word for a spirit of the forest, while 'mamiwater' refers to the well-known water spirit (also known as Mami Wata) who features in many West African traditions. Bayo's linking of Oto's ambiguously sexed body to these spirits is an illustration of the ways in which spirits in many African cultures are associated with gender ambiguity and fluidity. Although for Bayo this clearly is a negative association, at least potentially this spiritualization of the queer body can also be constructive. As Stella Nyanzi (2014: 67) has argued, 'cultural and indigenous understandings of gendered spirits of ancestors who may possess individuals offer socially appropriate notions of handling fluid, transient gender identities'. As we will discuss shortly, *An Ordinary Wonder* is concerned with exploring this queer potential of spirits. Yet, it does so against a background of popular beliefs in Christianized Nigeria today, that indigenous gendered spirits belong to the realm of the devil. One of the effects of missionary Christianity in many parts of Africa is that the spirits of indigenous religions were understood in a dualist Christian framework of good versus evil, God versus the devil. This is reflected in the way in which Oto's deeply Christian mother understands her child's condition. In a conversation with her cousin, she again compares Wura to Oto when saying: 'Wura is the joy of my life! Unfortunately she just won't accept that her brother's aim is her destruction. That he is being controlled by evil forces beyond her understanding. I do all I can to protect her from him, but it is never enough' (Papillon 2021: 46).

Oto's mother's understanding of Oto's condition is influenced by other people in her environment, in particular her own mother and the prophet of their church. Oto's grandmother, Mama Ondo, uses the explanatory framework of witchcraft to explain why Oto is 'abnormal down there' (44). A fervent member of a Pentecostal-type church, called Seraphic Temple of Holy Fire, Mama Ondo has successfully insisted that Oto's mother leaves the Baptist church she used to attend and joins the temple to seek spiritual protection against the spell put on her family. The difference between the two churches is profound: at Ezra Baptist Church 'people wore their Sunday best and sang softly from hymnals' (103), while at the Seraphic Temple of Holy Fire the four-hour-long services feature intense preaching, prophecies and deliverances performed by charismatic leaders, referred to with the Yoruba word *woli*, meaning prophet.[5] The senior prophet, Woli Omolaja, makes Oto's mother believe that Oto's condition is caused by the devil. Twice the prophet – with Oto's mother's consent – subjects Oto to a deliverance ritual, narrated in the novel in great detail to convey its traumatizing effect. After the first violent act of deliverance was performed, Woli Omolaja guarantees Oto's mother 'that the removal of the demon inhabiting this body and the restoration of your true son is only the beginning of Jehovah's miracles' (116). Mother's mind is put at ease, and Oto enjoys several months of peace at home, until another incident makes his mother doubt whether the demon has truly gone. She drags Oto to the temple again, for a second deliverance session with the prophet – in private and at night this time. This attempt is more forceful than the first one, complete with whipping Oto's back and a 'baptism' (in fact, a drowning) in a water stream to 'wash the filth of darkness from this sinner' (148). Seeing the burning eyes of the prophet cast upon him, Oto realizes that he 'wasn't meant to survive this. Not intact' (148).

What is significant in the deliverance narratives in the novel, is that in both cases, Oto experiences another spiritual presence that protects and saves his life. This female mermaid-type spirit first appears early in the novel, after his mother has beaten twelve-year-old Oto into hospital for putting on a dress of his sister: '*Call me Yeyemi*, she said without words. *You are safe. Here between worlds, at the parting of the veil, you may rest*' (11). Throughout the novel, Yeyemi – Yoruba for 'my mother' – is a symbol of maternal divinity appearing at the most critical moments when Oto is in trouble, such as when Bayo bullies him, and when his life is in danger. During the first deliverance, Oto has a vision of her while the prophet is spitting in his eyes: 'She caught me in her outstretched arms, looking every inch a goddess in a shawl of green and gold seaweed that floated around her as if it was alive. It wrapped itself around us. In that embrace, I breathed easy'

(115). During the second deliverance attempt, when the prophet is drowning Oto in the water, Oto screams for her – 'Yeyemi, save me!' (148) – and she comes again to his rescue, biting Woli Omolaja who is then forced to let Oto go. In the novel's closing chapter, when Oto – who by then has adopted the name Lori – is about to board a plane to America, heading towards freedom, Yeyemi appears again, with a word of encouragement and affirmation: '*I am the strength and fire in you, I am everything that is and was and ever will be*' (312).

The figure of Yeyemi is one way in which the novel suggests that indigenous religious beliefs can be life-affirming for queer people. Yet, the novel has yet another complementary way of making the same suggestion. Although Oto's father left the family soon after he was born, he does insist that Oto's mother – to her horror – takes the young Oto for regular visits to a *Babalawo*, which is a priest in the Ifa divination system (Ogundele 2007). It appears that when Oto and Wura were born, their parents brought them to the Babalawo for a naming ceremony intended to divine a child's *ori*, or destiny. For Oto, 'the results were ambiguous', although the priest discerned that 'his head is not cursed' (Papillon 2021: 27). After Oto has turned twelve, the Babalawo repeats the divination ceremony, this time with crystal clear insight: 'We have here a daughter whose *ori* made a most unusual selection in heaven before descending into the marketplace of life. … The form which best favours her destiny in this lifetime is female' (30). To explain Oto's condition, the priest shares a piece of Yoruba mythology, about how at the time of creation, the gods made a small oversight resulting in a body 'that looked neither fully male nor female', but that was adopted by the goddess Yemoja as falling under her female ori and receiving her protection and guidance (30). Oto is initially bewildered but also feels affirmed – 'the gods had pronounced me a girl!' – and is reassured by the Babalawo of being 'both normal and special' (31). The validation here is a declaration that Oto's embodiment inhabits sacred meaning – far from demon possessed, Oto is, indeed, 'an ordinary wonder' (5).

By including this scene, which is crucial to Oto's coming of age narrative, *An Ordinary Wonder* offers a literary illustration of the point that 'traditional societies in Africa possess myths that help them navigate daily social and political existence when it comes to gender and sexuality issues. … Gender and sexuality myths in Africa correspond to the lived realities of the peoples' (Olali 2022: 324). Thus, the novel suggests that indigenous religious traditions offer wisdom to understand and affirm gender ambiguity, while Christianity tends to demonize anything outside or in between the binary construction of male and female. The only nuance to the latter is a scene where a Catholic nun from England, who is a teacher at Oto's school, reassures him, like the Babalawo earlier, that there is nothing wrong with him. Sister Angelica uses language that merges Christianity and biomedical science when she tells Oto: 'You're just a child. God created us all in his image and the devil does not create but destroy. This likely has to do with your hormones' (Papillon 2021: 73).

It has been argued that 'cultural, and originally Christian, insistence on a binary opposition of maleness and femaleness is at the root of Western antipathy toward intersexuality' (Hiebert and Hiebert 2015: 31). *An Ordinary*

Wonder pushes this further by suggesting that in the current Nigerian context, Pentecostalism, in particular, delegitimizes the lived and embodied experiences of people such as Oto. Turning the Pentecostal demonization of the queer body around, Oto suggests that instead of him being demon-possessed, 'it was the people who whipped [him] till [he] fainted that were evil' (Papillon 2021: 147). In other words, it is the church prophets that need to be delivered from the evil of rigid cisgender heteronormativity and the subsequent violence against intersex and other queer bodies.

Reinterpreting Christianity in Under the Udala Trees

Hailed as the first 'Nigerian lesbian novel' (Manzo 2018: 151), *Under the Udala Trees* by Chinelo Okparanta (2015) stands out from the previous texts in a few ways. First, obviously it features a female protagonist (although, notably, the word 'lesbian' is never used in the novel, which is interesting given the ongoing debates about the limitations of Western LGBTQ+ identity categories in Africa). Second, not just religion as a social phenomenon, but faith as a personal matter, is a central theme, as already indicated by the epigraph, which is a quotation from the Bible (Hebrews 11.1). Indeed, this Bildungsroman can be read as a literary account of queering faith within Christianity through a process of biblical and theological reinterpretation that is woven through the narrative (Van Klinken and Chitando 2021: 165–80). The novel explicitly sets out to deliver Christianity from its investment into homophobic politics. It does so in the aftermath of the passing of the Same-Sex Marriage (Prohibition) Act in 2013 in Nigeria, with fervent support from the religious sector, which according to an author's note at the end of the novel was the direct occasion for writing this text. Third, this also makes the novel explicit in its political intentions, as it responds to an anti-gay bill and aims to 'give Nigeria's marginalized LGBTQ citizens a more powerful voice, and a place in our nation's history' (Okparanta 2015: 325). To recognize the place of LGBTQ people in Nigerian history, Okparanta chooses a significant historical context, as the story is set in the aftermath of the Nigerian Civil War, or the Biafra War (1967–70). The protagonist – named Ifeoma – is Igbo and loses her father in the war, with her mother ('Mama') being left traumatized and seeking comfort in her conservative faith. Fourth, different from the previous two texts, the scene of deliverance narrated in *Under the Udala Trees* is not set in the church but in a domestic space, and it is not a pastor but Ifeoma's mother who performs this drama onto her daughter. Thus, the novel also opens a conversation about parenthood of queer children.

When Mama finds out about Ifeoma's blossoming relationship with another teenage girl (a Hausa Muslim girl, for that matter), she subjects her daughter to a rigid programme of religious discipline because 'there's nothing more important now than for us to begin working on cleansing your soul' (65). This programme consists of daily Bible study lessons, where Mama and Ifeoma work through the whole Bible. Immediately from the first session, Mama uses the opportunity to explain that homosexuality, according to the Bible, is an abomination. Discussing the creation story of Genesis 1, she tells her daughter that clearly, God created man and woman to live as husband and wife, because 'if God wanted it to be otherwise, would He not have included it that other way in the Bible?' (68). So it continues, to the story of Sodom and Gomorrah, the laws in Leviticus and other so-called clobber verses which for Mama all centre around 'this issue of abomination' (80). Yet, Ijeoma is reminded of what her father once told her, about traditional folk-tales being allegorical, figurative commentaries on certain life situations; she wonders why the same might not be the case for biblical stories. Mama dismisses the suggestion, saying 'The Bible is the Bible and not to be questioned' (81), thus reinforcing the idea of a literalist interpretation of scripture. Ijeoma, however, has an independent mind and is not satisfied; she keeps questioning her mother's take on the Bible and comes up with alternative interpretations. For instance, regarding the story of Adam and Eve, she muses: 'Just because the story happened to focus on a certain Adam and Eve did not mean that all other possibilities were forbidden. … What if Adam and Eve were merely symbols of companionship?' (82–3).

For Mama, Ifeoma's sexuality is caused by the devil, and she prays for God's protection of her daughter: 'Protect this my child from the devil that has come to take her innocent soul away. … Protect her from the demons that are trying to send her to hell. Lead her not into temptation' (72). Yet, when the Bible lessons do not appear to show much effect – Ijeoma confesses that she is still thinking of the girl she fell in love with – Mama realizes that something stronger than a prayer for protection is needed: the devil, who clearly has entered her daughter's body and mind, needs to be cast out. In a dramatic scene, Mama performs a deliverance, praying over Ijeoma who is on her knees in front of her while sprinkling her with anointed water, and ordering the demon to come out and leave: 'Her voice was progressively louder each time she repeated it, but still controlled: "In the name of the Almighty God, I order you to leave my child alone"' (88). The repeated language and the volume of her voice are typical of the Pentecostal drama of deliverance, which is a performance of spiritual power. At the end her mother loses her self-control, crying for the devil to leave, with a piercing voice that causes shivers on Ijeoma's back. In the silence that follows this drama, Ijeoma realizes that the only way to get out of the situation is by giving in to her mother's prayers. Her response, saying 'I will be cured by the glory and power of God' (89), can be seen as a typical Pentecostal speech act of positive confession, where deliverance and healing are enacted by proclaiming it in faith (Adelakun 2021: 58).

Yet, Ijeoma is neither delivered nor cured, as she gradually comes to understand that her sexuality is neither an illness nor demonic but is a natural part of herself. As she puts it: 'By this time, a large part of me did not believe I had committed any type of abomination' (159). Instead of being delivered from an evil spirit, she is being liberated by giving in to a newly found love. While dancing together with her girlfriend Ndidi, Ijeoma 'felt a sense of liberation that I had not until then known' (193). Yet, this queer liberation is a process with setbacks. Still living with and influenced by her mother, Ijeoma keeps having doubts about whether she is doing the right thing, and even wonders whether she might be a 'witch under the influence of the devil' (196). Seeking consolation in a quiet church and asking God for a sign to help her recognize the evil in her heart, the sign comes in the form of her mother walking into the church space, from which Ijeoma concludes: 'If this was God's sign, then Mama was the evil in my heart' (197). It is a turning moment in this coming-of-age story, as Ijeoma learns to break away – be delivered – from her mother's watchful eyes and from her mother's homophobia that she has internalized. Yet, even this is not a straightforward process: after a violent and traumatizing attack on the community of queer women that Ijeoma, via her girlfriend, has become part of, she gives in to her mother's pressure to marry a childhood friend and lead a 'normal life' without fear of being found out (220). The marriage fails, and at the end of the novel Ijeoma returns to Ndidi. By then, even Mama finally, albeit reluctantly, accepts her daughter the way she is when she mutters: 'God, who created you, must have known what He did' (323).

Ijeoma herself, in this difficult journey of freeing herself from her mother and coming to terms with her sexuality, has not lost her faith, although she has had to reimagine it. Not only does she have to change her view of the Bible, recognizing the multiple ways in which it can be interpreted; she also grows in her understanding of God, moving away from the rigid image of a stern God that her mother taught her, and instead adopting a notion of God as an artist who is creatively and actively involved with the world, transforming it for the better:

> If the Old and New Testaments are any indication, then change is in fact a major part of His aesthetic, a major part of His vision for the world. ... Maybe God is still speaking and will continue to do so for always. Maybe He is still creating new covenants, only we are too deaf, too headstrong, too set in old ways to hear.
>
> (322)

These theological musings are a direct critique of a conservative form of Christianity which believes that God's laws as presented in the Bible are unchangeable. Yet, they also open up an alternative, progressive understanding of Christian faith in line with a humanistic vision of human diversity and freedom. This way, *Under the Udala Trees* creates 'a space for the Christian legitimacy of female same-sex love' (Frateur 2019) and helps to imagine a Christian social and political practice that is radically different from popular Pentecostal culture.

Conclusion

The Nigerian queer novels discussed in this chapter nuance, complicate and enrich the understanding of the relationship between queerness and religion in an African social and cultural context, and they gesture towards a postqueer, spiritualized understanding of sexual and gendered embodiment, be it indigenous, Christian or a combination of these two. By critically narrating the experience of deliverance of the queer body through violent religious ritual and discursive practices, they offer a unique African literary queer critique of religion, specifically in its Pentecostal Christian form, highlighting the intrusive and harmful nature of Pentecostal deliverance practices. Yet, importantly, none of these novels break with religion altogether.

Elnathan John and Àlàbá Ònájìn's *On Ajayi Crowther Street* is the most explicit and wide-ranging in its critique of Pentecostalism, not just centring on the Pentecostal demonization of queer bodies but also its broader moral hypocrisy and religious hollowness. Yet, as we have seen, in a more subtle way, the novel can also be seen as engaging in constructive religious thought. The name of the main gay character, Godstime, can actually be read as a suggestion that his coming out occurs at God's time. Buki Papillon's *An Ordinary Wonder* offers perhaps the most gripping narrative account of deliverance of the queer body in any Nigerian literary text so far. In this novel, the intersex protagonist, Oto, comes to terms with his condition after narrowly surviving a traumatic and intense attempt at deliverance by a Pentecostal prophet – a survival which he owes to the fact that the water spirit, Yeyemi, comes to his rescue. Papillon's narrative suggests that Yoruba religion has a rich mythology that helps to make sense and affirm Oto's condition, and thus is much more conducive of queerness than Pentecostal Christianity which can only demonize the queer body. Thus, this novel presents a literary example of reclaiming indigenous religion as a strategy of African (post)queer world-making. Different from *An Ordinary Wonder*, Chinelo Okparanta's *Under the Udala Trees* demonstrates that such world-making can also occur within the space of Christian symbols and meanings, yet the novel makes an effort to indigenize Christianity in the Nigerian Igbo context, suggesting that homophobia and heteronormativity are not intrinsic to Christianity but are linked to its colonial European kernel.

Through different strategies – exposing religious hypocrisy, reclaiming indigenous religion and reinterpreting Christianity – these three novels offer alternative modalities of African (post)queer world-making. Importantly, in each of these modalities, (post)queer world-making is not about breaking away from, but occurs within the realm of the religious, although it involves profound religious negotiations and transformations. In various ways, these novels subscribe to a frame in which sexuality is spiritualized but reimagine this spiritualization in a way that is affirming of queer bodies. Resisting a Eurocentric secular LGBT identities and rights framework, they explore the religious and spiritual resources that are relevant and meaningful in the Nigerian context and that can help to affirm queer existence. Doing so, they also contribute to postqueer theorizing. The queering (or postqueering, if you like) of queer Africa, to use Stella Nyanzi's (2014) phrase, is not about a wholesale liberation from religion as an oppressive force. Instead, it is about the continent being delivered from the evil of particular forms of religiosity that are harmful and destructive, in order for queer African bodies to flourish and be affirmed by the spirits and God(s) that gave them life.

Notes

1   *Walking with Shadows* is not the first Nigerian literary text with a gay character, yet it is the first that offers a characterization that 'is not only insightful but also deeply

sympathetic' (Dunton 2011: 208) and that renders visible 'the very possibility of a Nigerian homosexuality' (Zabus 2013: 95).

2	The Lord's Prayer is taught by Jesus in the gospels of the New Testament and is commonly prayed by Christians across denominations. Its last petition reads, 'Deliver us from evil.'

3	Our reading *for* deliverance is inspired by Gray's creative and thoughtful unpacking of deliverance as a methodological, ethical and theological category with queer potential.

4	*Emere* is a Yoruba term for a spirit-child believed to travel between the spiritual and visible world.

5	*Woli* is commonly used in Nigeria to describe prophets in indigenous Pentecostal-type churches.

References

Adelakun, Abimbola. 2021. *Performing Power in Nigeria: Identity, Politics, and Pentecostalism*. Cambridge: Cambridge University Press.

Anderson, Allan H. 2018. *Spirit-Filled World: Religious Dis/Continuity in African Pentecostalism*. New York: Palgrave Macmillan.

Azuah, Unoma. 2016. 'Whips', in Unoma Azuah (ed.), *Blessed Body: The Secret Lives of Nigerian Lesbian, Gay, Bisexual and Transgender*, 195–8. Jackson, TN: CookingPot Publishing.

Bademosi, Kehinde. 2016. 'Holy Anger', in Unoma Azuah (ed.), *Blessed Body: The Secret Lives of Nigerian Lesbian, Gay, Bisexual and Transgender*, 185–93. Jackson, TN: CookingPot Publishing.

BM. 2018. 'To Anyone Being Hated, Be Strong', in Azeenarh Mohammed, Chitra Nagarajan and Rafeeat Aliyu (eds), *She Called Me Woman: Nigeria's Queer Women Speak Out*, 210–27. Abuja: Cassava Republic.

Casciano, Davide. 2021. 'Popular Tales of Pastors, Luxury, Frauds and Corruption: Pentecostalism, Conspicuous Consumption, and the Moral Economy of Corruption in Nigeria', *Journal of Extreme Anthropology* 5 (2): 52–71.

Cassava Republic. n.d. 'About Us'. Available online: https://cassavarepublic.biz/about-us-4/ (accessed 8 July 2023).

Courtois, Cédric. 2022. 'Visibilizing "Those Who Have No Part": LGBTQIA+ Representation in Contemporary Nigerian Fiction in English', *Études anglaises* 75 (2): 175–91.

Dibia, Jude. 2011. *Walking with Shadows*. 2nd edn. Lagos: Jalaa Writers' Collective. (First edition published in 2005, with BlackSands Books, Lagos.)

Dunton, Chris. 1989. '"Wheyting be Dat?" The Treatment of Homosexuality in African Literature', *Research in African Literatures* 20 (3): 422–48.

Dunton, Chris. 2011. 'Afterword', in Jude Dibia, *Walking with Shadows*, 207–10. Lagos: Jalaa Writers Collective.

Dunton, Chris. 2023. 'Tuning into the Polyphony: The Emergence of LGBTQ+ Writing in Africa', *Research in African Literatures* 53 (4): 1–14.

Emezi, Akwaeke. 2018. *Freshwater*. London: Faber and Faber.

Frateur, Amber. 2019. '"Adam and Eve, not Eve and Eve"? Towards a Space for the Christian Legitimacy of Female Same-Sex Love in Chinelo Okparanta's Under the Udala Trees', MA thesis, University of Ghent. Available online: https://www.scriptiebank.be/scriptie/2019/adam-and-eve-not-eve-and-eve-towards-space-christian-legitimacy-female-same-sex-love (accessed 10 July 2023).

Gray, Biko Mandela. 2020. 'The Deliverance of Christian Queer', *Religious Studies Review* 46 (3): 321–4.

Green-Simms, Lindsey. 2016. 'The Emergent Queer: Homosexuality and Nigerian Fiction in the 21st Century', *Research in African Literatures* 47 (2): 139–61.

Hiebert, Valerie and Dennis Hiebert. 2015. 'Intersex Persons and the Church: Unknown, Unwelcomed, Unwanted Neighbors', *Journal of Sociology and Christianity* 5 (2): 31–44.

Homewood, Nathanael. 2020. 'Leaky Anuses, Loose Vaginas, and Large Penises: A Hierarchy of Sexualized Bodies in the Pentecostal Imaginary', in S. N. Nyeck (ed.), *Routledge Handbook of Queer African Studies*, 113–28. London and New York: Routledge.

Iweala, Uzodinma. 2018. *Speak No Evil*. London: John Murray.

Jackson, Jeanne-Marie and Nathan Suhr-Sytsma. 2017. 'Interview with Elnathan John', *Research in African Literatures* 48 (2): 89–93.

Jackson, Peter A. 2001. 'Pre-Gay, Post-Queer: Thai Perspectives on Proliferating Gender/Sex Diversity in Asia', *Journal of Homosexuality* 40 (3–4): 1–25.

Janson, Marloes. 2021. *Crossing Religious Boundaries: Islam, Christianity and 'Yoruba Religion' in Lagos, Nigeria*. Cambridge: Cambridge University Press.

John, Elnathan. 2019. *Be(com)ing Nigerian: A Guide*. Abuja and London: Cassava Republic Press.

John, Elnathan and Àlàbá Ònájìn. 2019. *On Ajayi Crowther Street*. Abuja and London: Cassava Republic Press.

KTN Kenya. 2014. 'Jeff Koinange Live with Valentine Njoroge and Binyavanga Wainaina (Being Gay in Kenya)', YouTube, 29 January. Available online: www.youtube.com/watch?v=CANd4G_ewBY (accessed 7 July 2023).

Manzo, Kerry. 2018. 'Queer Temporalities and Epistemologies: Jude Dibia's *Walking with Shadows* and Chinelo Okparanta's *Under the Udala Trees*', *African Literature Today* 36 (Queer Theory in Film & Fiction): 151–64.

Munro, Brenna. 2016. 'Locating "Queer" in Contemporary Writing of Love and War in Nigeria', *Research in African Literatures* 47 (2): 121–38.

Ncube, Gibson and Adriaan van Klinken. 2023. 'Abdellah Taïa and an Emergent Queer African Islamic Discourse: Texts, Visibility and Intimate Archives', *African Studies* 81 (3–4): 306–23.

Nyanzi, Stella. 2014. 'Queering Queer Africa' in *Reclaiming Afrikan: Queer Perspectives on Sexual and Gender Identities*, edited by Zethu Matebeni, 61–66. Athlone: Modjaji Books.

Obadare, Ebenezer. 2018. *Pentecostal Republic: Religion and the Struggle for State Power in Nigeria*. London: Zed Books.

Ogundele, Samuel O. 2007. 'Aspects of Indigenous Medicine in South Western Nigeria', *Studies of Ethno-Medicine* 1 (2): 127–33.

Okparanta, Chinelo. 2015. *Under the Udala Trees*. London: Granta.

Olali, David. 2022. 'African Traditional Religion, Sexual Orientation, Transgender, and Homosexuality', in Ibigbolade S. Aderibigbe and Toyin Falola (eds), *The Palgrave Handbook of African Traditional Religion*, 317–28. New York: Palgrave Macmillan.

Oloruntoba-Oju, Diekara. 2021. '"Like a Drag or Something": Central Texts at the Pioneering Forefront of Contemporary Nigerian Queerscapes', *Africa*, 91 (3): 418–33.

Otu, Kwame E. and Adriaan van Klinken. 2023. 'African Studies Keywords: Queer', *African Studies Review* 66 (2): 1–22.

Papillon, Buki. 2021. *An Ordinary Wonder*. London: Dialogue Books.

Quayson, Ato. 2003. *Calibrations: Reading for the Social*. Minneapolis: University of Minnesota Press.

Richman, Naomi. 2021. 'Homosexuality, the Created Body and Queer Fantasies in the African Deliverance Imaginary', *Journal of Religion in Africa* 50 (3–4): 249–77.

Robertson, Megan. 2021. 'Queer Studies and Religion in Southern Africa: The Production of Queer Christian Subjects', *Religion Compass* 15 (1): e12385.

Rowan, Kirsty. 2016. '"Who Are You in this Body?": Identifying Demons and the Path to Deliverance in a London Pentecostal Church', *Language in Society*, 45 (2): 247–70.

Ukah, Asonzeh. 2016. 'Pentecostal Discourses on Homosexuality in Nigeria', in *Christianity and Controversies over Homosexuality in Contemporary Africa*, edited by Ezra Chitando and Adriaan van Klinken, 21–37. London and New York: Routledge.

Ukah, Asonzeh. 2018. 'Pentecostal Apocalypticism: Hate Speech, Contested Citizenship, and Religious Discourses on Same-sex Relations in Nigeria', *Citizenship Studies*, 22 (6): 633–49.

Ukah, Asonzeh. 2020. 'Prosperity, Prophecy and the COVID-19 Pandemic: The Healing Economy of African Pentecostalism', *Pneuma* 42 (3–4): 430–59.

Van Klinken, Adriaan. 2013. 'Gay Rights, the Devil and the End Times: Public Religion and the Enchantment of the Homosexuality Debate in Zambia', *Religion*, 43 (4): 519–40.

Van Klinken, Adriaan. 2023. 'Pentecostal Plurality and Sexual Politics in Africana Worlds', in Michael Wilkinson and Jörg Haustein (eds), *The Pentecostal World*, 288–98. London and New York: Routledge.

Van Klinken, Adriaan and Ezra Chitando. 2021. *Reimagining Christianity and Sexual Diversity in Africa*. London: Hurst & Co.; New York: Oxford University Press.

Wariboko, Nimi. 2014. *Nigerian Pentecostalism*. Rochester, NY: University of Rochester Press.

Zabus, Chantal. 2013. *Out in Africa: Same-sex Desire in Sub-Saharan Literatures and Cultures*. Woodbridge, UK and Rochester, NY: James Currey.

Chapter 6

(NON)GENEALOGICAL RADICAL QUEERNESS: ON A SCHIZOPHRENIC READING OF FRIEDA EKOTTO'S *CHUCHOTE PAS TROP*

Naminata Diabate

'Peindre une liberté de cette sorte dans les sociétés peules du Cameroun revient à ourdir une révolution. Frieda Ekotto l'assume tranquillement' (To paint this kind of freedom in the Peul society of Cameroon amounts to starting a revolution and Frieda Ekotto quietly takes that on) (Nimrod 2006: 224; my translation). This is how novelist and literary-cultural critic Bema Nimrod frames Frieda Ekotto's first novel, *Chuchote pas trop* (2001), which was translated into English in 2019 as *Don't Whisper Too Much*. Is a revolution needed in representations of nonconforming sexualities in francophone sub-Saharan Africa? If yes, does the revolution require a novel reading praxis? What would the conditions of possibility of such a revolution look like? Although Nimrod does not answer these questions, I concur with his reading that Ekotto's novel is a radical departure from earlier imaginings of same-sex sexualities in francophone Africa, wherein oblique narrative strategies, albeit useful, end up marginalizing the subject. In *Chuchote pas trop*, multiple boundaries of sexual and intimate practices cross in extravagant ways, including racial, generational, familial and able-bodied. The first chapter of the novel, 'Affi ou la communion du corps', sets the stage,

At that moment, something inexplicable manifests itself in the connection between Affi and her mother. The girl shivers suddenly. Her head is raised by an irresistible force, and she moves her mouth closer, brushing her mother's chin with her forehead. Their lips meet in a kiss of uninterrupted violence. The rusty steel ring adorning the mother's lower lip opens and catches on Affi's tongue. A warm, salty liquid trickles from the girl's mouth. Holding her tighter and tighter in her arms, the mother continues her whispering: 'My blood and yours mix like two lovers signing a pact of union, a carnal contract linking life to death.'

(Ekotto 2019: 5–6)[1]

Adapted from 'Genealogies of Desire, Extravagance, and Radical Queerness in Frieda Ekotto's *Chuchote Pas Trop*', *Research in African Literatures* 47 (2) (Summer 2016): 46–65.

This passage of untrammelled and unrestrained connection – 'inexplicable', 'irresistible', 'uninterrupted' – posits that 'something', which remains unnamed or defies naming, is the force that ignores normative frameworks. The filial kiss becomes erotic with the mother's suggestion that they are 'like two lovers'. However, the simile indicates the impossibility of attaining that very union, leaving it incomplete. If the kiss is not uniquely filial, as one would expect, and if it is not fully romantic, then to what category does it belong? Perhaps, Ekotto seeks to imagine this kind of union as inhabiting a space that has yet to be carved out and named in imaginings of same-sex desire and pleasure. Perhaps, this kiss is a revamping of the familial staging of desire in that it echoes strongly the Oedipus/Electra complex with a queer twist. The mother/daughter bond and its nonconforming eroticism requires the need to rethink the conventional genealogy of desire between women, taking the familial roof as its starting point. This revamped (non)genealogy frames female filial pleasure as identification, given the kinds of violence to which the female body is subjected. The mother/daughter union, thus, more accurately reflects Kaja Silverman's concept of the negative Oedipus complex, in which the relation of desire is negative on two accounts: (1) the symbolic castration in which the mother is the object of desire, and (2) because of the cultural devaluation of the female position of/and nonheterosexuality (de Lauretis 1984, 1991; Silverman 1988). Parallels emerge between psychoanalytic theory, its extensions and postcolonial critique as represented by Ekotto's *Chuchote pas trop*.

Formally, the juxtapositions of the third-person narrator with italicized and indented quotations from the mother's unearthed diaries combined with the dizzying diversity of dissenting acts reflect Ekotto's political agenda of transcending multiple boundaries – race, age, family, educational level, able-bodiedness and location – and to rethink same-sex sexuality in relational terms. This sheer variety, what I call extravagance, of non-conventional sexual imaginings, lends itself to a schizophrenic reading praxis *à la* Deleuze and Guattari. This praxis consists in mobilizing often incompatible theories of (non)genealogy in order to imagine this post-independent and rural same-sex desire.

The exuberant restaging seems proportionate to the degree of violence brought to bear on female bodies under the Fulani heteropatriarchal regime. In that landscape of mangled bodies, one may expect the novel to perform the paradigm of victimization, however, the characters escape from that position and respond with queer practices, suicide and the transformation of dismembered bodies into subversive projects, producing what I argue is radical queerness. Thus, Ekotto's novel departs from an earlier and even a later tradition of homosexual figurations.

Francophone African cultural productions lag behind the anglophone context in taking up the difficult, yet generative, question of same-sex sexualities. Calixthe Beyala's *C'est le soleil qui m'a brûlée* (1987; *The Sun Hath Looked Upon Me*, 1996) represented, for some, a compelling opportunity to analyse the nexus between non-normative sexualities and literary fiction. However, the hopes that Beyala's novel fuelled about more fictional texts to supplement Yambo Ouologuem's *Le devoir de violence* (1966; *Bound to Violence*) are still to be fulfilled.[2] Perhaps, the protracted controversies around these earlier novels, often labelled outrageous and pornographic, explain both the scarcity of literary texts on the subject and the pervasiveness of oblique narrative strategies in existing ones. Thus, Frieda Ekotto's *Chuchote pas trop* is a welcome addition to the conversation.

I argue that whereas the novel departs from an earlier and even a later tradition of francophone African literature by tackling questions of disability, abjection, rurality, age-disparity, inter-filial and interracial nonconforming sexualities in a relational and excessive fashion, it weaves intertextual connections with Gertrude Stein's *Geography and Plays* (1922). As such, it establishes parallels between transafrican diasporic feminisms and North Atlantic queer theory although the author rejects the term 'queer'. I read *Chuchote pas trop* as paradoxically referencing a psychoanalytic development narrative, that of genealogy (desire and literary history) and that of non-genealogy (identity as in constant flux and charting a new literary lineage). Additionally, in portraying an interracial relationship, the novel strengthens the humanity of Africans and moves beyond the victimhood rhetoric about the un-Africanness of homosexuality. Making sense of these tensions (intentional or otherwise) necessitates the adoption of a schizophrenic, rhizomatic, reading praxis, which unfolds in four sections. While the first section provides a synopsis of the novel, the second explores its lines of literary inheritance and disavowal, leading to the discussion of the politics of naming as it intersects with diasporic genealogies in section three. The final section elaborates on radical queerness through a schizophrenic reading to demonstrate the novelist's investment in the logic of multiplication rather than that of bifurcation between Africans and the West.

Silences, Fragments, Records and Rediscoveries

A narrative about silences, fragments, records and rediscoveries, Ekotto's *Chuchote pas trop* imagines female characters who engage in filial, interracial and intergenerational same-sex intimacy, breaking the Lacanian law of the father – the prescriptive value of Fulani heteropatriarchal culture – that unsuccessfully attempts to silence them through institutional regimes of control: female genital surgeries, marital rape, bodily dismemberment, objectification and spectacle. First published in 2001 by Editions A3, the novel was reprinted in 2005 by L'Harmattan. In 2019, a translation into English by Corine Tachtiris as *Do Not Whisper Too Much* was published by Bucknell University Press. In the same publication is also a *Portrait of a Young Artiste from Bona Mbella* that Tachtiris translated from *Portrait d'une jeune artiste de Bona Mbella* (2010). The publishing history of the novel literalizes the notion of unofficial censorship. Given her daring and extravagant imagining of non-heterosexuality, it took Ekotto ten years to find a publisher.[3] In my interview with the writer-filmmaker-scholar, she explained that the challenges stemmed from the controversial nature of the text (Diabate 2010). Additionally, male chauvinistic practices, limited educational opportunities for women, intellectual imperialism and the need to discursively desexualize, read sanitize, the image of the African female body all contribute to explaining the scarcity of texts on homosexuality in francophone Africa.

In four chapters revealingly titled 'Affi ou la communion de corps' ('Affi or the Communion of Bodies'), 'Le boui-boui Garba' ('Garba's Poor Abode'), 'Ada and Siliki' and 'Ada', the narrative is set in contemporary northern Cameroon, specifically in a fictional Fulani village. The ambiguously identified speakers, continuous use of the present tense, even in the recounting of flashbacks, lack of any formal signposting or quotation marks, unmarked shifts in the progression and intermixed structure of the narrative turn any summary of the novel into a challenging task. The interweaving plot reads like the stream of consciousness of the third-person narrator in her struggle to stitch together bits and pieces of women's excavated stories. Told in a flashback, the coming-of-age story of Ada, the young female protagonist, is interlaced with the stigmatized stories of three generations of socially alienated women who practised nonconforming sexualities. Ada is on two quests: first, to uncover the history and identity of her deceased mother and, second, to unveil the mystery around her life and sexual partner, a dismembered old woman, Siliki.

One of the thirty wives of the village chief, Sita Sophie, Siliki's mother, becomes the symbol of stigma in the village for two reasons. First, for converting to Catholicism and, second, for entertaining an 'abominable' same-sex relationship with a Belgian Catholic nun, Soeur Gertrude, who taught her reading and writing. After the affair becomes public, Soeur Gertrude is excommunicated and sent back to Belgium, whilst Sita Sophie suffers physical and sexual abuse. These treatments seem to foreshadow the intent of current anti-gay legislation in several African countries. To avoid the insane asylum, she gives birth to a girl who becomes her beacon of hope. Following cultural prescriptions, when Siliki reaches adolescence, she is married off, but becomes a rebellious wife, flouting all heteropatriarchal cultural proscriptions. When Siliki becomes a mother, she secretly teaches her daughter, Affi, to read and write, while engaging in an erotic relationship with her. The seemingly secret relationship becomes the village's source of fables. While the daughter is subjected to clitoridectomy and infibulation at age twelve, Siliki is thrown down a well as punishment and loses her legs to the caimans. Reduced to a state of abject freak, she establishes a one-woman household outside the village for self-autonomy. Like all the young girls in her village, Affi is confined in Garba's Boui-Boui (her future husband's abode). But, she commits murder-suicide by starting a fire that burns down the Boui-Boui and all its inhabitants. However, her diary with her story and the rationale for the murder-suicide miraculously survives.

Similar to Siliki, Ada is also a social outcast because of the buried yet conspicuous story of her deceased mother. Stigmatized, the orphan is alienated from the community and from her father's compound. Specifically, she is not considered wife material because no man would ever marry her without a bride price. Already haunted by her experience, Ada's curiosity about and passion for Siliki is fuelled by rumours of witchcraft. During one of Siliki's impromptu wanderings into the village, Ada meets and falls in love with her, despite their age difference and the villagers' outrage. The narrative ends with Siliki's death and Ada still uncovering and compiling buried women's stories, which the narrator frames as women's sacred texts that are comparable to the Qur'an and the Bible. Just like Ada, Ekotto, through her novel, sheds light on these stories and gives voice to female characters and, by extension, rural francophone women who love women. On many levels, this novel represents also the coming-of-age story of fictional imaginings of female same-sex sexualities in francophone Africa. With *Chuchote pas trop* and its bold characterizations and extravagant poetics, a new-old tradition is in the making.

The themes of creating a new grammar, a new language, and excavating stories and histories to empower future generations, which structure *Chuchote pas trop*, are at the core of Ekotto's creative and intellectual projects. She reiterated the investment in 2023 in her column as president of the Modern Language Association (MLA). In 'Mapping Possibilities: The Poetics of Queering Blackness' (2023), Ekotto celebrates Audre Lorde for generating self-defining and self-sustaining linguistic and creative possibilities for Black LGBTQIA2S+.

Literary Inheritance and Disavowal

The choice of this novel for my analysis resides in its richness, in how it offers the opportunity to tackle questions of (non)genealogy and lines of filiation on both narrative and metanarrative levels. Until the mid-1990s, questions of dissident sexualities in francophone African literature were relatively marginalized. The novels that took up the subject emerged in the 1960 to 1970s. To what extent, can we produce lines of filiation with literary productions on the subject? What importance do we accord to categories of 'generation', 'filiation' and 'inheritance' in our tentative grouping? These questions are generative, as I claim that *Chuchote pas trop* departs from earlier and even later homosexual figurations. Through historical periodization and broad formal and topical aspects, I attempt a three-generation grouping of literary texts to understand the development of formal and thematic patterns in depictions of non-heterosexuality. The first generation concerns texts from 1960 to the 1970s, while the other two cover 1980 to the 1990s, and the 2000s onward, respectively. Like any periodization and grouping, overlaps and criss-crossings introduce ruptures.

Several pioneering analyses (Dunton 1989; Vignal 1983) have mapped out texts of the first generation. In 'L'homophilie dans le roman négro-africain d'expression anglaise et française' (1983), Daniel Vignal explores texts such as Camara Laye's *Dramouss* (1966, Guinea), Yambo Ouologuem's *Le devoir de violence* (1966, Mali), Saïdou Bokoum's *Chaîne* ([1974] 1997, Guinea), Abdoul Doukouré's *Le déboussolé* (1978, Mali), Cyriaque R. Yavoucko's *Crépuscule et défi* (1979, Central Africa), Cheikh C. Sow's 'Le rôle du tyran' (1980, Senegal) and Sony Labou Tansi's *l'état honteux* (1981, Congo). Chris Dunton's 'Wheyting Be Dat' (1989) builds on Vignal's exploration by identifying contexts from which the monothematic imagining of non-heterosexuality emerges. To Vignal's survey, Dunton adds

Mongo Beti's *Remember Ruben* (1974, Cameroon), William Sassine's *Wirriyamu* (1976, Guinea), Bernard Nanga's *La trahison de Marianne* (1984, Cameroon) and Caya Makhele's *L'homme au landau* (1988, Congo). Qualifying Vignal's and Dunton's surveys as 'embryonic attempts' to analyse the literary treatment of homosexuality, Chantal Zabus in 'Out in Africa' sets out to identify narratives that treat 'homosexuality as-an-identity rather than an occasional or ritualized practice' (2009: 251). Thus, she expands the list with *La révolte des galsénésiennes* ([1994] 2010) by the Malian, Dakar-based novelist Doumbi-Fakoly and Camara Laye's *Le regard du roi* (1954, Guinea).[4]

To these studies, Nathalie Etoke (2009) adds a feminist/womanist perspective with her analyses of texts that I consider literary progenitors of *Chuchote pas trop*, including the Guinean-Senegalese Mariama Barry's *La petite peule* (2000), the Senegalese Ken Bugul's *Riwan ou le chemin de sable* (1999) and the Franco-Cameroonian Calixthe Beyala's *C'est le soleil qui m'a brûlée* (1987) and *Tu t'appelleras Tanga* (1988). The list was relatively recently updated with narratives of the third generation by Boniface Mongo-Mboussa (2013) who added Sami Tchak's *La fête des masques* (2004, Togo), Max Lobe's *39 rue de Berne* (2013, Cameroon) and Berthrand Nguyen Matoko's *Le flamant noir* (2004, Congo-Vietnam). I expand these surveys with Congolese scholar-writer Valentin Mudimbé's *Le bel immonde* (1976; *Before the Birth of the Moon*, 1989), which is rarely mentioned in analyses of homoeroticism, Ken Bugul's *Le baobab fou* (1984, Senegal), Frieda Ekotto's second novel, *Portrait d'une jeune artiste de Bona Mbella* (2010, France-Cameroon), Calixthe Beyala's *Femme nue femme noire* (2003), Karim Deya's *J'attends mon mari* (2014, Côte d'Ivoire), Léonora Miano's *Crépuscule du tourment* (2016, France-Cameroon) and Mohamed Mbougar Sarr's *De purs hommes* (2018, Senegal).

These surveys and analyses allow us access to an archive with which I attempt a brief literary history of same-sex sexualities in francophone sub-Saharan Africa.

Most novels of the first generation (1960 to the 1970s) – Ouologuem's *Le devoir de violence*, Doukoure's *Le déboussolé*, Laye's *Dramouss* and *Le regard du roi*, Bokoum's *Chaîne*, Yavoucko's *Crépuscule et défi*, Mudimbe's *Le bel immonde*, Sassine's *Wirriyamu* and Beti's *Remember Ruben* – associate homosexuality with foreignness and deploy oblique narrative strategies in order to tackle the subject. Cameroonian political scientist E. H. Ngwa Nfobin (2014) goes as far as attributing problematically current homophobic sentiments on the continent to these texts. Until recently, these novels, when read for their treatment of homosexuality, have been considered outrageous, perhaps limiting the possibility of more literary fiction on the subject.

Works of the second generation (1980 to the 1990s) include Bugul's *Riwan ou le chemin de sable* et *Le baobab fou*, Doumbi-Fakoly's *La révolte des galsénésiennes*, Sony Labou Tansi's *L' état honteux*, Sow's 'Le rôle du tyran', Makhele's *L'homme au landau*, Nanga's *La trahison de Marianne*, and Beyala's *C'est le soleil qui m'a brûlée* and *Tu t'appelleras Tanga*. If these texts rely less on the trope of homosexuality as racial contamination, most of them rejoin the first generation in deploying oblique narrative strategies – fantasy, utopia, hallucination, surrealist tropes and literary allusions – albeit to a lesser extent. These strategies, which Chris Dunton first identified, have been called 'l'art du détour' (Mongo-Mboussa 2013: 129), 'ingenious literary devices, adroit techniques', 'narrative repression' (Etoke 2009: 176, 179), 'obliqueness' (Zabus 2009: 14) and having an 'ambiguous and metaphorical manner' (D'Almeida 1994: 95). With this generation, we already see bolder images, although the filiation seems to function without many ruptures. Of these narratives, Beyala's novels relaunched the debate on non-normative sexualities in African fiction, as her texts were considered pornographic and offensive.[5] Despite their bold imagining, the narratives still echo fantasy and hallucination, echoing strategies of the previous generation.

In the 2000s, the emergence of the third generation was inaugurated by the major cinematic production *Karmen Gei* (2001) by the Senegalese director Joseph Gai Ramaka, Ekotto's *Chuchote pas trop* and Mariama Barry's *La petite peule*. The film and novels presented the possibility of female homosexuality and several additional literary texts followed: Beyala's *Femme nue femme noire*, Tchak's *La fête des masques*, Nguyen Matoko's *Le flamant noir*, Ekotto's *Portrait d'une jeune artiste de Bona Mbella*, Lobe's *39 rue de Berne*, Deya's *J'attends mon mari*, Miano's *Crépuscule du tourment* and Sarr's *De purs hommes*. In several interviews with Ramaka, Beyala, Barry and Ekotto, one senses dissatisfaction with earlier images of homosexuality, which are then framed in terms of (in)visibility and the urgent need to do things differently. For instance, Ekotto criticizes the representational politics of *Karmen Gei*, arguing that it does not bravely advance the cause of women-loving women (Ekotto 2007; Ellerson 2013). In discussing her novel in my interview with her, Ekotto presents *Chuchote pas trop* as a political act, which was to bring female same-sex sexuality into mainstream conversation (Diabate 2010). By the time of her novel's publication in 2001, state-sponsored homophobic statements in several African countries had mushroomed. But women were discursively absent from the conversation, and their resistant sexualities were therefore subjected to imposed silence.

However, questions of (in)visibility are problematic because of the assumption of a correct form of representation of homosexuality. Expecting an adequate representational strategy burdens fiction with the task of correcting a mistake, of excavating queerness from obscurity, so that queers can be guaranteed basic rights – the right to civil society and the rule of law. The elusive understanding of (in)visibility and the complaints they incite emulate what M. Jacqui Alexander (1997) critiques in the western understanding of visibility. Speaking of the Caribbean context, Alexander notes that queer scholars in the West often repeat the imperialist gesture to the extent that they assume a defect in political consciousness and maturity regarding an absence of visibility of gay and lesbian movements in other contexts. Additionally, the assumption of a direct correlation between representation and life worlds, of the conflation of the real with the representational, is misguided, a point made by Annamarie Jagose (2002) in her analysis of North Atlantic lesbian studies. The point is not that homosexuals should not have these rights; the question is the normative and debatable account of (in)visibility and the role of fiction and literary criticism in the articulation of contemporary African identities. Additionally, invisibility, whether resulting from a limited mode of recognition or otherwise, should be understood as a paradox, for it offers these women the freedom to live out their sexuality outside the purview of oppressive social and political regimes. Dragging female corporeal intimacies out of invisibility may amount to exposing them to the wrath of the heteropatriarchal state. This paradox indicates that the relationship between silence and power is complicated.

Moments of dissatisfaction such as Ekotto's showcase a desire not to follow in the footsteps of literary forebears, but to write a new genealogy, both topically and formally. However, to start a new line of filiation is always already an impossible task, as traces of the past refuse to disappear completely once and for all. In many ways, the third generation of authors is bolder in its imagining, although at times it borrows oblique narrative strategies from the previous two. Several parallels exist between *Chuchote pas trop* and Barry's *La petite peule* in terms of intergenerational queer pleasure, the violence and trauma of female genital surgeries, the debilitating effects of forced heterosexual marriage and the use of Fulani communities as settings. Further, *Chuchote pas trop* shares similarities with Beyala's *C'est le soleil qui m'a brûlée* and *Tu t'appelleras Tanga* regarding filial, interracial and intergenerational intimacy and queer spatialization, and with Gertrude Stein's 1922 *Geography and Plays* relative to intertextuality, suggesting that the latter four provide a literary genealogy for Ekotto's representation of same-sex desire.[6]

In two novels, Beyala stages filial, interracial and intergenerational sexual intimacy as well as other practices. Suffice it to say that in *C'est le soleil*, Ateba's lesbianism works through her obsessive incestuous desire towards women: mother, aunt and friends (Asaah 2004). Ateba's desire for her mother, Betty, resonates with the mother/daughter dynamic in *Chuchote pas trop*, as analysed above: 'Elle [Ateba] aurait voulu s'introduire en elle [Betty], afin de purifier chaque veine, chaque artère du mauvais sang (des amants hétérosexuels de sa mère). Leur sang qu'ils déversaient en elle pour se décrasser' (90) (She [Ateba] would have loved to enter her [Betty] so as to purify each vein, each artery from that bad blood, that blood of theirs they poured into her to cleanse themselves'; 69). In *Tu t'appelleras* intergenerational and interracial connection is normalized. In a jail cell, Tanga, a girlchild-woman, offers Anna-Claude, a French woman who experienced a failed relationship with an African man, intimacy as a healing act. This reversal of the conventional power dynamic between Africans and Europeans resonates on several levels (race, age) to the relationships between Ada and Siliki, and Soeur Gertrude and Sita Sophie. In her exploration of female same-sex sexuality, Brenna Munro identifies several short stories and novels in 'Anglophone Africa' that include interracial lesbian desires. Munro traces the genealogy of that framework to Ghanaian Ama Ata Aidoo's novel *Our Sister Killjoy: Or, Reflections from a Black-Eyed* Squint (1977).[7]

Through the Belgian Catholic nun, Soeur Gertrude, *Chuchote pas trop* joins texts of the first and second generations in tracing the genealogy of homosexuality to foreignness. However, in imagining a relational and ebullient account of nonconforming sexualities, the novel constitutes a class of its own.

Chuchote pas trop's subversion of language, discussed below, which highly echoes the modernist tradition, is strengthened by a few parallels with the

American modernist writer Gertrude Stein, a seminal figure that fed queer theory. In the novel, Ada entertains a relationship with Siliki, and Siliki's mother, Sita Sophie, was involved with Soeur Gertrude, who taught her reading and writing. One cannot help noticing the possible intertextual connections with Stein and Alice B. Toklas. In *Geography and Plays*, Stein writes a portrait of Alice, her lover, which she titled 'Ada' and Ekotto's nun is named Gertrude. While Stein is part of the modernist canon, and most certainly had a role within the Paris avant-garde culture of the early twentieth century and the interwar years, she commented on the processes of reading and writing as heuristically similar to Soeur Gertrude's pedagogical relationship with Sita Sophie. Since Stein and Toklas spent over forty years of their lives together in the Left Bank of Paris, and given that Stein's work was translated into French, would Ekotto have known about this lesbian relationship and woven it into her text, albeit with a difference? This possible filiation with a figure of the modernist canon once again suggests the near impossibility of starting a new line of filiation.

With its myriad acts of alternative sexuality and corporeality, most constituted relationally, Ekotto's novel also gives us the opportunity to rethink the propensity to define and reify identities. Should that be a generative approach, what is the appropriate term to designate these characters in these three couples – Sita Sophie and Soeur Gertrude (racial), Siliki and Affi (age-disparate and bodily ability-divergent), and Ada and Siliki (filial)? Are they queer, homosexual, lesbian, women-loving or postqueer? It is in the strategies of representation and terminology that I see a dialectical relation unfold between current, North Atlantic, queer theory, African diasporic and African feminisms.

Lesbian, Women-Loving Woman, Homosexual, Queer, Postqueer: Diasporic and Transafrican Genealogies

Just as the rise of queer theory may have fed the publication of imaginings and literary criticism of same-sex sexualities, these texts also help expand the contours of conventional accounts of queerness as well as push back against the universalization of western gender and sexual identity terminology.[8] Similar to Beyala, who rejects the notion that she is writing about lesbianism but admits the existence of female same-sex erotic practices in Cameroon, Ekotto refuses to neatly translate all same-sex female intimacy into terms familiar to westerners.[9]

Moreover, the term 'homosexual', travelling through the centuries with a host of meanings, is a highly unstable term. For instance, in the nineteenth century, homosexual was primarily used to racialize and those deemed unfit for citizenship or human rights (Hoad 2007). As for the word lesbian, its so-called Eurocentrism, and reformulations – Cheryl Clarke's (1981) lesbians or Monique Wittig's (1981) materialist lesbians – to designate those who resist patriarchal and compulsory heterosexual economies,[10] breeds discomfort and subsequent rejection.[11]

By rejecting these 'Eurocentric' terms, Ekotto feeds a line of filiation with intellectuals of the African diaspora who have been invested in self-naming for decades.[12] Although the term women-loving women is at times appropriate and demonstrates the novelist's belief in the existence of multiple infused identities, it fails to account for other non-normative sexual behaviours in the novel. Cracks and fissures exist in what she considers her safe diasporic line of genealogy. In fact, the term is not organic to continental African communities. 'Women-loving women' was widely used in the United States in the 1970s and became racialized, designating same-sex erotic relationships between African American women and women of African descent.

Additionally, it was used to emphasize the emotional rather than the sexual aspect of relationships that often arose out of heterosexual frustration. Although conventionally euphemistic and all-encompassing, its original use conceives women-centred relationships as nonviolent, egalitarian, non-competitive and non-objectifying, the supposed opposite of heterosexuality (Segal 1994). From that perspective, female homoeroticism is not conceived in its own right but presented as derivative of heterosexuality, as more a gesture of powerlessness than a mark of active agency.

From Ekotto's naming project against perceived European ethnocentrism emerges a challenge. Just like 'lesbian' and 'homosexual', 'women-loving woman' fails to capture the characters' complexities as they do not engage in exclusively homosexual or lesbian practices or claim absolute sexual identities. The kiss in the first chapter of *Chuchote pas trop* opens up a space in-between the filial and the erotic and, along with the multiple subject positions the lead female characters hold, harbouring, as I claim, a kind of radical queerness. The identities of these characters should be considered relationally, that is, in tandem with questions of abjection, disability, rurality as well as interracial, intergenerational and inter-filial same-sex intimacy.

Indeed, there is danger in seeking to reify these characters with limiting labels because doing so suppresses the density of their identities as wives, daughters, mothers and rural community members, and isolates a defining characteristic from a wide range of possibilities. They give birth, get married and fulfil some of their naturalized functions, negotiating the complexities of their lived experiences. Their model of being and living resonates with Obioma Nnaemeka's (2003) notion of nego-feminism, a feminism of negotiation. In the narrative, Siliki 'oftentimes notices how possible it is to fit in the mold of tradition without observing it' ('la mère pense souvent combien il est possible de se glisser dans le moule de la tradition sans toutefois la respecter'; Ekotto 2005: 17). She is equipped with an ever-evolving and unstable identity, navigating social constraints in order to make a world possible for herself. Her radicalism stems from that fluidity.

Similar to the Deleuzian and Guattarian account of identity, she and others escape the stasis of categories used to define and capture them, becoming 'desiring nomads' in a constant process of becoming. They must not be uniquely identified as homosexual, lesbian, gay, women-loving women, heterosexual or bisexual, because their identities are in an unceasing process of transformation.

It is the constant becoming in the extravagant fashion that warrants the word 'queer', which unsettles any facile notion that Siliki or Ada are solely and/or forever

X, Y and Z. I use it not because of its salience as an umbrella term that subverts categorization but because it resonates more strongly with the variety of erotic desires and sexual practices in the novel: familial corporeal intimacy, compulsory heterosexuality and intergenerational same-sex love. In *Tendencies*, Eve Kosofsky Sedgwick's definition of 'queer' accurately describes the characters: 'One of the things "queer" can refer to: the open mesh of possibilities, gaps, overlaps, dissonances and resonances, lapses and excesses of meaning when the constituent elements of anyone's gender, of anyone's sexuality are made (or *can't be* made) to signify monolithically' (1993: 7).

Perhaps, one may argue for the term postqueer to designate these women and their practices. However, the term 'postqueer' (given the nature of its brittle contours) fails to account for practices in the novel because it seeks to move beyond the West. Despite the laudable goal of naming practices based on contexts, the term postqueerness still borrows from western categories. How non-Eurocentric is something called postqueerness? Are post and queerness indigenous terms to Africa? Is postqueerness another manifestation of the constant need for post-ness as a subjective sense of termination, or of post-ness as Kwame Anthony Appiah (1991) reformulates it as a space clearing gesture? How does one date postqueerness? Given the multiplication of questions, it is unclear how the word can enlighten the women's practices and identities.

In staging characters who epitomize excesses and escape the prison of limiting identity markers, even those imposed by so-called indigenous contexts, Ekotto invites, if not demands, an alternative reading praxis.

Towards a Schizophrenic Reading of Radical Queerness

Making sense of the excesses and fluidity dictates a reading method that I term schizophrenic. The praxis builds on the Deleuzian and Guattarian reformulation of schizophrenia (Deleuze and Guattari [1980] 1987), a profoundly desiring, decentred and revolutionary form of (non)subjectivity that is associated with the sublime. In that vein, the reader ought to borrow from seemingly incompatible frameworks to make sense of a novel that lends itself to multiple interpretive possibilities.

The style resists facile consumption, digestion and possibly disposability, thereby establishing the relationship between writing, sexuality and resistance. The difficulty of telling who is featured through the use of multiple and often undistinguished speaking and writing voices, reminiscent of Mikhael Bakhtin's (1981) heteroglossia; the multiple ellipses and unfinished sentences, paradoxically symptomatic of repressed thoughts, pregnant moments and economical ways of suggesting more than what is actually articulated (Derrida 1978); the continuous use of the present tense even in relaying flashbacks; and the novel's mixed structure and unmarked shifts in progression seem to reveal that the subversion of sexual norms is encoded through the subversion of textual norms. Ekotto's lyrical language and its defiance of conventional syntactical structures, including the rule of logic, turns *Chuchote pas trop* into a queer text that prevents the reader from imposing a limited number of meanings on it.

In relation to (non)genealogy, as I suggested earlier, Ekotto's preference for locating her characters within the category of women-loving women challenges the reader because the very characters resist categorization. This reader who draws on a queer framework finds herself at odds with the insights from an interview with Ekotto. The writer's attempt to connect with African diasporic, non-normative sexual practices seems counterintuitive to the association I uncovered between Gertrude Stein and *Chuchote pas trop*. Further, to deploy a hyper-critique of Freudian 'familialism' *à la* Deleuze and Guattari to explicate the dangers of reifying identities in a text that also draws on the Freudian model of desire (Oedipal/Electra) suggests some form of disjunction.

Given the timidity of earlier portrayals of female same-sex intimacy, *Chuchote pas trop* invests in a poetics of a somewhat manic exuberance, both formally and topically. It compounds multiple and interlocking forms: filial, interracial, bodily-ability-divergent and age-disparate intimacy that finds in abjection a source of pleasure, which then becomes subversive as compulsory heterosexuality is the established norm. Yet the interracial connection raises questions through a Fanonian reading. Departing from prevailing norms requires that the characters' investment in queer spatialization which is made possible, partly, through rural queerness. To close, I reflect on the so-called un-Africanness of homosexuality when several queer narratives restage cross-racial encounters.

No prevailing moral and social boundaries, no matter how prohibitive, succeed in curtailing the intergenerational love story between the young girl, Ada, and Siliki, the old woman. Through it, *Chuchote pas trop* flirts with what is multiply impermissible under local mores, bordering on what I call radical queerness. The blood oath and the intimate interaction between the mother and her daughter embody the dissolution of individual boundaries and belong to the realm of the queer that defies the normative construction of intimacy as life-giving, nonviolent and nurturing. The scene, a display of both violence and trust between the partners, is potentially offensive to the average reader's tastes. Yet, the narrative paints a pathology-free and uplifting image of age-disparate same-sex desire, presenting it as a haven of intellectual growth, empowerment and survival. That representation resonates with, but differs from, the 'mummy-baby' relationships observed in Lesotho. 'Mummy-baby' relations constitute important emotional and economic networks of support for women. But, while the novel suggests exclusive same-sex erotic acts between the parties and no prospect of heterosexual relationships, the 'mummy-baby' practice prepares the 'babies' to enter heterosexual relationships and marriage (Blacking 1978; Gray 1985).

The novel is radical even in the mainstream queer script as these age-disparate and familial corporeal intimacies, often, raise eyebrows. That is so because even consensual, such relationships frequently carry with them the stigma of paedophilia and pathology. Some have argued that the hysteria attached to children's sexuality results in the under-theorization of children and same-sex sexuality.[13] In *Homosexual Desire*, Guy Hocquenghem argues for '[young people's] right to dispose of their own sexuality' (1978: 141), and after him, in 'Thinking Sex', Gayle Rubin became a precursor on the question of children and sexual rights when she critiqued the hysteria over child pornography and spoke even of the need to sympathize with 'the community of men who love underaged youth' (1983: 7). The shifting nature of modes of judgement of the practice explains why mainstream queer theories interrogate the pathology attached to age-disparate erotic activity. Ekotto's deployment of a female-female dynamic behooves us to probe the texture of that conversation, which is often restricted to male-male intimacy. By imagining and de-pathologizing filial and intergenerational female-female eroticism, texts such as Ekotto's, Beyala's and Barry's allow a rethinking of the terms of this debate.

Chuchote pas trop's radicality also works through staging sexual pleasures between women, reprising Patricia McFadden's and others' proposition that 'sexual pleasure is fundamental to the right to a safe and wholesome lifestyle'[14] and should thus be considered political in its own right. In experiencing these pleasures, women tread men's jurisdiction, invading male terrains of fantasizing and possessing women's bodies metaphorically and literally. For instance, Ada finds pleasure in watching Siliki's dismembered body, which the Fulani heteropatriarchy finds abject. As Siliki emerges from the river after a bath, Ada describes her breasts as 'needle-like' ('pointus en formes d'aiguilles'), couching them in a rhetoric of vivacity and resistance (Ekotto 2005: 5).[15] The narrator dwells on the sexualized descriptions of female bodies, the roundness and fullness of buttocks and breasts, and the tight and exaggerated undulations.

Whether in reaction to the normalization of rape as heterosexual intercourse or sheer attraction, Sita Sophie and Soeur Gertrude's sexual intercourse opens a realm of pleasure unknown to them before as the former reaches her first sexual orgasmic state. In passing, the latter's act represents the most transgressive act within the context of her religious principles. Not only does she stray away from her vows, but she also savours the pleasures of the flesh with a same-sex partner of a different race. Soeur Gertrude's erotic fulfilment seems to take precedence over all her other affiliations. Ironically, although religious practices are supposed to wrest Sita Sophie away from her 'heathenish culture', her naturalized filiation, they end up losing her to her personal sexual desires.[16] Although the women's intimacy is both physically and intellectually fulfilling, their racial identities raise the question of authentic connection. To what extent is authentic love possible in this context?

A Fanonian reading questions that very possibility. In *Peau noire, masques blancs*, Fanon argues the impossibility of genuine love between a woman of colour and a white man (Fanon 1952: 25).[17] Although Fanon is not particularly concerned with same-sex sexual relationships, the dynamic he describes is transferable to Soeur Gertrude and Sita Sophie. It mimics the one between the Fanonian Black woman and the white man, for Soeur Gertrude is positioned with a phallic symbol (her clitoris is intact), while Sita Sophie is constructed as the female, the one lacking a phallic symbol, her visible clitoris. Soeur Gertrude's phallic position could also be determined by her membership in the Catholic Church, a patriarchal institution that also served as an instrument of colonialism in Africa through its missionaries. Given the possible transposition of the heterosexual dynamic to the couple, is Sita Sophie's relationship with Soeur Gertrude motivated by this desire for whiteness? Probably not, since the narrator overlooks Soeur Gertrude's whiteness and instead focusses on her religion. The invisibility of her whiteness potentially 'erases' Sita Sophie's blackness. The absence of confrontation between blackness and whiteness overrides the possibility of pathological blackness, which would have to be cured through mimicry. Genuine connection between them becomes a possibility in that Sita Sophie is immune from an inferiority complex created by her blackness.

Siliki's transgressive acts – disavowal of collective belief systems by entertaining intimate corporeal relationships with both her daughter and Ada – incite homophobic acts of violence, leading her to produce and enact an alternative mode of living, that of metaphorically removing herself from the suffocating social skin as quoted in the epigraphs. Siliki realizes that 'loving their fellow people disgusts everyone around her. It's simply unbearable to them' (Ekotto 2005: 25).[18] Further, she expresses her anti-humanist project thus: 'I abandoned the human race a long time ago. Here in this refuge, I breathe and live out my desires' (48).[19] By residing outside the community with Ada, she escapes compulsory heterosexuality, gives up the aspiration of normalcy, and as Julia Kristeva (1982) would say in her writings on abjection, found her existence on exclusion. Her decision bears out Michael Warner's (1999) suggestion that the introduction of normalcy goes hand in hand with that of compulsion. But Siliki goes even further, rejecting one of the imaginary foundational principles of so-called African societies, the essentializing communitarian ethos. Their pursuit of self-autonomy bespeaks of her determination that her life is not dependent on the activities, values, projects and goals of the community. However, Siliki's chosen form of being is too abrasive for her society, as she does not survive the duration of the novel. Thus, queer spatialization is a mixed victory because it contributes to the intolerance against sexual minorities.

That alternative spatialization, which often makes possible filial and age-disparate homoeroticism, connects several narratives. *Tu t'appeleras Tanga* and *Karmen Geï* stage intimacy between Tanga and Anna-Claude and between Karmen Geï and the warden, Angélique, in prisons. Placing practices of alternative sexualities in spaces twice removed from conventional communities reinforces their transgressive and shame-producing nature. It seems that female same-sex intimacy is already confined in unsociable spaces. Even though these characters are not incarcerated for engaging in queer activities, Tanga and Karmen are constructed as transgressive characters with a host of antisocial behaviours that land them in prison.

Siliki and Ada's ability to carve out a queer space owes a tremendous deal to the novel's underlining investment in rural queerness, moving beyond the expected figure of the educated, young, urban and frequently middle-class in queer fiction. Instead of the expected figure, the reader encounters women and girls with very limited educational opportunities and who live in rural areas, indulging, albeit not without consequences, in nonconforming erotic acts. With African American Sharon Bridgforth's *The Bull-Jean Stories* (1998), *Chuchote pas trop* exposes the limitations of our modes of recognition of rural queer women, moving between local and global understandings of desire between women as well as between contextual histories of women who live out alternative desires.

The Un-Africanness of Homosexuality: A Fact of Culture or Nature?

To conclude, let me address, reluctantly, the infelicitous question of the un-Africanness of homosexuality.[20] I entertain that much debated issue given the number of narratives of female queerness that include cross-racial intimacy.

As suggested earlier, *Chuchote pas trop* and its depiction of an interracial couple came out at a historical moment when much debate on homosexuality in Africa focussed around its construction as a colonial and a neocolonial import. How are we then to read a re-enactment of the dynamic of the European as the initiator of sexual pleasure and the provider of literacy in Ekotto's text? The couple's racial make-up recalls the trope of the helpless and infantile African woman positioned as receiver of queer pleasure and the white woman as benefactor. In other terms, since the Black man and woman have mutilated and raped the Black woman, the white woman is called on to rescue her emotionally and heal her wounds. This is a differential repetition of what Gayatri Spivak evokes as '[w]hite men saving brown women from brown men' (1988: 287). Ekotto's thought-provoking re-enactment seems counter-current to much work in postcolonial theories, which aims at deconstructing the paradigm of the European as the saviour.

Ekotto writes within a tradition as her interracial couple echoes previous novelistic and cinematic representations, turning these imaginings into a double-edged venture.[21] Whilst they show that same-sex desires escape the realm of the 'un-African', and other socially constructed variables, to become an expression of love, they also risk buttressing the dominant discourse of homosexuality as racial contamination.

Despite and perhaps because of that dynamic, these narratives participate constructively in the debate by making an argument about the humanness of same-sex erotic practices. They move beyond the mere restaging of the neurosis of victimhood – which certain corners of the decolonizing discourse seek to reverse – by featuring corporeal intimacy and writing as means of becoming. As a cultural product with a brazen radicalism and a poetics of extravagance, *Chuchote pas trop* makes a critical contribution to francophone queerness, mainstream queer theory, and decolonizing and decolonial practices. Ekotto refuses the either-or bifurcation of Africans against the West that sets Africans apart from other humans. In fact, she argues for a logic of multiplication by highlighting, if that was and is ever needed, the humanity of Africans.

Notes

1   'À ce moment-là se révèle quelque chose d'inexplicable entre Affi et sa mère. La fille ressent soudain un frisson. Une force irrésistible lui fait relever la tête. Elle approche

sa bouche, effleurant le menton de sa mère. Leurs lèvres se touchent en un baiser d'une violence ininterrompue. La boucle en acier rouillé qui orne la lèvre inférieure de la mère s'ouvre et accroche la langue d'Affi, la mère poursuit son chuchotement, 'Mon sang et le tien se mélangent comme deux amoureuses qui signent le pacte de l'union, contrat charnel qui lie la vie à la mort' (Ekotto 2005: 10).

2 On the later novels, see Dunton 1997.

3 Novelist, poet, short story writer and filmmaker, Ekotto is also professor of French and comparative literature at the University of Michigan, Ann Arbor. Currently, Ekotto serves as president of the Modern Language Association.

4 For a fuller attempt at periodization, see Zabus 2013.

5 For more on these comments, see Asaah 2004; Bjornson 1991; Chemain 1989; Jaccard 1989; Ndinda 1994; Nfah-Abbenyi 1997; Volet 1993.

6 Taking as his point of departure, multiple conferences and anthologies from the late 1990s onwards, on the relationship between homosexuality and globalization, Jarrod Hayes analyses several fictional texts, including Ekotto's *Chuchote pas trop*, to identify how queering francophone studies opens up intellectual possibilities for queer French studies. See Hayes 2020: 180–93.

7 Munro 2017.

8 For more on this debate, see Lorway 2008.

9 Beyala says: 'I think that those who see lesbianism in my writings are quite simply perverted, as tenderness between women doesn't necessarily mean lesbian- ism. How can you explain to Westerners that, in traditional Africa, intimate same-sex relationships are not defined as homosexual?' (quoted in Gallimore 1997: 199).

10 In 'One Is Not Born a Woman', Monique Wittig moves beyond lesbianism and argues for what she calls 'materialist lesbianism', which allows women to escape the category of 'Woman' by refusing to comply with the ideological, economical and political regime that created the categories 'man' and 'woman' (Wittig 1981: 9).

11 On such words as 'lesbian', 'gay', 'homosexual', 'queer', and so on, in African contexts, see Epprecht (2004) and Zabus (2013: 43–50, 251–68).

12 Explaining that terms such as 'lesbian' and 'gay' fail to capture their sexual identities and desires, several cultural critics and intellectuals have brought forward *mati* work (Suriname), mummy-baby relationships (Lesotho) and *zami* (West Indies) to designate corporeal intimacy among women in the African diaspora. Although most of these terms are organic to the communities in which they are applied, some have been creolized, such as *zami* from the French noun les amies (female friends). For more on terms, see Douglas et al. 1997; Lorde 1984; Tinsley 2010; and Wekker 2006.

13 For more on different ideological positionings on children and age-disparate same-sex sexuality, see Bruhm and Hurley 2004.

14 Awa Thiam's *La parole aux négresses* (1978) gives the floor to illiterate, literate, college-educated, and middle- or working-class women of Côte d'Ivoire, Guinea, Mali, Senegal, Ghana and Nigeria. In the interviews, women report and complain about the discursive and oftentimes physical violence of patriarchy and how they have been denied the possibility of enjoying sexual pleasures. Although relatively dated, Thiam's study remains compelling in explaining structures of oppression against women.

15 Barry's novel portrays a similar scene whereby a young girl fantasizes about female bodies in a bathing scene. 'Mon regard envieux fixa, pour ne plus s'en détacher, les beaux seins pointus aux mamelons foncés; la vue de cette nudité me fit toucher et caresser les miens, inexistants. J'aurais voulu m'attarder devant ces nudités, toucher

leurs seins, voir quel effet cela ferait dans mes petites mains' (Barry 2000: 198–9) (I threw an envious and sustained glance at their lovely, pointed breasts with dark nipples and brown aureolas; the sight of this nudity prompted me to touch and caress my own underdeveloped breasts. I would have liked to spend some time in the presence of these nude women, touch their breasts, see what effect my little hands would have'; Barry 2010: 137).

16   For more on the connection between colonialism and religion, see Mudimbé 1994 and Amadiume 1997.

17   Feminists have critiqued Fanon's masculinist proclivities; see Bergner 1995. However, Sharpley-Whiting (1998) disagrees with Bergner and constructs a profeminist Fanon.

18   'Le fait d'aimer ses semblables dégoute tout son entourage' (Ekotto 2005: 41).

19   'Il y a longtemps que j'ai abandonné la race humaine. Ici dans ce réduit je respire et je vis mes désirs' (Ekotto 2005: 73).

20   The debate led Fabien Eboussi-Boulaga to ask rhetorically: 'Ainsi, l'homosexualité n'est pas africaine? Est-ce du fait de la nature africaine ou de la culture?' ('So homosexuality is unAfrican? Is that the result of African nature or culture?') (2007: 8; my translation).

21   Sissie, the protagonist of Ama Ata Aidoo's *Our Sister Killjoy* (1977), was introduced to homoeroticism by the German Marija Sommers. *Tu t'appeleras Tanga* challenges that dynamic and that of *Chuchote pas trop* by depicting her protagonist as the active seducer in her relationship with the older French woman Anna Claude. *Karmen Gei* (2001) also features a mixed-race relationship.

References

Aidoo, Ama Ata. 1977. *Our Sister Killjoy*. London: Longman.

Alexander, M. Jacqui. 1997. 'Erotic Autonomy as a Politics of Decolonization: An Anatomy of Feminist and State Practice in the Bahamas Tourist Industry', in M. Jacqui Alexander and Chandra Talpade Mohanty (eds), *Feminist Genealogies, Colonial Legacies, Democratic Futures*, 63–100. New York: Routledge.

Amadiume, Ifi. 1997. *Re-Inventing Africa: Matriarchy, Religion and Culture*. London: Zed Books.

Appiah, Kwame Anthony. 1991. 'Is the Post- in Postmodernism the Post- in Postcolonial?' *Critical Inquiry* 17 (2): 336–57.

Asaah, Augustine. 2004. 'Lesbianisme dans *C'est le soleil qui m'a brûlée* de Calixthe Beyala', *Cahiers du centre d'études et de recherche en lettres, sciences humaines et sociales* 21: 25–43.

Bakhtin, Mikhael. 1981. 'The Discourse in the Novel', in Michael Holquist (ed.), *The Dialogic Imagination: Four* Essays, 259–422. Translated by Caryl Emerson and Michael Holquist. Austin: University of Texas Press.

Barry, Mariama. 2000. *La petite peule*. Paris: Mazarine.

Barry, Mariama. 2010. *The Little Peul*. Translated by Carrol F. Coates. Charlottesville: University of Virginia Press.

Bergner, Gwen. 1995. 'Who Is That Masked Woman? Or, the Role of Gender in Fanon's *Black Skin, White Masks*', *PMLA* 110 (1): 75–88.

Beti, Mongo. 1974. *Remember Ruben*. Paris: Union générale d'éditions.

Beyala, Calixthe. 1987. *C'est le soleil qui m'a brûlée*. Paris: Stock.

Beyala, Calixthe. 1988. *Tu t'appeleras Tanga*. Paris: éditions J'ai lu.

Beyala, Calixthe. 1996a. *The Sun Hath Looked upon Me*. Oxford: Heinemann Educational Publishers.

Beyala, Calixthe. 1996b. *Your Name Shall Be Tanga*. Translated by Marjolijn de Jager. Portsmouth, NH: Heinemann.

Beyala, Calixthe. 2003. *Femme nue femme noire*. Translated by Marjolijn De Jager. Paris: Albin Michel.

Bjornson, Richard. 1991. *The African Quest for Freedom and Identity: Cameroonian Writing and the National Experience*. Indianapolis: Indiana University Press.

Blacking, John. 1978. 'Uses of the Kinship Idiom in Friendships at Some Venda and Zulu Schools', in J. Argyle and E. Preston-Whyte (eds), *Social System and Tradition in Southern* Africa, 101–17. Cape Town: Oxford University Press.

Bokoum, Saïdou. [1974] 1997. *Chaîne*. Paris: Denoël.

Bridgforth, Sharon. 1998. *The Bull-Jean Stories*. Washington, D.C.: RedBone Press.

Bruhm, Steven and Natasha Hurley, eds. 2004. *Curiouser: On the Queerness of Children*. Minneapolis: University of Minnesota Press.

Bugul, Ken. 1984. *Le baobab fou*. Dakar: Nouvelles éditions Africaines.

Bugul, Ken. 1999. *Riwan, ou, le chemin de sable: Roman*. Paris: Présence Africaine.

Chemain, Arlette. 1989. 'L'écriture de Calixthe Beyala: provocation ou révolte généreuse?', *Notre libraire* 99: 162–3.

Clarke, Cheryl. 1981. 'Lesbianism: An Act of Resistance', in Cherrie Moraga and Gloria Anzaldua (eds), *This Bridge Called My Back: Writings by Radical Women of* Color, 128–37. Watertown, MA: Persephone Press.

D'Almeida, Irène. 1994. *Francophone African Women Writers: Destroying the Emptiness of Silence*. Gainesville: University Press of Florida.

De Lauretis, Teresa. 1984. *Alice Doesn't: Feminism, Semiotics, Cinema*. Bloomington: Indiana University Press.

De Lauretis, Teresa. 1991. 'Film and the Visible', in Bad Object Choices (ed.), *How Do I Look? Queer Film and* Video, 223–64. Seattle: Bay.

Deleuze, Gilles and Félix Guattari. [1980] 1987. *A Thousand Plateaus: Capitalism and Schizophrenia*. Minneapolis: University of Minnesota Press.

Derrida, Jacques. 1978. 'Ellipsis', in *Writing and* Difference, 294–300. Translated by Alan Bass. Chicago: University of Chicago Press.

Deya, Karim. 2014. *J'attends mon mari*. Éditions Textes Gais.

Diabate, Naminata. 2010. 'From Women Loving Women in Africa to Genet and Race: A Conversation with Frieda Ekotto', *Journal of the African Literature Association* 4(1): 181–203.

Douglas, Debbie, Courtney McFarlane, Makeda Silvera and Douglas Stewart, eds. 1997. *Má-ka: Diasporic Juks: Contemporary Writing by Queers of African Descent*. Toronto: Sister Vision Press.

Doukouré, Abdoul. 1978. *Le déboussolé*. Sherbrooke, QC: Naaman.

Doumbi-Fakoly. [1994] 2010. *La Révolte des galsénésiennes*. Paris: L'Harmattan.

Dunton, Chris. 1989. '"Wheyting Be Dat?" The Treatment of Homosexuality in African Literature', *Research in African Literatures* 20 (3): 422–48.

Dunton, Chris. 1997. 'To Rediscover Woman: the Novels of Calixthe Beyala', in Derek Wright (ed.), *Contemporary African Fiction*, 209–19. Bayreuth: University of Bayreuth Press.

Eboussi-Boulaga, Fabien. 2007. 'Editorial: L'homosexualité au Cameroon: problème politique', *Terroirs: revue africaine de sciences sociales et de philosophie* 1–2: 5–10.

Ekotto, Frieda. 2005. *Chuchote pas trop*. Paris: L'Harmattan.

Ekotto, Frieda. 2007. 'The Taboo of Female Homosexuality in Senegal', *Xavier Review* 27 (1): 74–80.

Ekotto, Frieda. 2010. *Portrait d'une jeune artiste de Bona Mbella*. Paris: L'Harmattan.

Ekotto, Frieda. 2019. *Don't Whisper Too Much and Portrait of a Young Artiste from Bona Mbella*. Translated by Corine Tachtiris. Lewisburg, PA: Bucknell University Press.

Ekotto, Frieda. 2023. 'Mapping Possibilities: The Poetics of Queering Blackness', *MLA Newsletter* 55 (2): 2–3.

Ellerson, Beti. 2013. 'Frieda Ekotto: For an Endogenous Critique of Representations of African Lesbian Identity in Visual Culture and Literature', *African Women in Cinema Blog*, 13 November 2013.

Epprecht, Marc. 2004. *Hungochani: The History of a Dissident Sexuality in Southern Africa*. Montreal and Kingston, London and Ithaca, NY: McGill-Queen's Press.

Etoke, Nathalie. 2009. 'Mariama Barry, Ken Bugul, Calixthe Beyala, and the Politics of Female Homoeroticism in Sub-Saharan Francophone African Literature', *Research in African Literatures* 40 (2): 173–89.

Fanon, Frantz. 1952. *Peau noire, masques blancs*. Paris: Éditions du Seuil.

Gallimore, Rangira Béatrice. 1997. *L'oeuvre romanesque de Calixthe Beyala: le renouveau de l'écriture féminine en Afrique francophone sub-saharienne*. Paris: L'Harmattan.

Gray, Judith. 1985. '"Mummies and Babies" and Friends and Lovers in Lesotho', *Journal of Homosexuality* 3–4: 97–116.

Hayes, Jarrod. 2020. 'Queer Desire on the Move: Resistance to Homoglobalization in World Literature in French', in Christian Moraru, Nicole Simek, and Bertrand Westphal (eds), *Francophone Literatures as World Literature*, 180–93. New York: Bloomsbury.

Hoad, Neville. 2007. *African Intimacies: Race, Homosexuality, and Globalization*. Minneapolis: University of Minnesota Press.

Hocquenghem, Guy. 1978. *Homosexual Desire*. Translated by Daniella Dangoor. London: Allison & Busby.

Jaccard, Anny-Claire. 1989. 'Des textes novateurs: la littérature féminine', *Notre librairie* 99: 153–61.

Jagose, Annamarie. 2002. *Inconsequence: Lesbian Representation and the Logic of Sexual Sequence*. Ithaca, NY: Cornell University Press.

Karmen Gei. 2001. [Film] Directed by Joseph Gaï Ramaka. Senegal, France and Canada: Arte France Cinéma.

Kristeva, Julia. 1982. *Powers of Horror: An Essay on Abjection*. Translated by Leon Roudiez. New York: Columbia University Press.

Laye, Camara. 1954. *Le regard du roi*. Paris: Editions Plon.

Laye, Camara. 1966. *Dramouss*. Paris: Editions Plon.

Lobe, Max. 2013. *39 rue de Berne*. Carouge, Switzerland: Editions Zoé.

Lorde, Audre. 1984. 'The Uses of the Erotic: The Erotic as Power', in *Sister Outsider: Essays and Speeches*, 53–9. Berkeley: Crossing Press.

Lorway, Robert. 2008. '"Where Can I Be Deported?" Thinking Through the "Foreigner Fetish" in Namibia', *Medical Anthropology* 27 (1): 70–97.

Makhele, Caya. 1988. *L'homme au landau*. Paris: L'Harmattan.

Mbougar Sarr, Mohamed. 2018. *De Purs hommes*. Dakar, Sénégal: Editions Jimsaan.

McFadden, Patricia. 1997. 'The Challenges and Prospects for the African Women's Movement in the 21st Century', *Women in Action* 1.

Miano, Léonora. 2016. *Le crépuscule du tourment*. Paris: Grasset.

Mongo-Mboussa, Boniface. 2013. 'Homosexualité et écriture en Afrique francophone', *Africultures* 6 (96): 128–37.

Mudimbé, V. Y. 1976. *Le Bel immonde: Récit*. Paris: Présence africaine.

Mudimbé, V. Y. 1994. *The Idea of Africa*. Bloomington: Indiana University Press.

Munro, Brenna. 2017. 'States of Emergence: Writing African Female Same-Sex', *Journal of Lesbian Studies* 21 (2): 186–203.

Nanga, Bernard. 1984. *La trahison de Marianne*. NEA.

Ndinda, Joseph. 1994. 'Ecriture et discours féminin au Cameroun: Trois générations de romancières', *Notre librairie* 118: 6–12.

Nfah-Abbenyi, Juliana Makuchi. 1997. *Gender in African Women's Writing: Identity, Sexuality, and Difference*. Bloomington: Indiana University Press.

Nfobin, E. H. Ngwa. 2014. 'Homosexuality in Cameroon', *International Journal on Minority and Group Rights* 21: 72–130.

Nguyen Matoko, Berthrand. 2004. *Le Flamant noir*. Paris: L'Harmattan.

Nimrod, Bema. 2006. 'Poésie urbaine de Yémy, poésie ultra-urbaine de Frieda Ekotto', *Africultures* 66: 223–7.

Nnaemeka, Obioma. 2003. 'Nego-Feminism: Theorizing, Practicing and Pruning Africa's Way', *Signs: Journal of Women in Culture and Society*, 29 (2): 357–85

Ouologuem, Yambo. 1966. *Le devoir de violence*. Paris: Éditions du Seuil.

Rubin, Gayle. 1983. 'Thinking Sex: Notes for a Radical Theory of the Politics of Sexuality', in Carole S. Vance (ed.), *Pleasure and Danger: Exploring Female* Sexuality, 267–319. Boston: Routledge & Kegan Paul.

Sassine, Williams. 1976. *Wirriyamu*. Paris: Présence Africaine.

Sedgwick, Eve Kosofsky. 1993. *Tendencies*. Durham, NC: Duke University Press.

Segal, Lynne. 1994. *Straight Sex: Rethinking the Politics of Pleasure*. London: Virago Press.

Sharpley-Whiting, Denean T. 1998. 'Fanon, Conflicts, Feminism', in *Frantz Fanon: Conflicts and* Feminisms, 9–30. Lanham, MD: Rowman & Littlefield Publishers.

Silverman, Kaja. 1988. *The Acoustic Mirror: The Female Voice in Psychoanalysis and Cinema*. Bloomington: Indiana University Press.

Sow, Cheikh C. 1980. 'Le ouv du tyran'. *Dix ouvelles de …* Paris: Radio-France-ACCT.

Spivak, Gayatri Chakravorty. 1988. 'Can the Subaltern Speak?', in Cary Nelson and Lawrence Grossberg (eds), *Marxism and the Interpretation of* Culture, 271–313. Urbana: University of Illinois Press.

Stein, Gertrude. 1922. *Geography and Plays*. Madison: University of Wisconsin Press.

Tansi, Sony Labou. 1981. *L'état honteux*. Paris: Éditions du Seuil.

Tchak, Sami. 2004. *La fête des masques*. Paris: Gallimard.

Thiam, Awa. 1978. *La parole aux négresses*. Paris: Denoël-Gonthier.

Tinsley, Omise'eke Natasha. 2010. *Thiefing Sugar: Eroticism between Women in Caribbean Literature*. Durham, NC: Duke University Press.

Vignal, Daniel. 1983. 'L'homophilie dans le roman négro-africain d'expression anglaise et française', *Peuples noirs, peuples africains* 33: 63–81.

Volet, Jean-Marie. 1993. 'Calixthe Beyala, or the Literary Success of a Cameroonian Woman Living in Paris', *World Literature Today* 67 (2): 309–14.

Warner, Michael. 1999. *The Trouble with Normal: Sex, Politics, and the Ethics of Queer Life*. New York: Free Press.

Wekker, Gloria. 2006. *Politics of Passion: Women's Sexual Culture in the Afro-Surinamese Diaspora*. New York: Columbia University Press.

Wittig, Monique. 1981. 'One Is Not Born a Woman', *Feminist Issues* 1 (2): 47–54.

Yavoucko, Cyriaque Robert. 1979. *Crépuscule et défi*. Paris: Editions L'Harmattan.

Zabus, Chantal. 2009. 'Out in Africa: Queer Desire in Some Anthropological and Literary Texts', *Comparative Critical Studies* 6 (2): 251–70.

Zabus, Chantal. 2013. *Out in Africa: Same-Sex Desire in Sub-Saharan African Literatures and Cultures*. Woodbridge, UK: Boydell & Brewer/James Currey.

SOUTHERN AFRICA

Chapter 7

TRANSLECTS: POSTQUEERING TRANSGENDER IN SOUTH AFRICAN AND NIGERIAN AUTOFICTIONS

Chantal Zabus

Of the following words – 'Aikane, arse-bandit, baby-dyke, bear, bent, berdache, bugger, bulldagger, butch, carpet-/rug-muncher, catamite, chaser, cherry-sister, chubby, cub, dandy, dinge-queen, dyke, femme, […] hijra, hungochani, […] gay, invert, jimbanda, john, kathoey, khawal, kiki […] mahu, maricon, mary, molly, nanshoku, otter, pillow-biter, poofter, […] quimbanda, Sapphist, shirt-lifter, […] stibane, stone-butch, straight, stud, that way, trade, trannie, tribadist, uranist […]' –, which Neville Hoad provided when reflecting on 'Queer Theory Addiction' (Hoad 2011: 128), some have gone global whereas others are definitely local. I am here interested in local African expression as it relates to transgenderism, or what I have called elsewhere 'translects', which allows for a gesturing towards a 'postqueer' movement.

Taking our cue from Elaine Showalter's (1991) definition of 'genderlect' to refer to a putative mother tongue 'spoken by the female population in a society, which differs significantly from the dominant language', Samir Kumar Das and I used 'translects'[1] to refer to 'transnational transgender terms' that some trans individuals in postcolonial societies use to refer to themselves, their body parts, sexual orientation, societal rituals and practices, usually not in the dominant or standard language and occasionally in a language form intelligible only to them (Zabus and Das 2020: 812).

Definitions of transgenderism in western contexts and academic milieus cover a broad spectrum: the term 'transgender individuals' refers to individuals ranging from 'non-operative' individuals who often live and identify as belonging to a sex different from that assigned at birth; to individuals who consider themselves a 'third sex' or 'two-spirit' and cultivate an often culture-specific gender liminality (genderqueer) to the extent of resisting the predominant view of gender categories as a male/female binary (nonbinary); on to transsexual individuals (transmen and transwomen) who, even though the term is questioned by the trans community, have changed their bodies (FTM or female to male; MTF or male to female)

To the memory of Zaen Nkabinde.

through sex reassignment surgery (SRS), more recently called *gender confirmation surgery.*

'Transgender' in turn is part of an ever-evolving spectrum – LGBPTIQ2A+ (lesbian, gay, bisexual, pansexual, transgender, intersex, queer/questioning, two-spirit, asexual, others/ friends/more). As the spectrum continues to incorporate imaginative routes around old impasses, some capitals are added or the meaning is enlarged, as in Q, for instance, which first designated 'queer' and came to mean 'questioning'. To the first 'A' another 'A' has been added to refer to 'androgynous' and/or 'ally'; the 'P' can also be seen after 'intersex' as in LGBTQIP2SA. More recently, as a result of decolonial movements among the First Nations, especially as of the 1990s, two-spirit came to hold prime of place: 2SLGBPTIQA+ (two-spirit, lesbian, gay, bisexual, pansexual, transgender, intersex, queer/questioning, asexual, others/friends/more), or a variant thereof. 'Transgender', however, remains topographically more or less in the middle as a result of its historical galvanization in the 1990s, when 'T' entered an arduous dialogue with 'Q(ueer)'. This temporal centrality, however, should not deter recognition of the fact that transgenderism – here understood loosely as the sum of all trans forms and subjectivities – is experienced differently in sub-Saharan African works and so is the suturing of social identity to the biological body. Another crucial difference lies in the use of translects.

To trans historian Susan Stryker, transgender refers to

> people who move away from the gender they were assigned at birth, people who cross over (trans-) the boundaries constructed by their culture to define and contain that gender. Some people move away from their birth-assigned gender because they feel strongly that they properly belong to another gender in which it would be better for them to live; others want to strike out toward some new location, some space not yet clearly defined or concretely occupied; still others simply feel the need to get away from the conventional expectations bound up with the gender that was initially put upon them. In any case, it is the *movement across a socially imposed boundary away from an unchosen starting place*—rather than any particular destination or mode of transition—that best characterizes the concept of 'transgender'.
>
> (Stryker 2008: 3)

This definition, which limns a movement away and across social boundaries and impositions, is key in theorizing American transgender history and in auguring a larger movement of undoing self, identity and disciplines. It was however criticized by other American scholars for its universalization as 'a capacitating story that is also a racial/ableist one' (Awkward-Rich 2022: 23). Yet, this capacitating story in a disabling environment is given another twist in some sub-Saharan African societies and their cultural production. The American trans individual may wish, in the best of circumstances, 'to strike out toward some new location', but in the texts under scrutiny, the location is not entirely new. As we shall see, the movement is not always *away from* society in that society always already holds enabling nexuses, some of them ancestral, that are receptive to gender variance and host translects.

I here examine these translects in two autobiographies or rather two autofictions from South Africa and Nigeria – *Black Bull, Ancestors and Me: My Life as a Lesbian Sangoma* (2008) by Nkunzi Zandile Nkabinde; and *Freshwater* (2018) by Akwaeke Emezi as well as Emezi's *Dear Senthuran: A Black Spirit Memoir* (2021), with which *Freshwater* is inexorably enmeshed. I also consider, for contrastive purposes, *Always Anastacia* (2016) by South African Anastacia Tomson. I deem these works 'autofictional'. 'Autofiction', a term originally deleted from French author Serge Doubrovsky's 1977 novel *Fils*, refers to a type of self-writing poised between autobiography and fiction (Groneman 2019: 2.6). It seems a better fit than the term 'autobiography' even though we retain the latter term's new meaning as being 'increasingly seen less as a literary genre or as a means of aesthetically presenting a certain vision of one's self, and more as a narrative modality endowed with the overbearing responsibility of grappling with facts, events, lives or simply history' (Schmitt 2020: 471).

In the context of a West-South African comparative take on transgenderism in literature, it is productive to consider this recent definition of autobiography as embedded in autofiction in its grappling with the 'event', 'facts' as well as 'history'. These new definitions have been applied to queering and transing the phenomenon of migration, but physical displacement is not a necessary condition in the sense that 'people transit among identities too' (Luibhéid and Chávez 2020: 6) and, in transgender contexts, *transition* amongst identity categories as well. The two autofictional accounts under scrutiny are linked through what I would venture to call a 'postqueer' form of transgenderism.

In *Sons of the Movement: FTMs Risking Incoherence in a Post-Queer Cultural Landscape* (2006), Bobby Noble refers to his own attempt at articulating and narrating trans life, which is marked by grammatical and logical 'incoherence'. One such example of postqueer 'incoherence' is found in his use of phrases such as 'lesbian man' and 'the guy who is half lesbian' (Noble 2006: 84), which instantiate his groping efforts at self-naming. This 'incoherence' Cameron Awkward-Rich has renamed 'lyric speech' for its capacity 'to sustain temporal and categorical paradox [which] has been continuously used by trans writers to represent the persistent form of trans subjectivity' (Awkward-Rich 2022: 137). In an African context, however, where 'queer' has been distributed unevenly and even erroneously over diverse personhoods and identities, the 'temporal and categorical paradox' which Awkward-Rich is referring to cannot fully obtain since the African continent has not been subjected to the same historicization of gender-related liberation struggles. We shall therefore here understand 'postqueer' as a general, post-secular approach to identities and personhoods which translate into various shades of postcolonial naming practices. In the South African and Nigerian autofictions under scrutiny, this postqueer form of transgenderism is imbued by belief systems involving ancestor worship and reincarnation. Both Nkabinde and Emezi draw on the cosmologies and epistemologies of the Zulu and the Igbo, respectively, to interpret their transgender status.

Susan Stryker's *Transgender History*, from which the above definition of transgender is excerpted, was published in 2008 in the same year Nkabinde published her autobiography. But, as would be expected, the two accounts passed each other like ships in the night for at least two reasons: as an MTF American historian Susan Stryker was conversant with American transgender history and, at that point in time, was only beginning to be aware of non-western conceptions of transgender;[2] Nkabinde did not read English-language transgender-related material and had not yet reached a self-perception as transgender. Additionally, Nkabinde resorted to an amanuensis, which gives her account an autofictional remoteness. Nkabinde's amanuensis, American, South African-based anthropologist, Ruth Morgan, was herself at the time grappling with the translation of African concepts.[3] Likewise, Nkabinde was looking for suitable English words to describe her gender core identity and at that stage, could only come up with the word 'lesbian', which features in her book title. Yet, another reason why Stryker's and Nkabinde's respective narratives would be at odds, besides the different genres they used, is that Nkabinde's account tellingly fails to outline such a burdensome societal and birth heritage as Stryker documents in the sense that some segments of South African society tolerate and oftentimes revere gender variance in the specific context of spirituality and healing.

Dis-Possession

Zandile Nkabinde's title, *Black Bull, Ancestors and Me: My Life as a Lesbian Sangoma* (2008) reads like a serpent swallowing its own tail as it is her occupation as a professional *sangoma* that validates the existence of Black Bull. *Sangoma* in IsiZulu and AmaXhosa means 'traditional healer' and relates to gender-differentiated spiritual possession cults and ancestor worship. Possession by 'dead' ancestors from the spirit world is common to most African ancestor worship systems, which antedate the advent of imported monotheistic belief systems. Ancestors remind the living of their presence among them through various processions, festivals, councils, sacrifice and other rituals. Additionally, the categories of 'the dead', as opposed to the living and the unborn, are, according to renowned Ugandan philosopher John Mbiti, 'determined by time depth and the capacity of the living to remember the dead' (1969: 83–4). Generally, in sub-Saharan African philosophical anthropology, personhood is subject to this re-membering of the dead and is mediated by gods and ancestors, with whom humans share some characteristics:

> Gods and ancestors alike are thought of as existing and acting in time and space, although they are not constrained in their actions by speed and geographical limits and are subject to at least most of the mores that guide humans. They are held in respect, and their friendship and favors are courted and sustained through a variety of symbolic acts such as those that constitute ritual and sacrifice.
>
> (Masolo 2010: 156)

Such belief systems therefore indelibly impact the notion of personhood and the sheer physicality of the body.

Nkunzi Zandile Nkabinde is a Zulu sangoma and a *male woman*, who cultivates a culture-specific gender liminality. She is dominated or 'possessed' by her male ancestor, Nkunzi or the Black Bull of the title. In Zulu spiritual possession cults, an ancestor can be a dead member of the family (here it is her great-uncle) and, if male and dominant, will be strong enough to inhabit the male woman, stop her menstruation and generally dictate her conduct, including her sexual preference, which he signals through roaring 'like a lion' (Nkabinde 2008: 69). In these cults, the body of the male woman is rendered 'neutral' and acts as the conduit for the male dominant ancestor, who renders it passive through possession, thereby locating agency outside of the subject. Such possession cults have a long colonial history of denigration.[4]

In the recent postcolonial and post-secular turn towards rehabilitation, ushered in by the 1996 South African Constitution, one might argue that, as Michael Lambek did in his work on Mayotte, colonial dispossession can engender a postcolonial repossession (Lambek 2014: 259). While being 'dispossessed' through the history of colonization and the apartheid regime, the sangoma male woman can be 're-possessed' by ancestors through an assertion over that colonial legacy and today's overly aggressive forms of Christianity. It remains, however, that sangomas commonly mix Christianity and Zulu ancestor worship in some sort of syncretism or 'bending' (Van Klinken and Otu 2017: 74); some of Nkabinde's relatives are members of the Church of Zion, where her grandfather officiated as a pastor (Nkabinde 2008: 28) and '[her] father combined traditional beliefs and Christian beliefs' (25). Moreover, the assumption of unilateral control in Nkabinde's possession by a dominant ancestor is belied by her later claims to be inhabited by a western-type transgender persona outside of ancestor worship.

As I have demonstrated elsewhere, ancestor dominance in female sangomas comes with an array of isiZulu ceremonial translects, associated with the call (*ubizo* or *ukuthwasa*) from the ancestors (*amadlozi*) generally through visions, bouts of fainting and dreams that act as communicating tools for the *Amathwasa* or trainees (literally: 'children of the ancestors'); as well as with the ceremonial training (*ukuthwala*) of male women by a spiritual mother; and the relationship which a male woman can have with her 'ancestral wife' (*unyankwabe*) or female sexual partner (Zabus and Das 2020: 5). The English term 'ancestral wife' is a judicious translation which Morgan and Reid (2003: 378–9) coined to refer to women who 'marry' female *sangomas* but the Zulu original word and potential translect for 'wife' – *unkosikazi* or *umfazi* or the etymon *umka* – is put under erasure. Although this is a relatively recent translation, the most common translects such as *amadlozi* and *sangoma* were translated in colonial times as respectively 'spirits' and 'witch-doctors' (Briault Manus 2011: 52). Ironically, the so-called witch doctors were deemed witches when in fact sangomas 'doing ngòmà' (Janzen 1992: 68) would often engage in witch-hunting and witch-smelling, which consisted in rooting out evil hosted in witches through a trance-like ritual.

A translect such as *umuthi* refers to medicine resulting from the sangomas' decoction in a pot during a process called *ukupehla*. Also known as *muthi*, the etymon derives from the Nguni root *thi* meaning 'tree' and designates Zulu traditional remedies as administered by sangomas to the average citizen. But it often connotes pseudo-medicine involving major health risks and is considered by born-again Christians as part of 'demonic forces' (Ashforth 2005: 135). Although the overarching term *umuthi* is only tangentially related to transgenderism, its general reduction to secret evil and poison(ing) (144) links it to colonial perceptions of sangomas as witches. Used in sports to heighten one's athletic performance, *umuthi* continues to be associated with witchcraft and the hateful screeds of bad science rather than being considered as a translectual part of indigenous knowledge systems (IKS), some of them involving water snakes, especially in sangoma practice.

The snake plays a decisive role when Nkabinde begins her sangoma training or *ekutbwaseni*:

> Suddenly the snake I saw at my aunt's house appeared between my legs and wrapped itself around me. They say that a powerful man's voice exploded out of my mouth.
>
> (Nkabinde 2008: 51)

Notwithstanding the quasi-biblical, erotic visitation of the snake 'between [Nkabinde's] legs', in Zulu religion 'it is common for ancestral spirits to manifest themselves in the form of snakes' (Chidester et al. 1997; quoted in Van Klinken and Otu 2017: 77). The snake's visitation motivates Nkabinde to take on her ancestor's name, Nkunzi. The snake will also surface in Akwaeke Emezi's novel, albeit in a different guise.

Even though tainted by various forms of Christianity, these IKS are also known as 'African science' (Ashforth 2005: 147). Some of its members such as the *inyanga* group of herbalist sangomas[5] clashed with Doctors for Life International (DFL), which considered doing ngòmà a form of malpractice. After the South African Parliament passed the Traditional Health Practitioners (THO) Act of 2004 (Act. 35) and its Bill (620/2007), *umuthi* was endorsed while the efficacy, safety and quality of traditional health services were ensured (Rees 2015). That the South African Medical Association backed THO points to a new, syncretic ecology of knowledges, which also contributes to the peaceful cohabitation of imported western-derived vocabularies and those indigenous translects which survived the shift to modernity in South Africa. This syncretism reinforced the popularity of the 220,000 sangomas whose employ was restored with the 1996 South African Constitution, and its amendments through 2012. These legitimate practitioners of ngòmà are consulted on a regular basis by 65 per cent to 80 per cent of the South African population, that is, an estimated 30 million citizens (Rees 2015).

Some of these translects as used by South African sangomas are also transnational in that they travelled and are known under cognate linguistic variants – for instance, 'doing ngòmà' in Zimbabwe. Historian Marc Epprecht in *Hungoshani* (2004) has contributed to the 'outing' of the lect *ngochani* in ChiShona, which is translated as 'homosexual' in Zimbabwe (see VaShona Project n.d.). The lect may have been borrowed via translation from the South African, often Bantu, mining milieus which, as of the 1860s, hosted 'mine-marriages', that is, intergenerational and initiatory male-male marriages between boss-boys and their boy-wives (Wa Sibuyi 1993: 36–57; Zabus 2013: 35–43) as well as cross-dressing and embryonic forms of contemporary transgenderism. Often considered 'secret', these translects and their corollary practices are now more of an open secret in that they have been mined and extracted through fieldwork by scholars, cultural anthropologists and specialists of theology, often with the help of the sangomas and other indigenous practitioners themselves.

The result of such syncretism is a proliferation of slippery contenders. To take only one example, the use of 'gay' has undergone a category crisis, as some women self-identify as gay women rather than lesbians (Morgan and Wieringa 2005: 65–75); same-sex between female 'gang bosses' and women inmates in the Soweto Women's Jail is called *snaganaga* (Nkabinde 2008: 134) but does not qualify as 'lesbian sex'; a South African 'masculine man' playing the dominant role in a relationship with another man is called 'a straight man' (126). Having said that, 'gay' served as the Litmus test for the 'modernity' of the new post-apartheid South African nation (Munro 2012). Today, I would posit transgenderism as the new trigger of visibility to test the postqueer, post-apartheid Rainbow Nation.

In the early twenty-first century, Nkabinde was wrestling with the translects she was familiar with and the new English vocabularies to which she was exposed through her education. As a result, she self-identified as a 'tomboy' in childhood (Nkabinde 2008: 37); at age 13, as a 'lesbian', which is a word she looked up in an English dictionary while being involved with a 'lesbian' social worker (Nkabinde 2008: 33); then as a 'butch', and much later, outside of her 'autobiography', as 'transgender'.[6] The conflation of 'lesbian', for instance, with sangoma, is however not always readily embraced. FTM Tebogo Nkoana, a sangoma as of age 15, who was first introduced to the word 'lesbian' when he was 11, titles his testimony 'My ancestor was living through me' (2009). But this is done tongue-in-cheek in a soft mockery of how his relatives perceive his condition. Moreover, he reports in 2008 (when he was 21) that he had to convince his girlfriend that he was not a lesbian:

> [My girlfriend] perceived me as a lesbian because she heard that her mother's trainee was lesbian. ... I then managed to convince her that I am not a lesbian; because she made it very clear that she doesn't date lesbians.
>
> (quoted in Morgan, Marais and Wellbeloved 2009: 122)

The relationship is, however, in the open, but the girlfriend is not identified as an 'ancestral wife'. Moreover, the translation of English terms in interviews carried out by Mkasi Lindiwe with sangomas reveals a certain level of translational loss or untranslatability:

i. Lesbian – A female sangoma who is possessed by a female spirit;
ii. Bisexual – A female sangoma who is possessed by a female and a male spirit;

iii. Transgender – A female sangoma who is possessed by a male (authoritative) spirit, or vice-versa;

iv. Hermaphrodite – A sangoma with both sexual organs. (Lindiwe 2013)

Confusion reigns when individuals claim, as Lindiwe reports, 'to be lesbian one day, the next day … bisexual; the following day … transgender' (quoted in Lindiwe 2013: 56). Transgender is, however, always associated with possession by a spirit in sangoma parlance.

To complicate matters further, one reason evoked by sangomas for being in same-sex relationships is that 'heterosexual sex is regarded as unclean and can weaken the medicine' (*umuthi*), while relationships between a male woman, who is too bossy, and a submissive ancestral wife 'are perceived to be male-female relationships rather than same-sex relationships' (Lindiwe 2013: 40). Generally, ordinary citizens take it for granted that the gender of sangomas 'is not fixed' (14). Could the Sacred then be 'the site of queer desire', queried Van Klinken and Otu (2017: 72)?

Taking their cue from Nkabinde's claim that she has not been 'contaminated by sex with a man' (Nkabinde 2008: 76) despite her having been raped at the age of 8, Van Klinken and Otu contend that 'the entanglement between Zulu spirituality and Christianity also functions to effectively suppress any turn to the erotic as a source of empowerment for Nkabinde' (Van Klinken and Otu 2017: 83). However, Nkabinde's 'wild' erotics, channelled through Nkunzi, her totemic Black Bull, also partake of the 'sovereign erotic' which Cherokee critic and two-spirit activist Quo-Li Driskill has suggested 'can be used as a Two-Spirit tactic for healing historical trauma and as a tool in decolonial struggles' (2010: 73). Earlier, Yupik (Eskimo) Anguksuar aka Richard LaFortune had already foregrounded erotics as central to Indigenous resistance, which is predicated on the recognition of multiple genders or at least 'the presence of both a feminine and a masculine spirit in one person' (LaFortune 1997: 221).

As a Zulu male woman, Nkabinde, in acknowledging that she is 'definitely two people' (Nkabinde 2008: 155), comes close to being a 'two-spirit', which is the translation of *niizh manitoog*, the Northern Algonquian term in vogue since the 1990s in Canada, which revealed the Indigenous peoples' or First Nations' distrust of the colonial nature of many LGBTQ+ movements in the United States and Canada. Such an indigenous translect as *niizh manitoog* and its English translation as two-spirit or 2(S), which has ousted L or G in recent charts, shows that translects and their corollary erotics are common to transatlantic indigenous belief systems which have undergone similar colonial policies of subjugation and dispossession, and have employed varied resistance tactics.

Nkabinde's erotics translates as sexual dominance, which is inspired by Black Bull. In that respect, the black-and-white picture of Nkabinde inserted in *Black Bull, Sangomas and Me*, shows Nkabinde, while working for the GALA Archive's queer tour of Johannesburg, as the 'butch' with shaven head dressed in dark trousers girdled with a leather belt, a leather jacket and a man's shirt. When I visited Nkabinde in Soweto in May 2017, he had renamed himself

Zaen Nkabinde; he was living as a 'trans man' with Felicity, his ancestral wife and a sangoma (who is not the same as in the 2008 autobiography). During that interview carried out in English and Zulu-inflected English,[7] Nkabinde acted as the dominant butch-like partner but did not call her 'ancestral wife' a *femme*; he called Felicity *nkosi*, from the Zulu term *umkozi* or wife which, because it is also used in heterosexual relationships, shows her internalization of some form of heteronormativity. In other words, Nkabinde occupies a grey zone between local, indigenous and western parlance, which precludes hir full-fledged membership in the international, western-inflected LGBTQ+ community and, generally, fails to locate her within the historically determined western skirmishes between FTMs and butch theorists in the 1990s (e.g. Halberstam 1998). At the time I carried out this interview, Nkabinde was dividing his life between his training of sangomas and his activist work at Constitution Hill. He had by then undergone a mastectomy in Bara Hospital in Soweto (as opposed to the more well-known Groote Schuur in central Johannesburg) and had asked the Administration for his identity card to match his recovered gender before his untimely death in 2018.

To offer a brief contrast with Nkabinde, South African Anastacia Tomson is a white MTF practising medical doctor in Johannesburg; she came out, shed her 'deadname' and the burden of maleness; her outing was quickly followed by *Always Anastacia* (2016), an 'autobiography' based on the diary form accounting for the personal trajectory, which has been the preferred genre for western transitioning individuals.[8] The text is conversant with the most up-to-date vocabularies that have trickled down from the West, as of the mid-twentieth century, as shown in this excerpt from Day-252 (that is, 252 before being Anastacia), on 22 October 2014:

> I heard about the support group from a friend I'd met at a dinner party. Originally, I had thought that *she* was a cisgender lesbian. I later learned that *they* (a chosen gender-neutral pronoun) were in fact genderfluid, and non-binary, and self-identified as 'hella queer'.
>
> (Thomson 2016: 7)

These are words that Anastacia/Staci had to learn and master, as her autobiography unfolds. Additionally, she learns 'to become skilled at avoiding the use of gendered pronouns or epithets when talking about [herself] and others' (Tomson 2016: 130). However, this capacity for adaptation does not preclude a degree of suffering and stigmatization in the Jewish orthodox neighbourhood of Johannesburg where she works as a general practitioner; her former boss no longer wishes to shake hands with her because 'Jewish law forbade him from social physical contact with a woman to whom he was not married or directly related' (125). Yet, her newfound friends make up for this display of heterodoxy:

> Straight ones, gay ones, pansexual, cisgender, transgender, Jewish, Asian, Greek and Anglo-saxon ones.
>
> (Thomson 2016: 149)

There is no mention of Black/indigenous Africans unless they are subsumed under other gender identities.

Seven years separate Nkabinde's from Tomson's self-writing and they have admittedly different gender identities (FTM vs MTF) and belong to a different class and ethnicity. But the divide also lies in the history of dispossession as well as the words used to approach transgenderism and transsexualism in English, which reveals what we might venture to call, not so much an 'apartheid of sex' (Rothblatt 1995) as an apartheid of gender. What is more, Anastacia Tomson does not envisage referring to herself with the gender-neutral pronoun 'they'/'them', and experiences 'euphoria that stems from being referred to with the correct set of pronouns' (Tomson 2016: 138): she instead of he, thereby entrenching a binary gender division.

Pronouns: We, They, She

In African languages, neutral personal pronouns can affect sex roles, as in woman-woman 'marriages', that is, ancestral nexuses whereby the 'female husbands', generally widows without a male offspring, take on 'wives' to produce heirs for their husbands' lineages. The wives then take in male lovers and have children who are in turn handed over to the female husbands. For instance, in Igboland in Eastern Nigeria, the grammatical erasure of the distinction between he and she (*ọ*) (see Logan February in this volume) as well as him and her (*ya*) facilitated woman-woman marriages (Amadiume 1987: 89–90). In Zulu, the third-person singular pronoun *yena* translates both he/she and him/her. This suspension of gender may also, along with the individual's vestment in the sacred, help delineate a stance beyond 'queer' in a space-clearing gesture whereby pronouns not always unequivocally stand for nouns with a stable meaning.

'They' and 'we' are yet another set of pronouns that initially refer to a split or a Spaltung in Nigerian, Igbo-Tamil writer Akwaeke Emezi. In her debut novel *Freshwater* (2018), Emezi foregrounds the Igbo myth of the *ọgbanje*, which is widespread in Southern Nigeria, amongst, for example, the Yoruba and the Urhobo, as well as in neighbouring West African nation-states. The *ọgbanje* (from the Igbo verb *-je* or 'to go'; *nje* means 'come on') is a spirit-child that dies repeatedly and is reincarnated to plague its mother's womb; it is often mutilated to facilitate its being recognized upon its return to the living and, when amongst the living, leaves behind an object or *iyi-ụwa*.

Spirit-children are 'born to die' in the sense that after their death, the cycle is repeated and they are reborn in the same families, often with the same serrated marks that the dibịa or traditional healer has imprinted on their dead body. This belief, which explained the high rate in infant mortality and may be linked to the sickle cell disease (Asakitikpi 2008: 61) was discouraged by Christian missionaries, colonial powers and then by UNESCO. This belief finds expression in such names as *Kokumo* (he will not die again) and *Malono* (don't die again) amongst the

Yoruba; *Onwubiko* (death, I implore you) amongst the Igbo; and *Akpoyoma* (the world is good) amongst the Urhobo, to persuade the child 'to stay' (60).

In both her autofictions, *Freshwater* (2018) and *Dear Senthuran: A Black Spirit Memoir* (2021), Emezi taps into the Nigerian literary tradition of foregrounding the *ọgbanje* (its Yoruba equivalent is the *àbíkú*), the most well-known instance being found in Chinua Achebe's *Things Fall Apart* ([1958] 1986), in which the main character Okonkwo's daughter, Ezinma, is an ọgbanje. So, when the non-Igbo, English-language readers read 'Perhaps she has come to stay' (Achebe [1958] 1986: 34), they are supposed to understand that the spirit-child has decided to remain amongst the living. Achebe's foundational novel features the elaborate retrieval of the *iyi-uwa*, the symbolic object that ties Ezinma to the spirit-world and which Emezi calls in *Freshwater* 'the oath of the world' (Emezi 2018: 15). The search for and the digging up of the *iyi-ụwa* is filmed in real time in the 1971 film based on Chinua Achebe's *Things Fall Apart*, which testifies to its potency.

Wole Soyinka and John Pepper Clark have written poems on 'Abiku', both of them in 1961. Whereas Soyinka sides with Abiku in the tug of war and love (Soyinka 1961: 7), Clark admonishes Abiku: 'No longer then bestride the threshold / But step in and stay / For good' (Clark-Bekederemo 1961: 4). Buchi Emecheta's ọgbanje girl in *The Slave Girl* (1977) is called Ojebeta, which contains the Igbo verb *je* which indicates 'urgency and the need for a response' (Ogunyemi 2002: 664) when beckoned for reunion with the spirit-world. Ben Okri's *The Famished Road* (1991), which takes its title from Wole Soyinka's poem 'Death in the Dawn' (1961: 64), also features the Yoruba *àbíkú* in the young character, Azaro, who has been interpreted as occupying Wole Soyinka's 'chthonic realm' or 'transitional gulf' (Soyinka 1990: passim), which is rendered as the road. Referring to his spirit-companions, Azaro remembers an episode from childhood when playing by the admittedly 'famished' road:

> One day, I was playing on the sand when they called me from across the road with the voices of my mother. As I went towards the voice a car almost ran me over.
>
> (Okri 1991: 8)

Incidentally, the risk of being run over materializes in Emezi's *Dear Senthuran* that features Emezi's sister being accidentally hit and then dragged by a truck, which leaves her with indelible scars.

The malevolence of the spirits' 'voice' and their cunning in Okri's novel is confirmed in *Freshwater*, in which Emezi's autofictional alter ego, Ada, is the ọgbanje whose 'foetus body, niched in her mother's "lining"' is expelled and is born despite the spirits' 'resistance' (Emezi 2018: 3, 2, 4). The spirits call Ada 'the Ada' to refer to her as a many-being, multiply birthed vessel, which they temporarily inhabit. Designated as 'we' or 'they', depending on who is narrating, or 'hatchlings' or 'godlings', these ruthless spirits are said to 'transition … from spirit to flesh' (6, 5) and then inhabit Ada to the point of ungendering her. Emezi uses the spirits' transitioning to Ada's flesh to reflect on her own trans liminality and, later, her various gendered worlds. She writes:

> The possibility that I was an *ogbanje* occurred to me around the same time I realized I was trans, but it took me a while to collide the two worlds.
>
> (Emezi 2021: 16)

and

> Ogbanje are as liminal as possible—spirit and human, both and neither. I am here and not here, real and not real, energy pushed into skin and bone. I am my others; we are one and we are many.
>
> (Emezi 2018: 225–6)

Like the early Nkabinde in *Black Bull, Ancestors, and Me*, Emezi binds her breasts and starts dating women. She then undergoes a mastectomy, starts wearing men's clothes and inhabits 'the *ogbanje* space', that is, 'the places we are suspended in, between the inaccurate concepts of male and female, between the us and the brothersisters slavering on the other side' (Emezi 2018: 193).

Emezi coins new translects, usually through compounding, to translate the *ogbanje* condition: the Ada's 'meatbody' that spirits have been forcibly shoved into, and which occasionally turn her into a 'beastself' (Emezi 2018: 24, 87); 'Ala's somethingborn'; 'spiritself'; 'the deityparents'; 'worldbend'; 'elderspirit'; 'godmemory'; and 'brothersister'(Emezi 2021: 57, 14, 69, 76, 119, 19). The translect that recurs the most is 'brothersisters' (e.g. Emezi 2018: 19), which recalls the 'sistergirls' and 'brotherboys' (*yimpininni*), among the Indigenous Tiwis in Northern Australia to refer to their trans status. But in Emezi's text, the spirits or brothersisters and Ada-as-ọgbanje are linked in siblinghood. As the spirits sink their roots into her, she becomes a 'beastself' at their sexual beg, and as a result becomes anorexic and mutilates her skin with a razor blade. Aware of her emerging condition as an ọgbanje, she searches over the internet 'things like disruption of identity, self-damaging impulsivity, emotional instability and mood swings, self-mutilating behavior and recurrent suicidal behavior' (Emezi 2018: 140). Yet none of these words opening the medical portal to pathology can adequately render her liminality. An exception could be the Dissociative Identity Disorder but poetic term 'alters',[9] which Emezi averts.

Emezi's body markings – she cuts her left wrist and has her forearm tattooed – can be related to 'the several small incisions with a sharp razor' that, in Igboland, are made by the dibịa to cut the ọgbanje's link with the other side (Achebe 1986: 44). The spirits relish in Ada's desperate self-harming:

> All these things she was doing to her skin made her closer to us; it was like an advertisement.
>
> (Emezi 2018: 210)

The eager spirits retaliate by further 'carv[ing]' the Ada's body into a curvature where they nestle and that they 'could truly call a home' (Emezi 2018: 188). The 'carving' then translates as her decision: 'we cut down the C cups of blatant mammary tissue to small As' (181).

True to the spirits' homing wish and ill at ease with the constant pull 'between girl and boy' (Emezi 2018: 123), Emezi undergoes a robot-assisted double mastectomy, which, exceptionally, involves not only the content of breast tissue, but her nipples as well. Put in rather clinical terms, the glandular tissue, the lactiferous duct via which the lobules of the aerolar complex drain, as well as 'the nerve supply to the nipple-areolar complex' were removed (Richards, Bowman and Braker 2017: 229). And thus was equally removed that which tied her to Saachi Emezi, their biological Tamil mother, the thin, bespectacled woman originally from Malaysia, whom Emezi called 'the human mother' (Emezi 2018: 188). The fraught biological relationship between mother and daughter confirms Ogunyemi's intuition that the metaphysics behind the Igbo *ọgbanje* or the Yoruba *àbíkú* may serve as 'a master narrative of the parent-child relationship in Pan-African socio-political contexts and literary texts' (Ogunyemi 2002, 663). What is more, Emezi trans-formed the scarred tissue into a tattooed triangle that recalls the 'inverted T or anchor-type pattern' (Richards, Bowman and Braker 2017: 236) that results from such surgery or chest reconstruction. The reassignment surgery is here re-read as an 'assignment as ọgbanje' (Emezi 2021: 16) and 'mutilation' is understood as 'a shift from wrongness to alignment' (20).

The removal of Ada's nipples, an erotic but also lacteal zone tied to the nurturing breast, is later completed by a bilateral salpingectomy (i.e. the removal of both fallopian tubes, which precludes pregnancy) and a hysterectomy which will lead to 'a new and bloodless life' (Emezi 2021: 19). Overall, she finds the reproductive, fertile female form 'unsatisfactory, too feminine, too reproductive':

> [F]ertility was a pure and clear abomination to us. It would be unthinkable, unbelievably cruel for us to ever swell so unnaturally, to lactate, to mutate our vessel. Could there be anything more human?
>
> (Emezi 2018: 187)

In unshackling the self from the flesh and relaying her trans status beyond humanness, Emezi uses the Igbo language, but it is suitably 'stunted' (Emezi 2018: 225). Unlike, for instance, Achebe who provided a Glossary at the end of *Things Fall Apart*, Emezi leaves a lot of Igbo words and whole sentences unglossed (61), especially the proverb-like epigraphs (notably to chapters 6, 9, 14 and 15), or tagged with their English translations. This 'cushioning' technique of tagging an explanatory English word or phrase onto the African one (Zabus 2007: 176) is applied to some Igbo expressions, for example 'slowly, slowly, newere nwayọ, take it slowly' (Emezi 2018: 42).

Despite such postcolonial techniques of linguistic reappropriation, Emezi is once removed from the Igbo language and Igbo ancestral knowledge, which she however seeks to repossess, as Nkabinde did, but with a twist: Emezi claims that there is 'no possession by an ǫgbanje' (Emezi 2021: 57), which is intrinsically nonbinary, for the 'spirit' and the 'human' are not perceived as binaries; hence the fusion of 'we' and 'they'. However, when faced with others' perceptions that she 'wasn't Nigerian enough', which finds its gender corollary in the allegation that she was not 'trans enough', Emezi has sought to restore 'Igbo ontology as a valid reality made unreal only by colonialism' (5, 13, 79). Likewise, the ǫgbanje cult has been revived through the Ogbanje Church of All Nations which opened in Nnewi, Anambra State in August 2023. For the first service, the cleric eulogized 'goddesses of some popular rivers in Nnewi' (Editor 2023).

Emezi's process of rehabilitation and repossession is sparked off by Saul Emezi, her father, who had dismissed the Igbo belief-system as 'mumbo-jumbo' (Emezi 2018: 13). To Emezi, in retrospect, her father's dismissal of things Igbo culminated in his albeit protective killing of a python coiled on the bathroom floor when Ada, in tears, was a mere child. This inaugural scene opens the novel's first chapter:

We
The first time our mother came for us, we screamed. We are three and she was a snake, coiled up on the tile of the bathroom, waiting.

(Emezi 2018: 1)

This scene is reminiscent of another in Achebe's *Things Fall Apart*, in which the Sacred Python, 'the emanation of the god of water' is killed by a zealous *osu* or outcast converted to Christianity (Achebe [1958] 1986: 112), which is redolent of the legendary Saint George triumphing over the dragon. Even though Emezi is not altogether dismissive of Christianity – one of the spirits is the meek Saint Vincent who creates a 'dreambody' for Ada, 'that of a boy complete with a penis' (Emezi 2018: 123) and another, the Christ-like Yshwa, who 'died in his own flesh form' (196) – the primary governing principle is Igbo cosmology.

In Nkabinde's *Black Bull*, one recalls that the sangoma's body hosts the ancestral snake: 'I take the form of a snake and I move this way and that way until I can identify the cause of the sickness' (Nkabinde 2008: 76). The slithering movement is here central to her divination (*ukubhula*) practice. In Emezi's autofiction, the freshwater of the title takes all its significance when translated from the Igbo (*oshimiri*; *Osun Oyi* in Yoruba) as that which flows out of 'the mouth of a python' (Emezi 2018: 9). In Igbo cosmology, Ala the Earth delivers her messages through the Sacred Python Eke, which was revered in pre-colonial times. Despite colonization and the demonization of snakes, starting with the book of Genesis, the python is still worshipped today; the Igbo Defender site muses: 'We still worship it because it was there before us' (see OzoIgboNdu1 2019).[10]

If the beginning of *Freshwater* testifies to the severance of 'we' from the biological mother, who is solely the spirits' chosen vessel for their birth – 'we were a distinct *we* instead of being fully and just *her*' – (Emezi 2018: 5), the end of *Freshwater* connects Ada with another 'she', the spiritual python mother, Nne. Ada, whose name means 'precious child' (218) and who embodies the Python's egg (lit. Awka-

Eke) is visited by Nne (lit. 'mother'), who admonishes her to '*find [her] tail*' (224), which is where the Python's sex is located. Ada/Emezi interprets their primordial mother's summon as an invitation to find their true gender core identity.

In Igboland, *Nne Mmiri* (the Water Spirit Deity) is the third category of spirits to whom the *ọgbanje nmiri* (Water Spirit being) owes loyalty (Achebe 1986: 28, 50–2). However, through her use of the *iyi-ụwa*, which is more connected to this other category, the *ọgbanje elu* (Earth Spirit being) than to the *ọgbanje nmiri*, Emezi seems to conflate the two categories under Nne Mmiri. Regardless of these subtleties, the ọgbanje condition is considered worthy of treatment. Chinwe Achebe, an Igbo clinical psychologist writes: 'Treatment ranges from (Afa) divination, "ogbome" (communicating with the spirits through an "innocent" young person), palmistry, mirror method etc' (Achebe 1986: 37). Ada/Emezi's consultation of the deity is therefore considered as pathological by Igbo clinical psychologists but not, for instance, by the Igbo widowed practitioner who helps guide Emezi to Ala's shrine in Umuahia, in a pilgrimage which is narrated in *Dear Senthuran* (2021: 133–5).

Nne Mmiri's oracle also prompts Ada/Emezi to find new meaning in Chi sayings, the Chi being the personification of an individual's fate. The Chi saying – 'ịchụrụ chi ya ka maba – One does not challenge their chi to a wrestling match' (Emezi 2018: 217) was famously used by Chinua Achebe to refer to Okwonko, the famous Igbo wrestler who, when faced with misfortune, 'could not rise beyond the destiny of his *chi*' (Achebe 1986: 92). Rebaptized 'guardian angel' by Christian missionaries, the Chi has since been variously interpreted as 'personal guiding spirit' (Achebe 1975: passim) or 'personal god' (Achebe [1958] 1986: 13) or as 'the God in Every Man' or even as 'destiny' (Chukwukere 1993: 519–34). The Chi's voice in *Freshwater* takes the form of the spirits' song beckoning Ada to '*Come home*' (Emezi 2018: 225). The end of *Freshwater* is marked by Ada's/ Emezi's surrender to their Chi, for 'You cannot wrestle with your chi and win' (225) as well as to the Supreme Mother, Nne, in an embrace of the snaky river 'full of [her] scales' (226). Yet, it is a differed surrender.

Emezi has thus trans-formed Igbo proverbs and words into translects to culturally sanction her own transitioning to a vessel they have been careful not to identify as male. As Ada is a remainer in the world of the living, 'they' and 'we' are rolled into one, and are reincarnated into each other, which is part of Emezi's lifelong project. By contrast, in a poem such as 'Some Kind of We', American-born poet Ari Banias develops a singular 'we' to refer to the trans subjectivity of 'a white dude / after having been a white girl' (Banias 2016: 1–3). Whereas Banias' 'we' is relationally awkward in 'dodging pronouns' amidst family members in 'Grandchild' (16), the pronouns 'we' and 'they' in Emezi's *Freshwater* are interchangeable through a flesh-transcendent type of relationality since Ada relates to the spirits in their various shape-shifting capacities. Yet, 'they' is Emezi's preferred pronoun, as stated in interviews and on their website (see Akwaeke 2024b).

The pronoun 'they' in its singular use usually refers to a neutral gender pronoun used by nonbinary, trans and other individuals familiar with trans life-worlds. But, as Cameron Awkward-Rich intuits, '*they* designates a range of particular gendered inhabitations' (Awkward-Rich 2022: 3). Emezi's use of 'they' certainly refers to this particular use of 'they' which flies in the face of contemporary identification technologies – from the passport to fingerprinting to 4D body scanning – but behind Emezi's 'they' also lies the presence of the 'many others', the 'brothersisters' and the spiritual mother – Nne – waiting for them to step in with both feet on the other side. In *Freshwater* and *Dear Senthuran*, we/they connect ancestor worship, as in Zulu *sangoma* Zandile/Zaen Nkabinde, and the western inclusive writing that is displayed by Anastacia Tomson, as well as reincarnation.

Trans-Migration

Despite their African trans status, Nkabinde and Emezi are fated to embrace different locations. Unlike post-apartheid South Africa, where Nkabinde was enabled, to some extent, to live hir transgenderism,[11] Nigeria, especially after its 2014 'Kill the Gays' bill, criminalizes homosexuality, with which transgenderism is often confused, and stigmatizes gender-variant individuals. This is sensitively rendered in Emezi's novel, *The Death of Oji Vivek* (2020), which traces the fictional life of a Nigerian transgender individual, who is brutally murdered and thereby lends credence to Nigerian MTF Miss SaHHara, who clamoured: 'I left Nigeria to save my life' (see 'Trans woman: "I left Nigeria to save my life"' 2016).

Born in 1987 in a remote Nigerian village, where she was abused as a trans child, Miss SaHHara found a way out through the demanding world of fashion, winning international beauty contests, gaining recognition in the West but also in countries such as Thailand and the Philippines, and defending transgender rights through her organization, TransValid. Miss SaHHAra's success story as a doubly refashioned body, rendered spectacular through the scopophilic gaze of cisgender people, also points to another fault-line, that is, her migration to the United Kingdom, a country that had and still has (neo)colonial bonds with Nigeria, thereby etching the North/South divide onto the very bodies of trans migrants, who have albeit unwittingly blurred the contours of binary M/F citizenship.

In *Dear Senthuran: A Black Spirit Memoir* (2021), which reads like epistolary autofiction, made of letters addressed to friends and relatives, Emezi muses on their status as a nonbinary transgender individual having undergone several surgical mutations in order to become 'finally sterile' (Emezi 2021: 14). At that point, after experiencing several births and flitting along the borders of multiple gendered selfhoods, Emezi can truly be Ala's avatar. Like this other version of Eke or Idemili (Achebe [1958] 1986: 13), 'the god who lives in the river … [and] comes on land as a python' (Emezi 2021: 127), Emezi is flat-chested and can better slither, slip and slide her way home, unhampered by pendulous mammary blobs.

This slithery spirit migration is experienced through multiple selfhoods in various 'alternate rogue centers' (Emezi 2021: 80): Bulgaria, Nigeria, Malaysia, Singapore, Tanzania, Trinidad, Vietnam. Unlike diasporic subjects, who hold on to their humanness when faced with de-subjugation and dehumanization, Emezi feels 'not even human'. More assertively than in *Freshwater*, Emezi is 'an embodied god' in *Dear Senthuran* (97) and a rapping 'deity' on her EP album[12] by virtue of her being the child of the Igbo python mother. Doomed to live for a while 'on multiple margins in a country that is not home' (104), they find a home, a 'Godhouse' (119) in swampy New Orleans.

From this 'temporary home' (2021: 219), Emezi is active on social media. As #the opulentogbanje, they tag photographs of themself in high fashion dresses and of their 'sixty-seven faces' or 'masks' (39–40) which herald ancestor embodiment through the 'masquerades' she witnessed as a child in Aba and Umuahia (see Logan February in this volume). In one picture depicting one of their sixty-seven faces, Emezi features themself sticking out their tongue in the attempt to reach the nose, the tongue in snakes functioning as the organ of smell. Their flayed away 'true skins' (221) conjure up more the snake shedding its skin than, say, the 'second skins' which Jay Prosser (1998) used to refer to transitioning in a British context. This episode in Emezi flaunting the embodiedness of 'God' is bound to be short-lived, as it is only 'a few decades before [they] go home' (2021: 230), intimating a pending death. This dying 'before death' (55) is also to be understood against the Igbo belief in reincarnation, inherent in the ogbanje myth, which is also explored in Nigerian-British novelist Okechukwu Nzelu's exploration of diasporic male same-sex desire in *Here Again Now* (2022). As for Emezi, they have several 'reincarnations left to go' (Emezi 2021: 63).

Whereas translects were ancestrally homebound and tied to doing ngómá in Nkabinde, Emezi's translects build on the ancestral myth of the ogbanje but 'travel' into diasporic contemporary subjectivity. Emezi's translects are thus unhoused. Unlike Nkabinde's translects, they come both from an indigenous language, that is, Igbo, and from English, yet a relexified, syncretic English coined by compounding. They are not land-transnational, the way Nkabinde's translects were because they crossed borders into other languages such as IsiXhosa, ChiShona and other Southern African nation-states such as Zimbabwe. But they travel through literature and translation; the ogbanje is also reincarnated algorithmically through social media and blogs, so many volatile gendered inhabitations that the original translects never thought they could call home.

Notes

1   'Translects' is also used in India to refer to second-language acquisition. See Pandey 2005.

2   In the first *Transgender Studies Reader* (Stryker and Whittle 2006), there was only limited reference to non-western societies. The second *Transgender Studies Reader* (Stryker and Aizura 2013) ventured further afield (e.g. 'Transsexing Transhumanimality') and beyond western epistemic borders (e.g. Lewis on gender variance in Latin America; Henry on cross-dressed male sex workers in early postwar Japan; and Aizura on Thai Reassignment clinics).

3   See, for instance, Morgan and Wieringa 2005.

4   The cult moved from being spiritually endorsed to being demonized with the advent of Christianity in 1799, amid the 1778 to 1781 wars between the Xhosas and the Europeans, and with the Witchcraft Suppression Act 3 of 1957 carried over from

1895, itself inspired by the British Act of 1735. Witchcraft was prohibited by a colonial clause referred to as the *Repugnancy Proviso*, which limited the recognition of customary law. Such limitation was recognized by the South African Commission Law of 1996 as 'a legacy of colonialism and a clear reflection of the ethnocentric bias in South Africa's legal system'. Chapter 3 under (e): 'the Repugnancy proviso' of the South African Law Commission 1996.

5	There are three types of sangomas/*inyanga* (or healers): diviners, faith healers and herbalists.

6	Zaen Nkabinde identified himself as 'transgender' on change.org in 2018 and in his personal email to me on 18 January 2018, that is some four months before he passed away on 24 May 2018.

7	I interviewed Zaen (also spelled Zane and Zean) Nkunzi Nkabinde on 27 May 2017 at 9148/61 Extension 12, Protea Glen, Soweto, Johannesburg, South Africa.

8	Jay Prosser argues that 'to write on transsexual narratives represents a displaced autobiographical act' (Prosser 1998: 4).

9	On 'alters', see, for instance, Salters-Pedneault 2023.

10	In post-apartheid South Africa, which boasts the most modern legislation in the world and contrary to its famed 9/3 sexual orientation clause of the Bill of Rights, male women and their ancestral wives are not united in a common identity based on a shared *sexual orientation* but rather are distinguished from each other according to gender difference, complicated by spirituality and its attendant erotics. Also, the new Constitution, written in English, has no room for Zulu translects as they pertain to sangomas' 'marriages'.

11	See and hear at: Akwaeke 2024a, c. 'Bànyě' as an active verb in Igbo means 'enter', 'get on board'.

References

Achebe, Chinua. [1958] 1986. *Things Fall Apart*. London: Heinemann.

Achebe, Chinua. 1975. *Chi in Igbo Cosmology*. London: Heinemann.

Achebe, Chinwe. 1986. *The World of Ogbanje*. Enugu: Fourth Dimension Publishers.

Akwaeke. 2024a. 'Banye', track 6, *Stop Dying, You Were Very Expensive!*. Available online: https://akwaeke.bandcamp.com/track/banye (accessed 15 April 2024).

Akwaeke. 2024b. 'Home'. Available online: https://www.akwaeke.com/home (accessed 4 December 2023).

Akwaeke. 2024c. 'Stop Dying, You Were Very Expensive!'. Available online: https://www.yungdeadthing.com/ (accessed 15 April 2024).

Amadiume, Ife. 1987. *Male Daughters, Female Husbands: Gender and Sex in an African Society*. London: Zed Books.

Asakitikpi, Alex E. 2008. 'Born to Die: the *Ogbanje* Phenomenon and Its Implication in Childhood Mortality in Southern Nigeria', *The Anthropologist International Journal of Contemporary and Applied Studies of Man* 10 (1): 59–63.

Ashforth, Adam. 2005. *Witchcraft, Violence, and Democracy in South Africa*. Chicago: University of Chicago Press.

Awkward-Rich, Cameron. 2022. *The Terrible We: Thinking with Trans Maladjustment*. Durham, NC and London: Duke University Press.

Banias, Ari. 2016. *Anybody*. New York: Norton.

Briault-Manus, Vicki. 2011. *The Emergence of a Tradition: Toward a Postcolonial Stylistics of Black South African Fiction in English*. Lanham, MD: Lexington.

Chidester, David, Chirevo Kwenda, Robert Petty, Judy Tobler and Darrel Wratten. 1997. *African Traditional Religion in South Africa: An Annotated Bibliography*. Westport, CT and London: Greenwood Press.

Chukwukere, Ibe. 1993. 'Chi in Igbo Religion and thought. The God in Every Man', *Anthropos* 78 (3–4): 519–34.

Clark-Bekederemo, John Pepper. 1961. 'Abiku', *Black Orpheus* 10: 4.

Driskill, Quo-Li. 2010. 'Doubleweaving Two-Spirit Critique: Building Alliances between Native and Queer Studies', *GLQ* 16 (1–2): 69–92.

Editor. 2023. 'Ogbanje Church Opens in Anambra', Info Daily, 6 August. Available online: https://infodailyng.com/ogbanje-church-opens-in-anambra/ (accessed 7 October 2023).

Emecheta, Buchi. 1977. *The Slave Girl*. London: Allison & Busby.

Emezi, Akwaeke. 2018. *Freshwater*. London: Faber and Faber.

Emezi, Akwaeke. 2021. *Dear Senthuran: A Black Spirit Memoir*. London: Faber and Faber.

Groneman, Claudia. 2019. '2.6 Autofiction', in Martina Wagner-Egelhaaf (ed.), *Handbook of Autobiography / Autofiction*, 241–6. Berlin: De Gruyter.

Halberstam, (Judith) Jack. 1998. 'Transgender Butch: Butch/FTM Border Wars and the Masculine Continuum', *GLQ* 4 (2): 287–310.

Hoad, Neville. 2011. 'Queer Theory Addiction', in Janet Halley and Andrew Parker (eds), *After Sex? On Writing Since Queer Theory*, 128–39. Durham, NC and London: Duke University Press.

Janzen, John M. 1992. *Ngoma: Discourses of Healing in Central and Southern Africa*. Berkeley: University of California Press.

Lafortune, Anguksuar/Richard. 1997. 'A Postcolonial Colonial Perspective on Western [Mis]Conceptions of the Cosmos and the Restoration of Indigenous Taxonomies', in Sue-Ellen Jacobs, Wesley Thomas and Sabina Lang (eds), *Two-Spirit People: Native American Gender identity, Sexuality, and Spirituality*, 217–22. Urbana: University of Illinois Press.

Lambek, Michael. 2014. 'Afterword: Recognizing and Misrecognizing Spirit Possession', in Paul Christopher Johnson (ed.), *Spirited Things: The Work of 'Possession' in Afro-Atlantic Religions*, 259–76. Chicago and London: University of Chicago Press.

Lindiwe, Makasi. 2013. 'A Threat to Zulu Patriarchy and the Continuation of Community: A Queer Analysis of Same-Sex Relationships Amongst Female Traditional Healers at Inanda and KwaNgcolosi, KwaZulu-Natal'. Dissertation. University of KwaZulu-Natal. Available online: https://researchspace.ukzn.ac.za/server/api/core/bitstreams/608da122-d75c-44e8-948d-cc8313cf131e/content (accessed 31 August 2024).

Luibhéid, Esther and Karma A. Chávez. 2020. *Queer and Trans Migrations: Dynamics of Illegalization, Detention and Deportation*. Urbana: University of Illinois Press.

Masalo, D. A. 2010. *Self and Community in a Changing World*. Bloomington: Indiana University Press.

Mbiti, John S. 1969. *African Religions and Philosophy*. London: Heinemann.

Morgan, Ruth and Graham Reid. 2003. '"I've Got Two Men and One Woman": Ancestors, Sexuality and Identity Among Same-Sex Identified Women Traditional healers in South Africa', *Culture, Health and Sexuality* 5 (5): 375–91.

Morgan, Ruth and Saskia Wieringa, eds. 2005. *Tommy Boys, Lesbian and Ancestral Wives: Female Same-Sex Practices in Africa*. Auckland Park: Jacana Media.

Morgan, Ruth, Charl Marais and Joy Rosemary Wellbeloved. 2009. *Trans: Transgender Life Stories from South Africa*. Auckland Park: GALA.

Munro, Brenna M. 2012. *Queer Sexuality and the Struggle for Freedom*. Minneapolis: University of Minnesota Press.

Nkabinde, Nkunzi Zandile. 2008. *Black Bull, Ancestors, and Me: My Life as a Lesbian Sangoma*. Auckland Park: Jacana Media.

Noble, Bobby. 2006. *Sons of the Movement: FTMs Risking Incoherence in a Post-Queer Cultural Landscape*. Toronto: Women's Press.

Nzelu, Okechukwu. 2022. *Here Again Now*. London: Dialogue Books.

Ogunyemi, Chinkwenje Okonjo. 2002. 'An Abiku-Ogbanje Atlas: A Pre-Text for Rereading Soyinka's *Aké* and Morrison's *Beloved*', *African-American Review* 36 (4): 663–78.

Okri, Ben. 1991. *The Famished Road*. London: Jonathan Cape.

OzoIgboNdu1. 2019. 'The Part of Igbo Land Where You Mustn't Kill a Python', Igbo Defender, 15 September. Available online: https://igbodefender.com/the-part-of-igbo-land-where-you-mustnt-kill-a-python/ (accessed 18 May 2023).

Pandey, Pramod K. 2005. 'Second Language Varieties have a Life of their Own: Hindi English', Invited paper for a Festschrift Volume, *Essays on Adegbija*, edited by Demola Jolayemi. (unpublished).

Prosser, Jay. 1998. *Second Skins: The Body Narratives of Transsexuality*. New York: Columbia University Press.

Rees, Anthony. 2015. 'Government intends regulating African Traditional Healers and their Medicine', The Traditional & Natural Health Alliance, 2 May. Available online: http://www.tnha.co.za/government-intends-regulating-african-traditional-healers-and-their-medicines/ (accessed 30 September 2023).

Richards, Christina, Walter Pierre Bowman, Meg-John Braker. 2017. *Genderqueer and Non-Binary Genders*. London: Palgrave Macmillan/Springer Nature.

Rothblatt, Martine. 1995. *The Apartheid of Sex: A Manifesto on the Freedom of Gender*. New York: Grown Publishers.

Salters-Pedneault, Kristalyn. 2023. 'Dissociative Identity Disorder (DID): Symptoms, Traits, Causes, Treatment', *Verywell Mind*, 7 July. Available online: https://www.verywellmind.com/dissociative-identity-disorder-425423#citation-2 (accessed 15 April 2024).

Schmitt, Arnaud. 2020. *The Phenomenology of Autobiography: Making It Real*. New York and London: Routledge.

Showalter, Elaine. 1991. 'Feminist Criticism in the Wilderness', *Critical Inquiry* 8: 190–205.

South African Law Commission. 1996. Issue Paper 4, Project 90. Available online: http://www.justice.gov.za/salrc/ipapers/ip04_prj_90_1996.pdf (accessed 31 August 2024).

Soyinka, Wole. 1961. 'Abiku'; 'Death in the Dawn', *Black Orpheus* 10: 7, 64.

Soyinka, Wole. 1990. *Myth, Literature and the African World*. Cambridge: Cambridge University Press.

Stryker, Susan. 2008. *Transgender History*. Berkeley, CA: Seal.

Stryker, Susan and Stephen Whittle, eds. 2006. *The Transgender Studies Reader*. New York and London: Routledge.

Stryker, Susan and Aren Z. Aizura, eds. 2013. *The Transgender Studies Reader 2*. New York and London: Routledge.

Tebogo (Nkoana). 2009. 'My ancestor was living through me', in Ruth Morgan, Charl Marais and Joy Rosemary Wellbeloved (eds), *Trans: Transgender Life Stories from South Africa*, 119–27. Auckland Park: Jacana Media.

Things Fall Apart. 1971. [Film] Directed by Peter Igho. Lagos: Old Nollywood Movies.

Tomson, Anastacia. 2016. *Always Anastacia: A Transgender Life in South Africa.* Jeppestown: Jonathan Ball Publishers.

'Trans woman: "I left Nigeria to save my life"'. 2016. BBC News, 29 April. Available online: https://www.bbc.com/news/av/world-africa-36168661 (accessed 4 December 2023).

Van Klinken, Adriaan and Kwame Edwin Out. 2017. 'Ancestors, Embodiment and Sexual Desire: Wild Religion and the Body in the Story of a South African Lesbian Sangoma', *Body and Religion* 1 (1): 70–87.

VaShona Project. n.d. s.v. 'ngochani'. Available online: http://vashona.com/dictionary/sna/ngochani (accessed 1 October 2023).

Wa Sibuyi, Mpande. 1993. 'Tinkoncana Etimayinini: The Wives of the Mines', in Matthew Krouse and Kim Berman (eds), *Invisible Ghetto: Lesbian and Gay Writing from South Africa*, 36–57. Johannesburg: COSAW.

Zabus, Chantal. 2007. *The African Palimpsest: Indigenization of Language in the West African Europhone Novel.* 2nd enlarged edn. Amsterdam and New York: Rodopi/Brill.

Zabus, Chantal. 2013. *Out in Africa: Same-Sex Desire in Sub-Saharan Literatures and Cultures.* Woodbridge, UK: Boydell & Brewer/James Currey.

Zabus, Chantal and Samir Kumar Das. 2020. 'Hijras, Sagomas, and their Translects: Trans(lating) India and South Africa', *Interventions: International Journal of Postcolonial Studies* 23 (6): 811–34. https://doi.org/10.1080/1369801x.2020.1784026.

Chapter 8

THE SARIMBAVY OF MADAGASCAR: BEYOND SEMANTIC BOUNDARIES AND THE POLITICS OF (IN)VISIBILIZATION

Alyette Rajaofera Andriamasinalivao

Introduction

'A soul has no gender', that is the motto of Emy Ga, a 24-year-old LGBT rights and environment activist from Toliara, Madagascar. It is also the title of a book by Denise M. Ajeto (2009), which tells the story of a mother who shares how she coped with her twins' nonconforming gender and sexuality. As the Malagasy proverb goes, 'A soul makes a human being', that is, the soul is what distinguishes a human being from an animal. The soul, in this context, is the ethical component of the human personality which makes one strive to abide by the norms established by society[1] and preserve one's status and *hasina* or 'the intrinsic or supernatural virtue that makes something/someone good and effective' (Webber in Ravelomanana 2006: 12). Holding a convenient place and being accepted in society are thus common concerns of the individual who has a soul. When it comes to gender-nonconforming individuals, namely the *sarimbavy*, there is a long record of the various ways in which these subjects were tackled in Malagasy society. While French doctors and colonial administrators tried to identify the 'most appropriate classificatory label for [*sarimbavy*'s] "true" sexological condition during the turn of the 20th century' (Palmer 2019: 92), later researchers argued that being a *sarimbavy* is more of a strategic means to circumvent bad luck (Allibert 1994) or presumably social duties such as tax payment and forced labour (Rencurel in Palmer 2019: 182). The perception of homosexuality as 'a highly suspicious import and contamination from the deviant West' (Zabus 2013: 15) as well as strong claims about the existence and tolerance of gender variance before the colonial period[2] shape contemporary understanding of nonconforming gender and sexuality in most African societies, including Madagascar. Though researchers on homosexuality in Africa argue that it is homophobia, not homosexuality, that has been imported by western culture (Hayes 2000; Hoad 1999; Tamale 2013), foreign and local media in Madagascar tend to echo international reports of homophobic or transphobic cases[3] as if the nation were not yet ready for western-imported homosexual practices.

It is within this context that the question about the visibility of gender-nonconforming individuals arises. The issue, however, is not so much the intensity of homophobia or transphobia as the concern about proper conduct required to be integrated in Malagasy society. To be visible has two translations, *hita* (adjective) and *miseho* (verb describing the action of making oneself visible) in Malagasy. The second translation, when duplicated as *misehoseho*, has negative connotations as it means showing off. As a matter of fact, gaining social recognition hardly rhymes with gaining visibility in the sense of *misehoseho*, especially for a community that is portrayed by the mass media and thereby perceives itself as a minority and marginalized group.[4] The present chapter focusses on a group of male-bodied, gender-nonconforming individuals based in Antananarivo who are generally called *sarimbavy* but whose personal experiences transcend 'Western, value-laden categories' (Palmer 2019: 143). Their strategic use of language in public spaces about matters that define their identity and social status contributes to their growing visibility in a way that promotes their social integration. The research is based on the analysis of social representations of *sarimbavy* and, by extension, sexual and gender nonconformity in general in contemporary Malagasy media and within Malagasy communities in Antananarivo. The four participants[5] in this study identify as women but their personal understanding of and affiliation to the *sarimbavy* category differ. Though based in Antananarivo, they come from different social, ethnic and religious backgrounds.

Sarimbavy *Argot: From a Sexual Minority*
Slang to an Urban Malagasy LGBT Code

Kinou[6] is the name given to the in-group sociolect (Palmer 2019: 4) that urban Malagasy LGBT people use. Its origin is credited to *sarimbavy* sex workers in Antananarivo, around the 1980s. The term *kinou* was not unanimously used nor understood by my four interlocutors.[7] Three of them, who self-identify as *sarimbavy,* are members of the association ONG réseaux Madagascar Solidarité,[8] formerly Solidarité MSM, led by Balou Chabat Rasoanaivo.[9] They referred to their in-group sociolect as *argot spécial* (special slang) for LGBT people. Lalatiana Virginie, a sixty-four-year-old *sarimbavy* from Antananarivo, somehow had a different understanding of *kinou:* 'it means gossip (*fosafosa*), *miknou* means gossiping (*mifosa*)', thus retaining the expression 'argot spécial' for their in-group sociolect. My fourth interlocutor, Emy Ga, who has settled for western concepts to define herself as a transgender woman, knew the term *kinou* but asserted that the phrase 'a secret code' for LGBT people is more common.

The perception of *kinou* as a sociolect for the LGBT community in Madagascar presupposes the existence of 'a homogenous community composed of lesbians and gay males, that shares a common culture or system of values and goals, perceptions, and experience' (Penelope and Wolfe in Kulick 2000: 250). Yet, such an assumption is problematic because gender-variant individuals in Madagascar, as in any other countries, do not form a unified, homogenous community.

They are mainly divided by social background, age, ethnicity and beliefs which influence their convictions about their gender identity and sexuality. Regarding the *sarimbavy*, Palmer contends that the sense of community and actual bonding is elusive.[10] My interlocutors somehow claimed that the use of *kinou* among sex workers does create unity if not sincere bonding. Tanamasoandro asserted that this 'secret code' used to unite LGBT people and give them a sense of belonging to a community. Lalatiana Virginie emphasized the fact that using this 'argot' created a bond between *sarimbavy* sex workers. She said that their argot enables them to help each other in various sexual contexts: when a client does not have much money, they call him 'cancrela' to warn their friends; they say 'manao maratra' (someone who harms) for a client who beats a *sarimbavy* and steals his/her money; 'boka io dog io' for a man with a genital wart or who is seropositive; and 'tsy piso' (lit. not a cat) for a client who does not know yet that the sex worker is a *sarimbavy*, not a woman.[11]

It would be misleading to focus on the constitution of a Malagasy LGBT community based on their use of language. Such an endeavour is bound to fail (Kulick 2000) provided as long as the grounds on which the community is constituted remains problematic. Instead, the focus should be shifted to the people or groups of people that use this 'special slang', their degree of knowledge of its codes and the purposes that it serves. This allows for a more accurate analysis of the politics of (in)visibility for gender minority groups in Malagasy communities. Indeed, though *kinou* is claimed as a 'special slang' for LGBT people, some of its codes are voluntarily adopted by heteronormative people.[12] As Tanamasoandro puts it, 'everybody is now familiar with the term *baoby* and uses it to refer to money'.[13] The circulation of *kinou* terms outside *sarimbavy* circles occurs thanks to their interactions with heteronormative people in various contexts. For instance, the clients of *sarimbavy* sex workers are familiar with the sexual terms for the services they request: 'tsaralalàna', a neighbourhood mainly occupied by Indo-Paskistanis in Analakely (Antananarivo) and infamously known as a sex workers' spot – typically on the pavement or at a street corner – refers to intercrural sex in *kinou* lexicon; 'Isotry' (the name of a neighbourhood on the outskirts of Antananarivo) is used for anal sex; and 'ravoniny' is the *kinou* word for fellatio.

Sarimbavy may also use *kinou* on TV shows and in interviews that are broadcast on national channels or radio stations. In 2019, *kinou* terms such as *dog* and *dognat* were already being widely used in Malagasy communities to designate sexual roles and/or gender identifications as is revealed in Tanamasoandro's interview with Mija Rasolo for the TV show *Takariva Mafana*. During this interview, Tanamasoandro first uses *lehilahy* to refer to men, but Mija Rasolo rephrases her statement, using *kinou* terms: 'she wished for a *nat* (woman) but it was a *dog* (man) that came out'. The use of *dog* and *nat* as the equivalents of the gender categories 'man' and 'woman' in this context differs from Palmer's explanation of the same terms: '*dog* refers to those who penetrate their male-bodied sexual partners and are understood to be normatively masculine' and '*dognat* refers to those who are penetrated' (2019: 55). Here, the terms refer to sexual roles. Significantly, *dognat*, as was used by my interlocutors, has become synonymous with *sarimbavy* in general.

The term *dognat* is also gaining popularity amongst the Malagasy diaspora in France. A film documentary directed by Mikael Rabetrano, a Malagasy director and camera operator based in France, bears the title *Dognat* with Balou Chabat Rasoanaivo on its cover. The 52-minute film, entirely in French and comprising translated testimonies and revelatory images of *dognat* subjects in the urban slums of Antananarivo, was released in 2014 and seems to have been limited to French-speaking audiences outside Madagascar so far.[14] *Dognat* in this film refers to 'effeminate men' and cross-dressers in Antananarivo, that is, to what is generally known in Madagascar as *sarimbavy*.

Considering these various uses of *kinou* in different contexts, we may agree with *Kulick* that 'not all people who engage in same-sex sexual practices, or who self-identify as gay or lesbian, use [the same slang] words, or even know them. And people who do not engage in same-sex sexual practices or self-identify as gay or lesbian … may be masters of the code' (2000: 257). However, the circulation of the terms amongst heteronormative people not only popularizes them but also slightly changes their meaning. The altered meaning does not contradict the initial meaning but rather complements it. Mija Rasolo's use of the words *dog* and *dognat*, for example, is more general compared to their meanings related to sexual roles as is explained by Palmer. These different usages and understandings of the same terms[15] point to the overlapping of Malagasy conceptions of sexual roles and gender identities, as is reflected in the interchangeable use of the terms by sarimbavy subjects in their interactions with their peers and heteronormative people. Here, the dissemination of *kinou* outside LGBT circles can be perceived as a form of cultural appreciation and mutual adjustment since the 'members of the dominant culture (in this case heteronormative people) are aware of and respect the origins of the term' (Laing 2021: 3) through an 'unproblematic process of cultural diffusion and blending' (Cruz et al. 2023: 2). The large use of *kinou* terms outside LGBT circles certainly enriches the Malagasy language but more importantly, it signals the recognition of the community that produces them, further supporting the idea that they are likeable.[16]

The popularization of *kinou* terms outside LGBT circles may also spring from the properties of the terms, following the dynamics of slang diffusion in the Malagasy context: 'people from rural areas create their argot lexicon by drawing from their activities and environment whereas people from urban milieus probably get their inspiration from their relationship with the West' (Rakotomalala 2012: 71). Nevertheless, some *kinou* terms are still embedded in widely known, often ordinary elements of Malagasy culture. For instance, the word *tsaralalàna* for intercrural sex evokes the small alleys where people throng to attend to their daily occupations around the thriving Indo-Pakistani shops, bus stops and street markets. Some *kinou* expressions seem to be a transformation of the meaning of older argot words and expressions. The expression *tsy anahazana* refers to a particularly handsome and attractive partner, which may have come from the root word *manahy* (lit. 1. Caring or 2. Letting dry). It is the second literal meaning which is commonly used in the expression *manahy vary* (lit. letting rice dry) to describe someone as a yokel, the rice probably denoting farm life and peasantry.

The expression *tsy anahazana* thus expresses the opposite of the older expression *manahy vary* and dissociates it from its pejorative meaning in a different urban context.

Finally, analysing sexual and gender-variant Malagasy individuals' understanding of the LGBT acronym sheds light on the local reception of a transnational queer rhetoric. Be they *sarimbavy*, transgender, MSM, *dossier*,[17] homosexual, lesbian or *travesti*, gender-nonconforming individuals in Madagascar unanimously refer to themselves as members of the LGBT community. The LGBT acronym is largely used in local media, though its understanding does not entirely correspond to its usage in western countries. In Malagasy TV programmes such as Alalino and the iBC investigation documentary series on *sarimbavy*, LGBT is used as an umbrella term for gender-nonconforming individuals. The hosts of these programmes explicitly refer to LGBT people as individuals with 'disability' (*kilema*)[18] and LGBT is even called a disability/disease in one instance. LGBT is thus perceived as a disease that affects people who are thereby called LGBT.

Each letter in the acronym has its respective meaning or equivalent, based on how my interlocutors understood them. The letter L, which stands for lesbians, is understood as women dating or having sex with women, regardless of their sexual preferences and sexual roles, but my interlocutors said that they have another word, *lily*, for lesbians from the upper and middle classes, and *ndiky* or *sarindiky* for lesbians from the lower class. Further, same-sex relations between women are called *nat+nat* (women+women) in *kinou* terms. What was also striking is the original understanding of the T in the acronym. Lalatiana Virginie said that initially, the members of the association NGO Réseaux Madagascar Solidarité thought that it stood for *travesti* but now it means transgender. This, however, did not prevent the members from using the LGBT acronym as an umbrella term for all gender-nonconforming people. The letters IQ+ have been recently added. Lalatiana Virginie proudly showed me her T-shirt for HIV prevention work with the new acronym LGBTIQ+. When I asked her what the IQ+ meant, she said: 'These are people who are in between, neither *sarimbavy* nor *sarindahy*, neither men nor women, and people who don't like sex.' This simplified definition of 'queer' and 'intersex', which captures the fluidity and expansiveness of local perceptions of gender and sexual matters which hardly fit into clear-cut, rigid categories, seems to match Sedgwick's definition of 'queer' as 'the open mesh of possibilities, gaps, overlaps, dissonances and resonances, lapses and excesses of meaning when the constituent elements of anyone's gender, of anyone's sexuality aren't made (or can't be made) to signify monolithically' (1993: 8). It can further be argued that the association's adoption of these western terms[19] corresponds to a process of localization whereby local actors, that is, Malagasy *sarimbavy*, 'actively construct … foreign ideas … [to develop] significant congruence with local beliefs and practices' (Acharya 2004: 245). In that sense, the local actors acknowledge the possible limitation or inadequacy (245) of their existing naming system when it comes to defining the identity and experiences of a wider gender-nonconforming public. However, the new terms do not displace the local perceptions of and beliefs about gender variance characterized by fluidity and inclusiveness. The new terms serve to 'broaden and strengthen [existing beliefs and approaches] with the infusion of new ideas' (245). Significantly, one of the principal missions of *sarimbavy* peer educators in this association is to sensitise *olon-tsahala* (individuals who are like them) about safe sex practices and LGBT rights and encourage them to join the association. More importantly, adhering to this global community inevitably enhances their visibility in Malagasy society. While the representations of the members of the LGBT community on Malagasy media are still imbued with an underlying rejection of homosexuality, the fact that local TV channels broadcast special programmes featuring LGBT people signals an attempt to make them known and visible to the public, to give them an opportunity to share their views and experiences.

Social Responsibility and the Language of Inclusiveness

'Claiming one's rights requires duty and responsibility … When you are a *sarimbavy*, it's not just about showing off your beauty and youth and being fashionable and all, there are duties and responsibilities that the community requires from you when you claim your rights.' Those are Tanamasoandro's words during her interview with Mija Rasolo in 2019.[20] Apart from being grounded in the transnational discourse of human rights and LGBT rights activism, they emphasize the importance of the community in Malagasy society. As Malagasy proverbs make it clear, 'it is better to be hated by kings than to be hated by the crowd' and 'If only one person doesn't like you, grind some rice to get fat, but if a whole crowd hates you, drink poison to die.' In other words, it is not the individual but the crowd, that is, the members of the community, that stands at the heart of the social system that guarantees harmony. Tanamasoandro adds: 'that's the problem with the LGBT community in Madagascar. They want to blindly follow Western practices. Yet, Malagasy customs do not tolerate this yet.'[21] Her statement taps into global issues faced by the LGBT community who want to gain more visibility in a country that is allegedly hostile to same-sex relations and non-normative gender identities. The actions undertaken by *sarimbavy* subjects take various forms, which can be perceived as subtle attempts to gain social recognition and integration, rather than an outright cry to gain visibility.

In the mid-2000s, a group of *sarimbavy* subjects going by the stage name 'Sarimbavy tena izy'[22] (authentic *sarimbavy*) made a public performance at the Roxy cinema in Antananarivo. Back then, they were also known as *travesties*, male-bodied individuals who cross-dressed and behaved like women. In 2015, the same event was described on the local gay bar's website[23] as the 'grand coming out' of *sarimbavy* in Antananarivo. One of the remaining members of the group, Tanamasoandro, also used the expression 'coming out' when she talked about this event. She insisted that the aim was 'to show that sarimbavy are like any other human beings, not just a subject to laugh about.'[24] The expression 'coming out' is mainly used by urban-dwelling Malagasy youth who search the internet to learn more about their gender identities and sexualities.[25] The expression is also used by project managers and local actors in HIV prevention work, along with other western vocabulary for non-normative gender identities and sexualities.[26] This testifies to the large diffusion of western queer sexual identities and culture, gradually changing local perspectives and practices.

Lalatiana Virginie did not know the meaning of 'coming out'. When I explained its meaning as is generally understood in a western context, she said that she did not have to proclaim publicly that she is a *sarimbavy* because everybody already knows it from the way she looks and dresses every day. Most of the *sarimbavy* that I interviewed at the early stage of my research[27] claimed that their families and the people in their neighbourhood were already aware of their 'effeminacy' when they were children.[28] Significantly, Lalatiana Virginie told me that she is 'a woman on her national identity card'. She explained that she had no problem changing her name at the courthouse as she convincingly displays the appearance of a woman. This process, which is perceived as a form of legal transition by my other interlocutors,[29] is not easy because, as they put it, 'it is still illegal to change one's gender identity in Madagascar'. Still, it should be noted that there is no indication of the individual's sex on the Malagasy identity card, which may have facilitated Lalatiana Virginie's name changing process.

Despite the globalization of 'coming out' and other components of western culture, the distinctive features of the *sarimbavy* subculture show that 'globalization has an uneven impact across the globe … globalized practices are located within distinctive national social, economic, cultural, and political formations' (Massey in Binnie 2004: 25). Contact with the West neither displaces nor eradicates existing practices and beliefs. As Acharya puts it, 'the idea recipient's chief goal [is] to strengthen, not to replace existing institutions' (2004: 246). Indeed, there is in Madagascar a strong sense of a Malagasy identity which is often conveyed in nationalistic aphorisms such as 'Gasy ka Manja' or 'Za Gasy' expressing the pride of being Malagasy. *Sarimbavy* subjects are particularly concerned about preserving and reflecting this Malagasy identity in their own experiences, including their effort to gain social recognition and integration.

Following the 'Sarimbavy tena izy' show and *sarimbavy* subjects' participation in other public events,[30] there has been a major shift from public claims for *sarimbavy* rights to a more subtle plea for recognition and social integration through the engagement in HIV prevention work and the collaboration with international non-governmental organizations (NGOs) that seek to defend LGBT rights. Global actors that are proponents of universal ideas about public health and social activism are well aware that in order to succeed in importing their ideas, they have to collaborate with 'credible local actors [who are] seen by their target audience as upholders of local values and identity and not simply "agents" of outside forces or actors' (Acharya 2004: 248). *Sarimbavy* subjects, who somehow reproduce their representations by French colonial doctors and administrators in the early twentieth century[31] by engaging in feminine activities, such as modelling,[32] fashion designing[33] and hairdressing,[34] are currently largely associated with HIV prevention work. This testifies to the prevalence of sex work and the growing presence of *sarimbavy* in this sector. Conferences and workshops are co-organized by global and local actors of public health development and LGBT rights protection to familiarize 'vulnerable groups' with safe-sex practices but also to train them how to behave in society. A Malagasy website, dognat.mg, has been created to provide extensive information about HIV prevention, the associations throughout Madagascar that are involved in the protection of MSM rights, as well as explanations about homosexuality and stigmatization. The website even includes a glossary for *kinou* or *sarimbavy*/MSM argot. The content includes Malagasy texts translated from French websites such as *passportsanté, bibamagazine,* and videos in French or in Malagasy, along with contemporary videos by foreign queer artists. The website also provides practical information about the public places where Malagasy MSM usually meet, including bars, nightclubs and outdoor sites such as public parks, the beach and some well-known public places. Nevertheless, the relatively small content in the forum section where internet users are supposed to exchange about various subjects related to MSM identification and experiences, indicates that only a few of them have access to these contents. The website mainly targets heterosexual or homosexual people who have regular access to the internet. It is the physical meetings at conferences and workshops that enable the association to reach out to the majority of lower-class *sarimbavy.*

My interlocutors mentioned that apart from receiving training about HIV prevention, the members of the association are taught how to behave in society to promote social integration. They emphasized that self-respect is essential if one wants to be integrated in the community. Self-respect or one's capacity to preserve one's *baraka*[35] is observed in the way one speaks, behaves and dresses. Three of my interlocutors (Balou Rasoanaivo, Tanamasoandro and Lalatiana Virginie) have all opted for what they call a 'classic' dressing style which connotes elegance and respectability.[36] They thus avoid wearing provocative clothes such as miniskirts and tight-fitting trousers. During their public appearances, they use a formal register and only introduce their argot when their interlocutors start using them. Behaving appropriately within the community also means avoiding *mipelipelika* (too much agitation), instead, respectability springs from tangible efforts to be decent by fulfilling duties in the community, including contributions to the development of the neighbourhood, social and community services. The job title 'project manager' or 'president of an association' confers authority and invites respect. Balou Rasoanaivo, for instance, is called by everyone in her neighbourhood and amongst her circle 'Madama', a title which not only connotes respect but also shows the acknowledgement of her gender identification. Amongst the significant actions undertaken by the association to put an end to discrimination against *sarimbavy* sex workers is the use of positive vocabulary which signals 'a burning need for words that [do] not denote them pejoratively' (Cory in Kulick 2000: 249). The expression *mpampanofa vatana/fahafinaretana* (someone who rents their body/pleasure) in official Malagasy language substitute for pejorative and vulgar words such as *koetra, kox, mpivaro-tena* (prostitute) or *makorela*, which all mean sex workers. In *kinou* terminology, the expression *maman'i Gaby* (Gaby's mother) is used alongside with MSM, which do not indicate their status as sex workers.

Finally, my three interlocutors who self-identified as *sarimbavy* explained that adopting their relatives' children is a common practice amongst them to 'have their own descendants'. They literally adopt the role of a mother to these children. As Tanamasoandro explained, she was a real mother to her elder sister's daughter when the latter had a baby in her place: she took care of her, prepared food, provided physical and emotional comfort, and helped to look after the baby. Similarly, Lalatiana Virginie has raised several relatives' children who are grown up now and who keep in touch with her. Balou Rasoanaivo also talked about her 'children' who still live with her. In this context, the conventional conception of motherhood is altered as it is detached from an experience defined by blood relationships. Motherhood in Malagasy society is not always defined by blood relationships, nor is the status of being a parent or *raiamandreny*. Rabenoro contends that in traditional Malagasy society 'women with no children born of themselves may benefit from the same status as "natural" mothers' (2003: 2) through adoption. Similarly, 'the eldest [people] who are closest to the ancestors' (Dahl 1993: 96) are generally acknowledged as *raiamandreny*. These show that *sarimbavy* subjects' concern[37] about perpetuating their names through their descendants is deeply rooted in Malagasy traditions.

Sarimbavy *and Sexual Visibility*

Speaking about Malagasy nationalism and sexuality in his introduction to the 45th volume of the *Etudes océan indien* journal, Rakotomalala writes that 'nationalism consists … in only revealing what deserves to be revealed, precisely normative sexuality, that which does not "sully" the Malagasy's [reputation]' (2010a: 2). This presupposes some reserve regarding what Malagasy people are ready to make public about their sexuality, the latter being generally perceived as a 'private affair, belonging in the private sphere' (Binnie 2004: 14). The changes brought about by the liberal regime in Madagascar during the Third Republic somehow led to the gradual presentation of public talks about sexual matters on local media.[38] Articles and videos about Malagasy same-sex relations are also being gradually produced in local newspapers, social media and most notably on the previously mentioned *dognat* website. On the *Takariva Mafana* show, Tanamasoandro made open statements about her sexual life. When the host asked her if, as a biologically male person with a penis, she ever has an erection, she openly stated that she has never had one in her life.[39] Furthermore, when prompted to talk about the impact of having a penis on her sexual relations, she said: 'I am not embarrassed at all by my sex organ … and the men who are with me know where my anus is so they can get in, that's all that matters'. Such talks mirror the growing interest in and curiosity about sexual dissidence in a modern context that is constantly marked by 'the antagonism between what is convenient … and the inevitable evolution of society' (Rakotomalala 2012: 44). However, what is convenient is defined by the subjects' capacity to incorporate global practices within ancestral beliefs and customs. Merina or Malagasy people from the capital are indeed well known for their syncretism. As Rakotomalala puts it, 'the adoption of external elements … is done … with precaution: the Merina make sure that they do not disrupt the identity that they have previously created. They take [the elements] that could enrich the local, refrain from proceeding to the opposite and silence the local to put to the fore elements that come from abroad' (44).

The desire to know more about the sexual lives of the *sarimbavy* was also shared by the Europeans who wrote about them in the early nineteenth century, though their main concern was to provide a 'more nuanced sexological classificatory system given the increasing accounts of "inverts" whose diversity defied standard sexological typologies' (Palmer 2019: 168). At times depicted as 'asexual inverts',[40] at others as 'sexual perverts'[41] (Palmer 2014) by these foreigners, *sarimbavy* elicit public speculations and rumours about their sexual lives, most of which are transpositions of global notions about same-sex relations. In this last section, I examine the ways in which the *sarimbavy* who participated in my study trigger processes that make them visible and recognized in society through the language surrounding their sexuality and sexual practices. Their use of language in the realm of sexuality is embedded in social, cultural and historical practices that constitute 'sexual behaviour as an element of the social system' (Rakotomalala 2012: 12).

Sarimbavy's sex-related language creates linguistic spaces that gradually signal and enhance their presence and belongingness in physical spaces. Many sex related *kinou* terms refer to geographical places: *tsaralalàna, Isotry* and *antanim-boanjo* (lit. peanut field but in reality, the areas in which sex workers find their clients). The neighbourhood of Antaninarenina in the vicinity of the Bank of Africa down to the French Embassy in Ambatomena is the main spot for *sarimbavy* sex workers whose clients look for anal sex. Lalatiana Virginie said that female prostitutes rarely go to this area because they are afraid of anal sex. The use of language in this context ties in with *sarimbavy*'s appropriation of physical space. In French photographer Philippe Gaubert's words, 'the city is not endured but contributes to [the] evolution [of social life whereby the *sarimbavy*] play with territories to exploit them, get through them and stage themselves in them so that the architecture becomes the backdrop of this transformation'.[42] Though their presence in these spaces is limited to the evening, the popular consciousness of these territories as specific spots for *sarimbavy* sex workers marks them as their *antanim-boanjo*, that is, areas that are reserved for a specific group that provides specific sexual gratifications.

Sarimbavy sex workers are aware that doing *tapis vert* (lit. 'green mat'; having sex in public places such as the outskirts of bars and secret alleys) is prohibited.[43] When their client does not have enough money to go to a brothel or to rent a hotel room, or when they want to protect their reputation by avoiding being seen in these places, they opt for what *sarimbavy* sex workers call *trano maizin'i Bakoly* (Bakoly's prison/dark house), which refers to secret and safe places for sex that only *sarimbavy* gangs know of. This enables them to avoid having sex in the client's car, which means running the risk of being found by a *dadatoa* (policeman) who fines the client for doing *tapis vert*. Furthermore, in an overt attempt to dissociate the sexual act from the vulgar expression *milely* (fucking), *kinou* users opt for more neutral expressions such as *andoro fiangonana* (burn a church) and *dona dona* (knock knock). The first, a euphemistic yet profane expression that attenuates the crude sexual act behind the transgression of Christian values, probably constitutes an indirect move against homophobic and transphobic individuals who deploy Christian beliefs to condemn sexual and gender nonconformity. The second, on the other hand, is an onomatopoeic and metaphorical expression that creates the image of the sexual act in the users' minds. It may be related to the expression *dona kely*, a small punch between two people to say hello or to express mutual agreement on something. In the sexual context, the duplicated word *dona* conveys the idea of simultaneous action, just like the expression *dona kely*. The 'ancestral perception of physical love as food' (Rakotomalala 2012: 70) is also preserved in *kinou* terms for sex, namely *mikepoka* (biting) as a substitution for the infamous argot *milely*. The *kinou* term *ravoniny* for oral sex may come from the root word *voniny*, which is the female organ of a flower. Here, in the context of a sexual relation between men, the figurative association of the oral stimulation of the penis with a female organ suggests a discarding of the symbol of masculinity signified by the terms *tabory* (penis) and *vôtabory* (balls) from the sexual act. At the same time, the association of oral sex with the female organ of a flower also blurs gender and sexual roles during same-sex sexual relations.

Furthermore, sexual roles in same-sex relations are subject to public scrutiny. *Sarimbavy* are familiar with the French terms *actif* and *passif* but their sexual practices transcend these linguistic boundaries. For a *dog* or a male client who is both *actif* and *passif*, they say 'asesy sy manesy ny dog'.[44] Being active or passive, however, is subjective. Though my interlocutors self-identified as *sarimbavy* in the sense that they cross-dress and behave like women, their sexual practices seem to disregard the penis as a male sexual organ associated with masculinity. For Lalatiana Virginie who claims to be passive in the sexual act, passivity means being penetrated. However, she explained that she experiences erection and ejaculation while being penetrated. For Balou Rasoanaivo who also claims to be passive and to play a feminine role, sexual acts include sucking her partner's penis and having her penis sucked.[45]

Malagasy researchers on sexuality assert that these sexual practices result from the 'contact with the West [which] introduced new forms of erotic games' (Andrianetrazafy 2010: 20). Rakotomalala emphasizes the fact that fellatio is 'highly prohibited in Malagasy ancestral culture'[46] but 'people start to transgress taboos' (2010a: 2). Nevertheless, beyond this general assumption, the subjects' agency should not be neglected. In their sexual narratives, my interlocutors stressed the importance of what they called the 'Malagasy touch'. Emy Ga voiced her preference for Malagasy men, whose smell, the 'Malagasy smell', she adores, as opposed to the smell of *vazaha* (foreigners) and *karana* (Indo-Pakistanis). Lalatiana Virginie explained that *sarimbavy* sex workers have specific expressions for common sexual situations that may be embarrassing and require specific reactions. The expression 'maty ny trano' (the house is dead) means that the *sarimbavy* sex worker's bottom is filled with excrement, which spoils the *revy* (lit.

dream, here, the sexual act) and results in the client's dissatisfaction and refusal to pay. Lalatiana Virginie said that this usually happens when the client takes drugs and it takes him at least one hour to ejaculate, which is not only painful for the sex worker but also causes excrement to come out of the anus. To avoid being a *tsinain-kena* (bowels for sausages), that is being taken advantage of and not being paid, *sarimbavy* sex workers resort to masturbation[47] and fellatio. Thus, sex-related language among *sarimbavy* circles not only enables the appropriation of spaces that take on more meaning than the usual pejorative connotations associated to sex work but also invites positive perceptions of *sarimbavy*'s sexual experiences.

Conclusion

The circulation of *sarimbavy* argot or *kinou* amongst Malagasy LGBT circles and heteronormative people endows it with contextualized, multiple layers of meaning that depict *sarimbavy* subjectivity in a more positive light. *Sarimbavy*'s fluid and expansive self-definitions and experiences are captured in this argot which enhances *sarimbavy* visibility and their strategic adherence to transnational collective actions related to HIV prevention and human rights. However, sexual and gender nonconformity are not flaunted as distinctive identity markers through a process of visibilization. Rather, *sarimbavy* subjects engage in a subtle process of visibilization by drawing from traditional values and cultures, which, instead of being discarded, are reinforced through norm localization. The latter refers to the precautious reception of global ideas and their adaptation to local beliefs and practices. The limitations of the present study reside in the difficulty to deeply explore the ethnic differences between the participants who may have been subsumed under the category of *sarimbavy* or LGBT. Future studies may investigate ethnic and cultural differences amongst *sarimbavy* subjects residing in Antananarivo. Spirit possession[48] is one of the components of *sarimbavy* subjectivity that could be explored in this light.

Notes

1   In a folk-tale drawn from the same proverb, a Malagasy orator and storyteller says that the verb *miahy* or caring derives from the word *fanahy*, which implies that 'having a soul means caring, being careful not to do things that might ruin the reputation of one's relatives or harm the community'.

2   Molet writes that 'Malagasy people do not hold any moral condemnation against transvestites (*saikatra*) [and] the female status of these *sarim-bavy* … is acknowledged in informal settings and even in the field of tax payment …. [Furthermore, their homosexuality] … is not subject to blame, being considered as attributed by God' (Molet 1967).

3   RFI reported on 4 July 2021 that 'the Malagasy government cancelled an LGBT party at a pub in Antananarivo … which is a big blow to the [LGBT] community in a country that is hostile to sexual minorities'. The Malagasy website Koolsaina called

a Malagasy deputy's initiative to draft anti-homosexual legislation 'an attack against the LGBT in Madagascar' (Schermerhorn 1964).

4	Schermerhorn (1964) defines a minority group as 'any group smaller than half the population of a society whose life history and culture differs significantly from the remainder; this group, in the process of social change, becomes differentiated from the surrounding population so as to assume a status of subordination. This status is defined by a dominant group (and sometimes by the minority itself)'.

5	They have been singled out because of the frequent interactions with them in various formal and informal settings. Other informants have been interviewed only once at the headquarters of ONG Réseaux Madagascar Solidarité, headed by Balou Chabat Rasoanaivo.

6	The variants *knou* and *knoa* were used by my interlocutors.

7	I use the pronoun she/her to refer to my interlocutors. They all identified as women despite the conflating meanings of *sarimbavy*, *travesti* and *transgenre* that each of them partially associated to their self-identification.

8	It is recognized as the only legal LGBT association in Madagascar. It has several branches in the different regions of Madagascar (Mahajanga, Toamasina). One of my interlocutors, Tanamasoandro, a public figure known as a *sarimbavy*, has her own association regrouping sex workers from Antananarivo and collaborating with foreign NGOs engaged in human rights activism and HIV prevention work.

9	Balou Chabat Rasoanaivo also calls herself a *transgenre*, using the now widely popular term within NGOs engaged in HIV prevention human rights activism. At some point during our interaction, she referred to herself as a *lehilahy transgenre* (transgender man) to signify her position as a male-bodied person identifying as a woman. This obviously contradicts the literal meaning of the category 'transgender man' which, in western terminology, refers to female-bodied individuals transitioning into men.

10	Palmer acknowledges that 'outside of MSM activist work, [*sarimbavy*] are unlikely to voice themselves as belonging to a bounded "community"' (2019: 99).

11	In this case, either the client ends the contract, or he decides to try and experience the sexual relation with the *sarimbavy*.

12	Palmer speculates that the Malagasy TV series *Vola*, which features a *kinou*-speaking *sarimbavy*, constitutes 'the first exposure that heteronormative Malagasy had to the sociolect' (2019: 28).

13	Samy Atsika.

14	The film was screened in 2022 in several cultural institutions and libraries such as Lespas St Paul, Le séchoir, Château Morange in Reunion.

15	One might here consider the idea from discourse analysis and/or rhetoric studies that the meaning of an utterance can only be fully understood if one takes into account who is speaking, to whom and in what context (a famous example would be 'Ba-a-a-d nigger!' which can be used as a term of approbation by an African American, even when speaking to a white person).

16	Analysing the representations of transgender and transsexual subjects in Malagasy humour, Zoly Rakotoniera (2021) posits that 'the fact that … queer characters make the audience laugh in a way informs the audience that they are not harmful, that on the contrary, they are likeable … [and] such a situation marks a shift in Malagasy people's perception of queer body modification'.

17	*Dossier* is 'an identity category which is used by speakers of the "secret" in-group sociolect *kinou* to synonymously refer to *sarimbavy*' (Palmer 2019). My interlocutors said that *dossier* is also their term for *koetra* or *sarimbavy* sex workers.

18   Lalatiana Virginie also said that being a *sarimbavy* is a *kilema* although she claims, like Tanamasoandro, that for her, being a *sarimbavy* is natural or *voa-janahary* (as the Creator made her).

19   Chantal Zabus writes how '[a]ncestral beliefs and local naming practices often vie with Western-influenced parlance for the ownership of African sexualities' (2014: 153).

20   See the talk show with Mija Rasolo on YouTube, Takariva mafana an'i Mija Rasolo 2019.

21   She alluded to other public figures, namely Zatia Rocher, the first Malagasy transsexual woman, who is widely criticized for his/her exuberance and wholesale appropriation of foreign ideas and practices.

22   The group is reported to have been created by Balou Chabat Rasoanaivo in the early 1990s (Palmer 2019).

23   Nocomment.mg.

24   Public representations of *sarimbavy* during that period were mainly based on humoristic performances by Malagasy comedians who cross-dressed in the TV sitcom *Torak'hehy*.

25   Emy Ga was quite familiar with the expression and gave a detailed account of her 'coming out', which was not well received by her father who repudiated her, whereas her friends and most people she is in touch with respected her choice.

26   Palmer underlines how 'sarimbavy … would reconvene after having been exposed to the language of HIV prevention and MSM rights or after socializing with other dossier from across the island' (2019).

27   On my first encounter with Balou Chabat Rasoanaivo, I was introduced to around eight *sarimbavy* and one *sarindahy* who were members of her association in Antananarivo. They agreed to answer the questions on my questionnaire. The interview took place in Ambohidroa, Antananarivo on 18 May 2022.

28   Most of them reported that they preferred playing dolls and 'house' with girls rather than cars and little soldiers with boys. Some said that their preference for female clothes was already marked at that early age. It should be noted, however, that Malagasy children's games are not limited to gendered stereotypes and generalizations like playing with dolls for girls and playing with cars for boys. These may be true of children that come from middle-class families and whose parents can afford to buy these toys. In most cases, traditional games are less gendered. Varieties may be observed in the different regions but not always along gender lines. For example, collective games such as *avy mangataka izahay* (we have come to request someone …) are played by girls and boys alike, and so are individual games such as *tantara vato* (inventing and staging stories by using small pebbles as characters). See *Folklore oral des enfants malgaches* (1988) by Sambo Clément for more details on traditional games.

29   A female-bodied interlocutor who identified as a transgender man said that he has completed the social transition and looks forward to going abroad since legal transition is not possible in Madagascar.

30   The football match between female journalists and *sarimbavy* in 2009 was quite memorable. The latter's victory was immortalized by the final goal scored by a *sarimbavy* whose wig was blown off in the process.

31   Rencurel notes that *sarimbavy* 'engaged in the traditional economic activities of Merina women: sewing, carrying water, lace making, and weaving' (Rencurel in Palmer 2019).

32   Balou Chabat Rasoanaivo and Emy Ga are former models.

33 Emy Ga is a fashion designer collaborating with foreign associations that defend
human rights and denounce gender-based violence.

34 Lalatiana Virginie is a hairdresser. Tanamasoandro and Balou Chabat Rasoanaivo
dress famous artists' hair and do their make-up as a second occupation, outside their
role as project manager or president of LGBT rights associations.

35 Losing one's *baraka* means being humiliated as if being naked in public (Rabenoro
2012).

36 Lalatiana Virginie told me that there are three categories of *sarimbavy* sex workers:
the first one, to which she claims to belong, is what they call 'classe' or high-ranking.
This category is for *sarimbavy* who know how to respect themselves by dressing
correctly and speaking in a respectable manner. They can be paid up to 100,000
ariary. Those who belong to the second category are average, they are said to accept
any price. The last and lowest category is for *sarimbavy* sex workers from the lower
class who are commonly referred to as 'vulnerable'. Lalatiana Virginie said that people
in this category are vulgar, and they usually accept very low pay (500–600 ariary),
some of them are also said to be pick-pockets.

37 This concern is not shared by westernized gender-nonconforming Malagasy youth.
When I asked Emy Ga about her views on marriage and children, she answered that
these are not part of her plans; rather, her project is to create a 'house' for LGBT
people who have been rejected by their families like herself. Her idea of a 'house' is
inspired by the ballroom culture, whereby the members have a sense of belonging to
a community. It should be noted that French colonial doctors also stressed *sekatra/
sarimbavy*'s lack of desire for reproduction (Roux 1905).

38 Iconic programmes related to sex on Malagasy media from the 1990s to the early
twenty-first century include a radio programme and a TV programme which
screened sex-related debates. The TV programme featured Malagasy female
prostitutes (Rakotomalala 2012). The same author mentions that 'nowadays, some
Malagasy newspapers no longer hesitate to talk about sex … sometimes illustrating
their articles with the photos of Europeans' (Rakotomalala 2012).

39 One might relate her to gynandrians, who are described by Felix Bryk as 'impotent
fellows with feminine manners' or 'men whose penis has died', and who are
'construe[d] as passive pederasts' (Bryk in Zabus 2013: 50).

40 Note also Flacourt's description of the *secats* as feminine presenting men who
'travelled from place to place, among the Great, to entertain them … the Great loved
them and protected them because they gave them pleasure, flattered them with their
songs' ([1658] 2007). This is probably what Emy Ga had in mind when she said that
'homosexuals have existed in Madagascar before colonisation. They were called
sekatra and people loved them'. Lalatiana Virginie also said that '*sarimbavy* used to
entertain kings in the olden days, everyone liked them'.

41 Dr Roux suggests that *sarimbavy* paid for their male partners' sexual favours, which
dissociates them from their contemporary representation as sex workers.

42 Exhibit of Gaubert's work at the IFM (Institut Français de Madagascar), 2013.

43 This echoes Rakotomalala's description of social norms that regulate sexual practices:
'The sexual act doesn't occur at anytime, anywhere, in any manner one wants, and
with anyone' (2012).

44 It is difficult to translate this sentence because the word *asesy*, a passive verb and
its active form, *manesy*, do not have precise equivalents in English. *Manesy* can be
described as acting on someone from behind and thus putting them in front of
oneself. *Asesy* refers to the opposite, being acted upon.

45   In her words, heterosexual men prefer having sex with her precisely because they
     have the privilege to do things that they can never do with their female partners, that
     is, sucking another man's penis.
46   He also mentions the colonial symbolism of fellatio, which is flagrant in the sculpture
     of a woman performing oral sex on a character wearing European clothes in Mangily,
     in the south-western part of Madagascar.
47   The *kinou* term is *mitoto sakay* (crushing chilli with a mortar and pestle).
     Traditionally, individual masturbation is perceived negatively (Rakotomalala 2012).
     Here, it is done for someone else.
48   Some of my interlocutors refused to discuss this subject with me, saying that they
     believe in spirit possession but do not engage in it. Others said that it is similar to
     being possessed by the devil. Balou Chabat Rasoanaivo developed the subject a
     little more by drawing a parallel between Christian beliefs in saints and Malagasy
     beliefs in *tromba* (spirit possession). See Palmer for comprehensive research on spirit
     possession and *sarimbavy* in the north-western part of Madagascar.

References

Acharya, Amitav. 2004. 'How Ideas Spread: Whose Norms Matter? Norm Localization and
    Institutional Change in Asian Regionalism', *International Organization* 58 (Spring):
    239–75.
Allibert, Claude. 1994. 'Les Sekatse de Flacourt: réflexion sur un comportement. Déviance
    ou contournement social ?', *Cahiers ethnologiques* 22: 106–21.
Andrianetrazafy, Hemerson. 2010. 'Notes sur la représentation de la sexualité dans la
    société sakalava du Menabe', *Etudes Océan Indien* 45: 13–49. https://doi.org/10.4000/
    oceanindien.901.
Binnie, Jon. 2004. *The Globalization of Sexuality*. London, Thousand Oaks, CA and New
    Delhi: Sage Publications.
Cruz, Angela G. B., Yuri Seo and Daiane Scaraboto. 2023. 'Between Cultural Appreciation
    and Cultural Appropriation: Self-Authorizing the Consumption of Cultural Difference',
    Journal of Consumer Research 50 (5): 962–84. https://doi.org/10.1093/jcr/ucad022.
Dahl, Øyvind. 1993. *Malagasy Meanings*. Stavanger: Centre for Intercultural
    Communication School of Mission and Theology.
Flacourt, Etienne de. [1658] 2007. *Histoire de la grande isle Madagascar*. Paris: Karthala.
Hayes, Jarrod. 2000. *Queer Nations: Marginal Sexualities in the Maghreb*. Chicago:
    University of Chicago Press.
Hoad, Neville. 1999. 'Between the White Man's Burden and the White Man's Disease:
    Tracking Lesbian and Gay Human Rights in Southern Africa', *GLQ: A Journal of
    Lesbian and Gay Studies* (5): 559–84. https://doi.org/10.1215/10642684-5-4-559.
Kulick, Don. 2000. 'Gay and Lesbian Language', *Annual Review of Anthropology* 29:
    243–85. https://www.jstor.org/stable/223422.
Laing, Rachel E. 2021. 'Who Said it First?: Linguistic Appropriation of Slang Terms Within
    the Popular Lexicon'. PhD diss., Illinois State University.
Molet, Louis. 1967. 'Cadres pour une ethnopsychiatrie de Madagascar', *L'Homme* 7 (2)
    (Spring): 5–29.
Palmer, Seth. 2014. 'Asexual Inverts and Sexual Perverts. Locating the Sarimbavy of
    Madagascar within Fin-de-Siècle Sexological Theories', *Transgender Quarterly*:

Decolonizing the Transgender Imaginary 1 (3) (August): 368–86. https://doi.org/10.1215/23289252-2685642.

Palmer, Seth. 2019. 'In the Image of a Woman: Spirited Identifications and Embodied Interpellations Along the Betsiboka Valley'. PhD diss., University of Toronto.

Rabenoro, Mireille. 2003. 'Motherhood in Malagasy Society: A Major Component in the Tradition Vs. Modernity Conflict', *Jenda: A Journal of Culture and African Women Studies* 4: 1–11.

Rabenoro, Mireille. 2012. 'Le mythe des femmes au pouvoir, arme de l'antiféminisme à Madagascar', *Cahiers du Genre* 52 (1): 75–95.

Rakotomalala, Malanjaona. 2010a. 'Amour et sexualité du côté de l'océan indien occidental', *Etudes Océan Indien* 45: 1–8. https://doi.org/10.4000/oceanindien.123.

Rakotomalala, Malanjaona. 2012. *A cœur ouvert sur la sexualité merina (Madagascar)*. Paris: Editions Karthala.

Rakotoniera, Zoly. 2021. 'Hilariously Queer: The Transgender and Transsexual Body in Malagasy Culture', *CODESRIA Bulletin* (1) (July).

Ravelomanana, Jacqueline. 2006. 'Regards croisés: la femme malgache vue par l'étranger à travers le temps', *Tsingy. Revue de l'Association des Professeurs d'Histoire et de Géographie de Madagascar. Les femmes dans l'océan indien* (5) (September): 51–73.

Roux, Paul. 1905. 'Note sur un cas d'inversion sexuelle chez une Comorienne', *Bulletins et Mémoires de la Société d'anthropologie de Paris* 5 (6) (April): 218–19.

Schermerhorn, R. A. 1964. 'Towards a General Theory of Minority Groups', *Phylon* 25 (3): 238–46.

Sedgwick, Eve K. 1993. 'Queer and Now', in *Tendencies*, 1–20. Durham, NC: Duke University Press.

Takariva mafana an'i Mija Rasolo. 2019. 'takariva mafana TANAMASOANDRO', YouTube, 1 June. Available online: https://www.youtube.com/watch?v=4P239Q6Hhtg&t=1186s&ab_channel=Takarivamafanaan%27iMijaRasolo (accessed 1 September 2024).

Tamale, Sylvia. 2013. 'Confronting the Politics of Nonconforming Sexualities in Africa', *African Studies Review* 56 (2) (August): 31–45.

Zabus, Chantal. 2013. *Out in Africa: Same-Sex Desire in Sub-Saharan Literatures and Cultures*. Woodbridge, UK: Boydell and Brewer & James Currey.

Zabus, Chantal. 2014. 'Trans Africa: Between Transgendered "Possession" and Transsexuality in South African Experiential Narratives', in Chantal Zabus and David Coad (eds), *Transgender Experience: Place, Ethnicity, and Visibility*, 153–69. New York and London: Routledge.

Chapter 9

THE ECO-QUEER TREE OF SOUTH AFRICAN CONSTITUTIONALISM

Francois Lion-Cachet

Introduction

What is regarded as (un)natural? How is this portrayed in the institution at the heart of South Africa's constitutional project? After apartheid, the country's depiction and understanding of law was reimagined. The central iconic shift from colonial and apartheid law to constitutional democracy in 1994 led to the portrayal of constitutionalism as a tree, instead of the erstwhile imported symbols of Lady Justice, the scales of justice and a reliance on classical courtroom architecture. This decolonial shift, of rooting post-apartheid justice as an indigenous practice through the image of a tree, signals a moment of law in reaching a higher cosmological consciousness in the context of the Anthropocene. Given the law's inherent reliance on being seen, this significant act of fundamentally changing its portrayal can be considered as an eco-queering of the legal system. Central to the apartheid project was the creation of separateness through spatial policies, a totalitarianism that has left much to be transformed. The design of the Constitutional Court of South Africa, as is discussed further on, reflects how people of all races, genders and sexualities are to be treated and protected as equals in the environment that all humans share.

The apartheid state used difference to divide society: race and gender were used to subordinate, and queers were condemned. A prominent member and champion of the LGBTQ+ community, retired justice of the Constitutional Court of South Africa, Edwin Cameron, writes that this Court's most vivid jurisprudence resulted in response to cases brought before it by gay and lesbian activist groups, as the Court could spell out the meaning of constitutional equality and protection from discrimination (Cameron 2012: para 83). As much as the court cases that granted full moral citizenship to queers in South Africa were watershed moments, humanity is faced with a new rights frontier regarding difference – the Othering of nature – that requires vivid jurisprudence more than ever.

I locate the tree symbolism within the burgeoning eco-queer movement and consider it as a critique of anthropocentrism. Understood within the framework of queer ecology, the tree of law is read as a rejection of human exceptionalism or the granting of a greater legal position to humans above all other things. As an act of eco-queering, I frame this constitutional aesthetic as a challenge to the perceived divide between humankind and nature, which constitutes a pressing challenge to the limitations of dualistic thinking. Eco-queer theory transcends human concerns by locating that which affects us in a much broader, universal context. As a form of post-humanism, I look beyond human laws and their disastrous impact, by drawing from the natural world's 'biosocial constitution' (Sbicca 2012: 34–9). This involves a challenge to human systems of authority that have caused a deluge of destruction. At play is a politics of awareness and legal activism with(in) nature that goes against the dominant legal discourse and hegemonic, western knowledge systems. I argue that the fight for queer equality has been subsumed to the much greater struggle for restoring our natural interconnectedness, drawing from Afropolitanism and the image of the tree of law.

In this chapter, I will be exploring how the image of a nondescript tree has been deployed at the Constitutional Court of South Africa in its emblem, architecture and artworks – all forming part of a strategically crafted jurisprudential identity – imagery that reveals the ideological premises and ideals of post-apartheid law. I further survey the cross-continental origins and the South African construction of the concept of justice under a tree. I proceed to plant it as an ecological and spiritual marker of humanity's environmental dependence, drawing from African ontological cosmology. I relate the tree to environmental law scholarship that advocates for giving rights to natural objects, as part of an eco-conscious shift, in order to establish ecological integrity as a fundamental legal norm. In conclusion, I ascertain what visual precedent the image of the tree sets regarding law's anthropocentric positioning, within the project of transformative constitutionalism in South Africa and beyond.

Where Trees Are Planted

The logo of the Constitutional Court (Figure 9.1) depicts a tree with eleven branches, sheltering eleven human figures standing under it. The tree's trunk and the branches that spread from it mimics the Y-shape that is found in the South African flag when shown vertically. The South African Constitution and its guardian, the Constitutional Court, are depicted as a tree that provides shelter and protection. The humans under the tree are depicted in altering shades of white and black, thus foregrounding race and diversity while emphasizing inherent equality. The front four figures have alternating manly and womanly properties, while the figures to the back are left nondescript in terms of sex and gender. The implication is that race, sex and gender are predicated as central considerations of equality under the rule of law (under the tree).[1] The number eleven serves as a signifier of diversity,[2] and references South Africa's eleven official languages and the eleven justices that serve on the Court's bench.

Justice Albie Sachs, who was part of the first bench of this Court, stated that as much as the tree protects the people, the people also look after the tree,

Figure 9.1 Logo of the Constitutional Court of South Africa (CCSA). Courtesy of the CCSA.

thereby establishing an interconnected relationship between the Constitution and its subjects, but also between nature and humankind (Constitutional Court of South Africa n.d.). Furthermore, the metaphor of justice under a tree is ascribed to traditional African societies' rituals where people would meet under trees to resolve disputes, referring to customary law practices in southern Africa. Sachs states that the logo had to reveal the Court's ethos and culture 'as a source of protection for all', and it had to root the Constitution in the historical struggle for human rights. In the spirit of a new democracy, the image was a move away from the 'clichéd images of the scales of justice and Roman columns' (Constitutional Court of South Africa n.d.). It was a deliberate decision to not only depict a tree or people in the logo, but also to combine the two elements. The logo is circular – like a planet – and thereby conveys a sense of cyclical wholeness. A multiplicity of meanings is united in the circle, making it a universal and recognizable icon. However, the circle is not closed off with a solid line, it remains open to outside (cosmological) influences. All of the logo's elements have been given a harmonious space within the image and each part makes up the whole. No specific tree is represented in the logo of the Constitutional Court or in its architecture; therefore I argue that the image corresponds and reflects the collective beliefs of society in equal terms as it is not confined to a specific geographic area only. The image is imbued with something like an aura, a halo or a surplus of meaning beyond what it depicts. It returns our gaze, reflecting our individual and collective desires. In this light, Richard Sherwin (2012: 28) writes how humans think with visual objects, with what they might radiate. Whether an image evokes a sublime presence, or an empty delight depends on the extent to which, and in which circumstances, it is regarded. We need otherness to think otherwise and thus to experience an image 'one must look and think with the image, beyond oneself' (29). In this way, I proceed to study the theme of justice under a tree that underpins the design of the Constitutional Court's purpose-built building, that opened its doors in 2004.

The foyer of the Constitutional Court building (Figure 9.2) features pillars stretching up diagonally to the roof, their slanted appearance evoking the idea of trees reaching up to the sky. The pillars, which stand in contrast to the use of straight and imposing columns in classical courtroom architecture, are decorated by mosaic designed by the artist Jane du Rand (Figure 9.3a). Du Rand used reds and ochres for the bottom parts of the pillars, denoting soil and other organic material, and blue-greens for the top parts, referring to greenery and the sky. The chandeliers that hang overhead, by the artist Walter Oltmann, are woven in wire in the shape of leaves (Figure 9.3b), creating the idea of a forest canopy overhead. The roof skylights let in dappled sunlight throughout the day, further adding to the simulation of standing in the clearing of a forest.[3] As one walks to the court chamber from the foyer, one encounters the Court's logo, reaffirming that as a visitor you and all others in the space are enacting what is depicted in the logo: gathered under the trees to engage with the ideals of justice, as part of a journey to the great tree.

Thenjiwe Mtintso, who was on the Constitutional Court's architectural competition jury, and who had been imprisoned on the site known today as

Figure 9.2 A section of the foyer of the Constitutional Court of South Africa. Photograph by Ben Law-Viljoen, courtesy of the Constitutional Court Trust.

a

b

Figure 9.3 a and b Detail of the pillar mosaic by Jane du Rand (a) that includes a variety of arboreal shapes such as seedpods, thorns and leaves; and detail of the chandeliers representing a canopy of leaves (b), by the artist Walter Oltmann. Photographs by Ben Law-Viljoen, courtesy of the Constitutional Court Trust.

Constitution Hill that houses the Court, states: 'The building had to project a notion of a protective tree, which in the rural areas is usually used as a court under which elders sit and resolve the problems of the village or villagers sit in community. It had to be like an imbizo' (2006: 32). *Imbizo* is an isiXhosa word that refers to a gathering that is usually called by a traditional leader, while the Sotho and Tswana communities of southern Africa have an equivalent in the terms *kgotla* and *lekgotla*, being a gathering of the people of a village or community to discuss important issues, or to serve as a judicial court. The court and tree are layered in complex inclusion, superimposed upon one another in a singular space, creating a hybrid narrative of tree as court (Noble 2011: 138).

The idea or practice of justice under a tree is not unique to South Africa, or to any cultural or ethnic group. Trees, especially the old and large ones, have for ages been markers in landscapes that offer a sense of place for important gatherings. Somali pastoralists' traditional culture of arbitration is known as 'xeerka geedka', which translates as 'the law of the tree', that refers to the traditional practice of legal proceedings that are given symbolic weight as it mostly happens under acacia trees (Mansur 2011: 185–7). Teutonic and Celtic courts were at first held outside, on top of hills under trees,[4] often with stones forming a sacred circle (like a *kraal*), a historical practice that was common in the documented ancient history of Europe and North America, as in Africa (Mulcahy 2010: 15–17). Despite their love of litigation, ancient Athenians had no buildings dedicated solely to law, and hearings often took place outside (15–17). In common law jurisdictions, court proceedings that were held in a field under a tree have been recorded as recently as the nineteenth century, while in Australia the judiciary and policymakers are experimenting with outdoor trials involving aboriginal community members (7). In Rwanda, '*gacaca* courts' refer to the practice of communities meeting in an open, outside landscape (Geraghty 2020: 590). The new Benin National Assembly building that is under construction, designed by Francis Kéré, takes inspiration from the palaver tree and 'the age-old West African tradition of meeting under a tree to make consensual decisions in the interest of a community' (Kéré Architecture n.d.). The palaver tree is described as a timeless generational symbol that inspires respect for the majestic forces of nature (Kéré Architecture n.d.). In 1960s Indonesia, the changing depiction of law through Lady Justice with scales to a banyan tree 'represented a quickening of the process of transformation of the heritage of Dutch colonial law into Indonesian law' (Lev 1965: 282).[5]

What Trees Come to Signify

Laura Rival (2020: xiii) asserts that anthropology has long been interested in studying how cultures derive meanings largely from natural elements which then find expression in symbolic systems. The tree of law expresses the envisioned post-apartheid social order in visual form, analogous to the natural world. Bryson bases this approach on 'the drive inherent in all societies to "naturalise" the reality they have constructed and to transform a world produced by a specific socio-historical activity, into a World given from the beginning, a Creation, natural and unchanging' (1983: 14). Further, Bryson writes that humans' habitus extends beyond the physical environment to an assemblage of 'maxims, morals, proverbial lore, values, beliefs, and myths' – also including codes of justice, articles of faith and the socially institutionalized domain of art – which ensures coherence of experience in a social formation (14). 'Trees provide some of the most visible and potent symbols of social process and collective identity', writes Rival (2020: 1). A shared object of focus, such as a tree, can reveal a collective sentiment that has become conscious of itself, in this case the purpose of constitutionalism.

From ethnography we understand that trees are used symbolically to concretize and materialize the abstract notion of life; trees are ideal for this symbolic purpose because they remain ambiguous as life forms. Rival posits that arboreal symbols elicit two essential qualities, vitality and self-regenerative power, biological particularities which make trees 'life-reaffirming and death-denying cultural representations' (2020: 1). Early humans worshipped trees and other life powers as everything was at once material and spiritual, with little division between the animate and inanimate. Studies in comparative religion highlights the symbolic significance of trees in classical mythology, in the religions of ancient civilizations, and in contemporary cultural beliefs and rituals. Tree worship shows how most religions had originated from personifying nature (4). In many African folk-tales, totemic trees are considered as living beings that are comparable to humans through their morphological features. Associations include the trunk and the human body, bark and skin, limbs and arms, roots and legs, wood and bone, sap and blood, leaves and hair. Furthermore, Rival points out that the androgynous nature of trees – a pervasive view in ancient and classical mythologies – has captured the popular imagination (10, 21).[6] The symbolism of the tree could also be seen as representing the sources of South African law by equating the roots and branches of the tree to legal pluralism.[7]

There are many archetypal figures who, in close association with a tree, attained enlightenment or special power and insight: Augustine's religious conversion under a tree in his garden; Isaac Newton who discovered gravity under an apple tree; the Buddha sitting in enlightenment under the Bodhi (sacred fig or banyan) tree; the tree of the knowledge of good and evil (and the tree of life) in Judaism and Christianity; and in the biblical book of Judges, the prophet Deborah, a judge of Israel, rendered her judgements beneath a date palm tree. All of this orienting thought in culture, amongst many other examples, finds resonance in the understanding of South Africa's constitutional aesthetic, and what is signified by the tree as a place of meeting, judgement and connection.

An African Seed in a Universal Forest

I posit that the tree contains in it a universality, and points to a burgeoning legal consciousness that has sprouted from South African soil, signalling an awareness that western colonial and apartheid legal systems did not have, and their present-day avatars continue to lack. Denis Ekpo and Pfunzo Sidogi (2021) have concerned themselves with the notion and achievement of post-African aesthetics. Their provocative book contains in its opening a quote from Frantz Fanon, who wrote in the conclusion to *The Wretched of the Earth*: 'let us decide not to imitate Europe; let us combine our muscles and our brains in a new direction. Let us try to create the whole man, whom Europe has been incapable of bringing to triumphant birth' (1963: 313). It is from a spirit of Black enlightenment that a ravaged Africa's societies and institutions are reimagined, not out of nostalgia but in the interests of moral advancement.

Ekpo (2021a) writes that Africa's modernity consciousness is an essentially aesthetic phenomenon, and that what is often loved about Africa is 'mostly precisely those things that Europe had badmouthed and condemned as the very sources of Africa's barbarity and non-evolution' (3, 6). An over-compensatory love for Africa, drawing from Ekpo, may include a view that 'Africans' are morally superior on account of their pre-colonial living relationship with nature. However, South Africa's current constitutional imagery does not harken back to a nativist or fundamentalist way of living and engaging with the world, but takes what works for Africa as a matter of universal concern, and discards that which is harmful. What is found at the Constitutional Court is an ingenious and hybrid aesthetic. Including in building technologies, architectural design, art movements, court procedure, convention and sources of law, much of the South African legal system's Roman-Dutch and common law influences have been adopted into the Constitutional Court's physical and jurisprudential design. It does not rely only on what Africa has to offer but also draws liberally from a wide array of local and international influences.

Ekpo (2021b) encourages transcendence into a greater consciousness, by recognizing humanity's common historical foundation (of a close connection to nature) and our bounded future trajectory. The transcendence out of a conquering mindset (of each other, of other nations and of nature) can be achieved by the reaching of a higher consciousness that entails realising the interconnectedness of all things (Ekpo 2021b: 32–3). What the tree of law represents of Africa should be read not as a utopia lost or to be regained, but as a call to action for socio-environmental justice. It demands a recognition of our shared responsibility to the planetary project. It is a statement of interconnectivity, not of exclusive 'Africanness'. The concept of justice under a tree, I argue, is an example of the re-universalization of Africa in that it breaks free from colonialism and apartheid's aesthetic world-view and anthropocentric images of the law, whilst taking care not to root an identity in indictment of the West, but for the cause of universal benefit. The arboreal aesthetic sets a visual precedent for regarding the need of human development in the same picture as the environmental cost of that development – pertinent issues in a globalised economy that is based on extraction and commodification.

Michael Onyebuchi Eze (2017: 624) outlines what in Africa can be of benefit to the global community, in an effort to articulate a theory of African environmental ethics outside of the western intellectual framework as point of departure. Eze frames an African world-view as being rooted in universal vitalism, that regards community as encompassing the physical and metaphysical universe, recognizing the fluid interactivity of all things (625). By holistically understanding the world of forces like a spider's web, no one being is superior in importance or prior in necessity (626). For Eze, African ontology regards no 'object' as dead matter, everything radiates a life force, from a pebble to a pelican. Nature is sacred because of this all-pervading vital force, making the environment constitutive of humanity (626–7). This ontological holism finds expression in totemism, as in portraying the law as a tree.

Eze (2017: 627–8) considers how modernity and industrialization brought rapid development and increased production of food, goods and services, whilst this phenomenon has destabilized, if not destroyed, ecologically harmonious ways of life. Eze does not dismiss the need for African socio-political and economic progress, and does not frame this as arcane or anachronistic to the African experience. Rather, Eze argues for a balance between the eco-community and materialistic civilization. 'Respect for the environment is not a slavish or impractical submission; it is a view grounded in metaphysical realism and ontological holism' (629). The earth community should thus be understood as being both material and spiritual. It is needed to ground law in spirituality, a radical shift from all 'isms', thereby transcending constitutionalism as an ideology to a way of life (631). Read in this way, the tree of law challenges the very system in and by which it was planted.

South Africa's legal aesthetic, while influenced by foreign systems of law, is infused with local insights. It sets out a philosophical approach to higher growth consciousness that is historically and ecologically imbued, framed universally. Chielozona Eze's (2021: 88) rendition of such a 'higher consciousness' finds itself in the term of 'Afropolitanism', denoting openness as an ethical attitude in and to the world.[8] Cosmopolitanism in Africa does not opt for essentialist and traditionalist identity configurations, but remain receptive to all influences that can be applied to the benefit of the (inter)nationalist project. Furthermore, it does not diminish the spiritual and cultural intelligence developed in the African region, but seeks to test cultural practices against those of others, and is open to being changed in whatever way beneficial (89–90). In South Africa, the portrayal of the law had to break free from past imposed imagery, and the new aesthetic had to signal a consciousness that transcends reactionary impulses and moves towards a state of universality. Considered in its broad context, the tree and humans' relationship with it may perhaps be the most effective, provocative and conscious image of law that has emerged globally.

A Universal Law beyond Anthropocentrism

I want to focus on what the image of the tree demands of us humans, as a type of visual legal precedent, adding to justice-under-a-tree potency. The effects of living in the Anthropocene, marked by the crises of climate change and rapid ecological decline, as a result of human activity, necessitates a reconsideration of the law today. The following discussion will consider law's anthropocentric positioning and why the human–nature divide is no longer tenable, proceeding to advocate for ecological integrity's inclusion as a constitutional *grundnorm*.[9]

The new climatic regime has irrecoverably disturbed the political imaginaries of modernity (Matthews 2019: 3). The challenge we are presented with is an aesthetic one, as we are becoming aware of 'that to which we are rendered sensitive and insensitive, that which is included within or without the various framing devices that structure our modes of perception' (3). Colonial and apartheid law, in its efforts to separate racial groups and humans from nature, can be considered as a type of anaesthetic, that which cuts off feeling to the body and world, whereas the post-apartheid conception entails an aesthetic reorientation of law to attune legal thinking to our ecologically complex, living planet (3–4). It is through the law that the societal premise is set, through legal concepts, theories and fictions that are enforced (5–9). In this vein, the field of earth jurisprudence is concerned with developing law that is good for the earth community, by seeing the task of human law to be the harmonization with the broader laws of nature (6). Constitutionalism should be concerned with planetary wholeness instead of environmental apartheid.

Nicholas Mirzoeff (2014: 216) argues that a planetary counter-visuality to global financialization has begun to develop in the Global South. Mirzoeff equates the Anthropocene to a battlefield that is too complex and extensive for any one individual to physically see, and states the need to make use of our imagination to create images which will make the all-pervasive effects of this epoch visible (216). The Anthropocene is regarded as a colonized form of the imagination, that rendered the earth into a *terra nullius* ('territory without a master') to be made into the domain of the West/Man, through the conquest of nature and those living in harmony with it (218–19). In this sense, seeing the world differently/otherwise equates to a postqueer legal vision.

As our senses have become accustomed to the capitalist aesthetic of consumption and pollution, a counter-aesthetic to challenge the modern imperial imagery is needed. The idea of the commons should be embraced and thereby be expounded in the law's visual representation. Mirzoeff writes that 'climate change is the polite name for the robbing of the commons' (2014: 226). Harking back to the South's resistance to domination, Mirzoeff asserts that contesting Anthropocene visuality 'is a decolonial politics that claims the right to see what there is to be seen and name it as such: a planetary destabilization of the conditions supportive of life, requiring a decolonization of the biosphere itself in order to create a new sustainable and democratic way of life that has been prepared for by centuries of resistance' (230).

Environmental law scholar Louis Kotzé states that the use of the term 'Anthropocene' is no longer limited to its role as a cautionary rhetorical device, but now goes to the core of epistemological and ontological enquiries about the legal systems that govern human behaviour on earth (Kotzé 2017a: vii). Contemporary legal discourse needs to be concerned with the system that has enabled ongoing environmental degradation, in order to determine the purpose of the law going forward. With the emerging biospheric conditions of this age, the societal ordering maintained by environmental law under former Holocene conditions is no longer tenable (viii). Tim Stephens refers to how Enlightenment humanist thinkers saw a separation of the natural and human domains, but that it is now clear we have always been in a socio-ecological system that is intermixed, interdependent and inseparable (Stephens 2017: 32). According to Andreas Philippopoulos-Mihalopoulos, law's confidence in the old yet sustained world order has been replaced by an 'Anthropocene-turn', providing scholars (lawyers and curators too) with new insights to shape the legal system (Philippopoulos-Mihalopoulos 2017: 117). Indigenous peoples' cultures and world-views also offer valuable insights that may help root the law in a more sustainable way.

A change in perspective leads humanity back to the understanding of our environmental embeddedness and, by extension, how non-human entities and things have standing and power of their own (Vermeylen 2017: 143). Actors of nature – fauna, flora and entities such as rivers, mountains, fields, the sky – form part of the Other that challenges humanity to think beyond ourselves. The tree is a useful symbol to infuse alterity – otherness, eco-queerness – into the law. Saskia Vermeylen advocates for the need to think through natural, non-human subjects to challenge western views about society and the law, as a way of transcending the great divide between human culture and nature (143). This need to think of natural entities as subjects rather than objects, outside of legal tradition that assigns ownership of nature is a direct challenge to law's deep entwinement with anthropocentrism that always puts humans first, even to their own detriment. Such thinking seeks to address the violent use of law against nature by decentring the human in the systems we employ to arrange our world, in a paradigm shift that regards the ecological field as a continuum (152).

Such a shift in human thinking about the law requires the broadening of the language that is used in formulating and employing the law: by limiting the law to human language, nature is excluded from political life and legal agency. Nature communicates through its own way of signification, requiring our attentiveness. According to Vermeylen, by accepting non-linguistic representations[10] as forms of legal language, new possibilities for extending sovereignty beyond the state and the human is made possible (Vermeylen 2017: 161). Dead fish in a polluted river scream of a crime, so does a tree felled without just cause, and so do declining, diseased and decimated populations of natural life forms and their habitats. The aesthetic turn in law is a revolution away from anthropocentrism – through communication of the senses the law can be developed in a more sustainable way.

As part of challenging unbridled human development in relation to the global socio-ecological crisis, a healthy environment is not only a universal concern, but it is also a precondition for the existence of human rights, and queer rights for that matter (Kotzé 2017b: 190–1). South Africa's constitutional aesthetic signals the need for greater jurisprudential regard – by the Constitutional Court and the legal fraternity at large – to be paid to the need of employing constitutionalism as an inherently environmental force. In South African law, the constitutional dispensation is based on three fundamental values: *human* dignity, freedom and equality, the first of which enjoys international support as a *grundnorm*.[11] These values relate to the human person and not to the environment. There is growing support for the hypothesis that 'ecological integrity must attain the same fundamental normative status in law as human rights, the abolition of slavery, the rights of women [and queer people] and the rule of law' (Bosselmann 2017: 242). If and when ecological integrity is established as a legal norm, it would be read in conjunction with human rights, and when required would need to be balanced against existing anthropocentric norms. Such a change to the underpinnings of the rule of law will enable the shaping of a new legal story, in line with depicting the law as people standing under a tree. As Klaus Bosselmann writes, '[u]nder the prevailing story of economic growth, people will continue to live unsustainably, until they can no longer do so' (264). As the law structures society, systemic change is dependent on a jurisprudential embrace of the natural world of which we form a part, marking a shift from human arrogance to humility in the Anthropocene. Humanity already functions on an ecological *grundnorm*, but this is yet to be widely acknowledged, calling for a legal paradigm shift.

In a seminal article, Christopher D. Stone sets out a case for granting the environment legal rights, both in its parts – rivers, forests, oceans – and as a whole, arguing that it is neither fanciful nor devoid of operational content, and that it can and should happen (Stone 1972: 456–7, 464). As a fundamental premise, nature should have legally recognized dignity and worth in its own right, and should not merely be regarded as being there for the benefit of humans (463). This means that natural objects should be able to institute legal proceedings in their own names, and that injury to them would need to be considered by the courts, and remedy or relief must be to the benefit of the natural entity itself (458). Legal action would no longer be dependent on humans being able to show an invasion of their rights and choosing to instate legal action against a polluter or another infringing party (459). Following environmental damage, a suitable order of court could be the cost and action of making the environment whole again, and not just paying out an aggrieved human individual or group that might not enact environmental reparation.[12] Making the environment whole again would entail all the costs that are associated to successfully rehabilitate or recreate the damaged ecosystem, or making a comparable contribution that restores ecological integrity. However rude an estimate of restoring 'priceless' natural life might be, this would still amount to a more balanced and sustainable world environment than by ignoring harmful practices (478).

Stone posits that corporations, states, estates, infants, those left incompetent and institutions in a wide sense cannot speak for themselves, even though they have legal personhood, and that there is thus no reason that representatives (lawyers) cannot also be appointed to represent the natural world (Stone 1972: 464). Anyone who regards themselves as a friend of a natural object should be able to apply for the guardianship of it, through a court of law, that will give them rights of inspection or visitation to determine the environment's condition to make a case on its behalf (466). In a sense, humans speaking for the rights of nature does not dismantle the idea of the Anthropocene, but owns up to our collective responsibility as custodians of nature, in the interests of nature – while 'nature' implicitly includes our own interests. Stone posits that giving nature rights will open up the possibility of instigating litigation where traditional class and

a   b

Figure 9.4a and b Sandile Goje's artwork Making Democracy Work (1996) (a) represents how the artist envisaged democracy in the nascent years of universal suffrage in South Africa. The artwork is remarkably similar to the design of the Constitutional Court, as the Court architects identified and drew inspiration from it at the conceptual design stage of the building (Law-Viljoen 2006: 60). In metaphorical contrast, a towering London plane tree (b) is found outside the front entrance of the Supreme Court of the United Kingdom. In the case of the latter, nature is something kept outside of court proceedings, as the law there draws its glory and authority from neo-Gothic architecture. With the example set by South Africa's highest court, legal proceedings are framed as something that happens in harmony with nature, thereby challenging Anthropocentric subordination, separation from, and the abuse of the natural world. Artwork (a): Sandile Goje, Making Democracy Work, 1996, linocut on paper, 525 x 365 mm. Constitutional Court Art Collection. Courtesy of the artist and the Constitutional Court Trust (CCT). Photograph by Ben Law-Viljoen © CCT. Photograph (b): Taken by Francois Lion-Cachet, courtesy of the author.

individual action suits may not have arisen (475). Making the environment – in its parts and as a whole – the carrier of rights and the beneficiary of a judgement would also curtail the practice where human litigants or agencies agree not to enforce rights they hold, to achieve economic growth based on environmental pillaging (480). This is not to say that all human development will be blocked, but that human interests will not be the only and primary consideration. Such a legal shift would lead to the development of case law and accompanying legislation, and aid the concomitant growth of environmental law. By establishing ecological integrity as a *grundnorm*, judges will be enabled with new explanatory rhetoric to reach decisions that might not have been possible before, enabling the development of new legal insights and a viable body of law (488–9).

Nature does not exist for 'man'. The health and well-being of humankind is dependent on a healthy environment, making ecological integrity not an imposition to 'our' interests but a crucial factor in advancing prosperity. Therein lies the irony of law's anthropocentric approach to othering nature – we are already a part of the natural world but have to become conscious of this to stop the depletion that harms us as much as it does nature. A higher consciousness will require excesses to be curbed, and possibly for the human population to be stabilized (Stone 1972: 492). Thereby, a rhetoric of law that will speak to a newfound jurisprudential cosmology can emerge, regarding the earth as an interconnected organism where consciousness is not owned or unique to humankind, as it vests in fauna and flora, and may transcend our planetary boundaries (499). As Stone puts it:

> Before the forces that are at work, our highest court is but a frail and feeble—a distinctly human—institution. Yet, the Court may be at its best not in its work of handing down decrees, but at the very task that is called for: of summoning up from the human spirit the kindest and most generous and worthy ideas that abound there, giving them shape and reality and legitimacy.
>
> (500)

Conclusion

In this chapter, the arboreal symbolism found in the Constitutional Court was explored in the context of the broad cultural and legal significance of the image of a tree (Figure 9.4a and b). Race, sex and gender are pointed out as forming a part of this constitutional aesthetic, whilst underscoring the equality principles of non-racialism and non-sexism, and holding space for gender neutrality. But more importantly, the tree has become a poignant representation of humankind's relationship with the natural world in the context of the climate and biodiversity crises, thus planting a constitutional rhetoric of our environmental dependence. Furthermore, the arboreal imagery speaks to an othered nature, challenging humanity to think beyond ourselves as a way of infusing restorative alterity and eco-queerness into the law. The tree symbolizes an existential concern as the 'planet veers toward environmental catastrophe driven by forces that elude visualization' (Hariman and Lucaites 2016: 1). Moreover, James W. Fernandez writes that '[t]rees, by certain associative purposes, can excite the moral imagination concerning the health or disease of corporate bodies, bodies corporeal and bodies politic as it were, and are thus powerful or power-associated imaginative devices' (2020: 85).

Drawing on post-African aesthetic theory, I find that the tree is a symbol that points to but also summons a universality of the law, thereby making it an effective marker of law in the Anthropocene. I emphasize the fact that the tree must be framed and understood as a universal symbol, and not one that rehashes traditional cultural practice without conceding to the globally beneficial, but also the detrimental developments of modernity. In this way, a romanticized contextualization of postcolonial law may be avoided.

As a core finding, a visual precedent is set by visualizing South African constitutionalism as a tree that shelters but is also left vulnerable to the actions of humans. The spiritual imagery speaks to our interrelationship with nature and demands that the human legal system has to develop to harmonize with the natural laws on which human society is dependent. As an act of (up)rooting the law, South Africa's constitutional aesthetic is connected to scholarship advocating for the recognition of environmental integrity as a fundamental legal norm. The judiciary will increasingly be called into question about their environmental policies and the execution thereof, just as gender and racial transformation has been called into question. The tree is a signpost to that which law must become consciousness to preserve, restore and advance earthly vitality and health. This symbol therefore marks how constitutionalism can be better understood, developed and executed both in South Africa and across the world, as an enlivened universal symbol of conscious law.

Notes

1   The racial element in the Constitutional Court's logo speaks to one of the Constitution's founding provisions, non-racialism (listed alongside non-sexism). This value carries irony in a country where gross inequality is still very much marked along the lines of race. Kevin Minofu considers the Constitutional Court's jurisprudence on race in a historical context, within the larger constitutional scheme, and puts forth an argument that substantive non-racialism 'does not stand as an impediment to race-conscious redistributive efforts – it instead rejects colour-blindness and acts as a powerful licence to dismantle all forms of racial hierarchy by being actively attentive to race in decision-making' (2021: 301).

2   This reminds us of the motto on the South African National Coat of Arms, that is drawn from the /Xam expression '!ke e: /xarra // ke', which literally means 'diverse people unite' and commonly referred to as 'unity in diversity'.

3   The foyer, furthermore, makes use of tree stumps and wooden benches that give the impression of sitting on tree trunks. A shadow-patterned carpet also forms part of this exhibition area. The flooring of the foyer is made of different levels, that mimics the topography of a natural amphitheatre.

4   A practice that circles back to Constitution Hill in Johannesburg, the site of the Constitutional Court, where justice is symbolically performed under trees, atop a hill.

5   The banyan tree symbol seems to have since been replaced with an unremarkable crest, resembling the coat of arms of a state.

6   One might recall the Ents of *Lord of the Rings*, the fourteen-foot-tall humanoid tree creatures, that have left a mark on popular culture.

7   The sources of law in South Africa are the Constitution, legislation, common law, judicial precedent, customary (indigenous) law, religious personal laws, international law and authoritative writings.

8   Chielozona Eze also refers to popular support of cosmopolitanism in the African
    context; see: Mbembe (2001) and Appiah (2006).
9   *Grundnorm*, a German term created by Hans Kelsen in *Pure Theory of Law*, refers to
    the underlying rule or order that forms the unitary basis for a legal system.
10 Vermeylen refers to an example of non-linguistic communication: a wolf pack does
    not recognize the sovereign nation-state and its declared laws, but does recognize
    human markers of territoriality, and makes judgements about insiders and outsiders
    accordingly. The politics of sovereignty and territoriality are communicated in a
    wide variety of natural registers, involving a complex set of bodily gesture, visual and
    pheromonal signals, and various forms of (aesthetic) vocalizations (Vermeylen 2017:
    161).
11 Article 1 of the Universal Declaration of Human Rights declares that '[a]ll human
    beings are born free and equal in dignity and rights' (United Nations 1948), whereas
    the preambles of both the International Covenant on Civil and Political Rights
    and the International Covenant on Economic, Social and Cultural Rights state that
    'recognition of the inherent dignity and of the equal and inalienable rights of all
    members of the human family is the foundation of freedom, justice and peace in the
    world […] these rights derive from the inherent dignity of the human person' (Office
    of the High Commissioner for Human Rights 1966a, b).
12 'The costs of making a forest whole, for example, would include the costs of reseeding,
    repairing watersheds, restocking wildlife – the sorts of costs the Forest Service
    undergoes after a fire. Making a polluted stream whole would include the costs
    of restocking with fish, water-fowl, and other animal and vegetable life, dredging,
    washing out impurities, establishing natural and/or artificial aerating agents, and so
    forth' (Stone 1972: 462).

References

Appiah, Anthony. 2006. *Cosmopolitanism: Ethics in a World of Strangers*. London: Allen
    Lane.
Bosselmann, Klaus. 2017. 'The Imperative of Ecological Integrity: Conceptualising a
    Fundamental Legal Norm for a New "World System" in the Anthropocene', in Louis
    J. Kotzé (ed.), *Environmental Law and Governance for the Anthropocene*, 241–65.
    Oxford: Hart Publishing.
Bryson, Norman. 1983. *Vision and Painting: The Logic of the Gaze*. London: Macmillan.
Cameron, Edwin. 2012. 'What you can do with rights', The Fourth Leslie Scarman Lecture of
    the Law Commission of England and Wales, 25 January. Available online: https://lawcom.
    gov.uk/lectures-talks/what-you-can-do-with-rights/ (accessed 1 September 2024).
Constitutional Court of South Africa 'The logo'. Available online: https://www.concourt.
    org.za/index.php/about-us/the-logo (accessed 8 July 2023).
Ekpo, Denis. 2021a. 'Africa Mis-traveling to Modernity: From Modern African Art to
    African Modernism', in Denis Ekpo and Pfunzo Sidogi (eds), *The De-Africanization
    of African Art: Towards Post-African Aesthetics*, 1–20. Abingdon and New York:
    Routledge.
Ekpo, Denis. 2021b. 'Manifesto for a Post-African Art', in Denis Ekpo and Pfunzo Sidogi
    (eds), *The De-Africanization of African Art: Towards Post-African Aesthetics*, 21–53.
    Abingdon and New York: Routledge.

Ekpo, Denis and Pfunzo Sidogi, eds. 2021. *The De-Africanization of African Art: Towards Post-African Aesthetics*. Abingdon and New York: Routledge.

Eze, Chielozona. 2021. 'Africanity, Litigation Aesthetics, and Openness to Being', in Denis Ekpo and Pfunzo Sidogi (eds), *The De-Africanization of African Art: Towards Post-African Aesthetics*, 77–95. Abingdon and New York: Routledge.

Eze, Michael Onyebuchi. 2017. 'Humanitatis-Eco (Eco-Humanism): An African Environmental Theory', in Adeshina Afolayan and Toyin Falola (eds), *The Palgrave Handbook of African Philosophy*, 1st edn, 621–32. New York: Palgrave Macmillan.

Fanon, Frantz. 1963. *The Wretched of the Earth*. New York: Grove Press.

Fernandez, James W. 2020. 'Trees of Knowledge of Self and Other in Culture: On Models for the Moral Imagination', in Laura Rival (ed.), *The Social Life of Trees: Anthropological Perspectives on Tree Symbolism*, 81–110. Abingdon, London and New York: Routledge.

Geraghty, Mark Anthony. 2020. 'Gacaca, Genocide, Genocide Ideology: The Violent Aftermaths of Transitional Justice in the New Rwanda', *Comparative Studies in Society and History* 62 (3): 588–618.

Hariman, Robert and John Lucaites. 2016. *The Public Image: Photography and Civic Spectatorship*. Chicago: University of Chicago Press.

Kéré Architecture. n.d. 'Benin National Assembly'. Available online: www.kerearchitecture.com/work/building/benin-national-assembly (accessed 31 October 2022).

Kotzé, Louis J., ed. 2017a. *Environmental Law and Governance for the Anthropocene*. Oxford: Hart Publishing.

Kotzé, Louis J. 2017b. 'Global Environmental Constitutionalism in the Anthropocene', in Louis J. Kotzé (ed.), *Environmental Law and Governance for the Anthropocene*, 189–218. Oxford: Hart Publishing.

Law-Viljoen, Bronwyn, ed. 2006. *Light on a Hill: Building the Constitutional Court of South Africa*. Parkwood, South Africa: David Krut Publishing.

Lev, Daniel. 1965. 'The Lady and the Banyan Tree: Civil Law Change in Indonesia', *American Journal of Comparative Law* 14 (2): 282–307.

Mansur, Abdalla Omar. 2011. 'The Tree of Wisdom: Tradition and Modernity', in Mara Frascarelli (ed.), *A Country Called Somalia: Culture, Language and Society of a Vanishing State*, 185–193. Turin: L'Harmattan Italia.

Matthews, Daniel. 2019. 'Law and Aesthetics in the Anthropocene: From the Rights of Nature to the Aesthesis of Obligations', *Law, Culture and the Humanities* 19 (2): 227–47.

Mbembe, Achille. 2001. *On the Postcolony*. Berkeley: University of California Press.

Minofu, Kevin. 2021. 'Non-Racial Constitutionalism: Transcendent Utopia or Colour-Blind Fiction?', *Constitutional Court Review* 11: 301–22.

Mirzoeff, Nicholas. 2014. 'Visualizing the Anthropocene', *Public Culture* 26 (2 (73)): 213–32.

Mtintso, Thenjiwe. 2006. 'Site of Pain and Renewal', in Bronwyn Law-Viljoen (ed.), *Light on a Hill: Building the Constitutional Court of South Africa*, 32–45. Parkwood, South Africa: David Krut Publishing.

Mulcahy, Linda. 2010. *Legal Architecture: Justice, Due Process and the Place of Law*. Abingdon: Taylor & Francis.

Noble, Jonathan Alfred. 2011. *African Identity in Post-Apartheid Public Architecture: White Skin, Black Masks*. Farnham: Ashgate.

Office of the High Commissioner for Human Rights. 1966a. International Covenant on Civil and Political Rights. Available online: https://www.ohchr.org/en/instruments-mechanisms/instruments/international-covenant-civil-and-political-rights (accessed 1 September 2024).

Office of the High Commissioner for Human Rights. 1966b. International Covenant on Civil and Political Rights. Available online: https://www.ohchr.org/en/instruments-mechanisms/instruments/international-covenant-economic-social-and-cultural-rights (accessed 1 September 2024).

Philippopoulos-Mihalopoulos, Andreas. 2017. 'Critical Environmental Law in the Anthropocene', in Louis J. Kotzé (ed.), *Environmental Law and Governance for the Anthropocene*, 117–35. Oxford: Hart Publishing.

Rival, Laura, ed. 2020. *The Social Life of Trees: Anthropological Perspectives on Tree Symbolism*. Abingdon, London and New York: Routledge.

Sbicca, Joshua. 2012. 'Eco-queer Movement(s): Challenging Heteronormative Space Through (Re)imagining Nature and Food', *European Journal of Ecopsychology* 3: 33–52.

Sherwin, Richard K. 2012. 'Visual Jurisprudence', *New York Law School Law Review* 57: 137–65.

Stephens, Tim. 2017. 'Reimagining International Environmental Law in the Anthropocene', in Louis J. Kotzé (ed.), *Environmental law and Governance for the Anthropocene*, 31–54. Oxford: Hart Publishing.

Stone, Christopher D. 1972. 'Should Trees Have Standing – Toward Legal Rights for Natural Objects', *Southern California Law Review* 45: 450–501.

United Nations. 1948. Universal Declaration of Human Rights. Available online: https://www.un.org/en/about-us/universal-declaration-of-human-rights (accessed 1 September 2024).

Vermcylcn, Saskia. 2017. 'Materiality and the Ontological Turn in the Anthropocene: Establishing a Dialogue between Law, Anthropology and Eco-Philosophy', in Louis J. Kotzé (ed.), *Environmental law and governance for the Anthropocene*, 137–62. Oxford: Hart Publishing.

Part II

TESTIMONIES

Chapter 10

1995, READING THE SIGNS OF THE TIME

Philippe-Joseph Salazar

In Memoriam Koos Prinsloo

In October 1995 the First Colloquium of Gay and Lesbian Studies in Southern Africa conference (hereafter 'the Event') took place at the University of Cape Town (UCT). The timing was right as South Africa was moving swiftly to do away with both the colonial, and religious, denunciation of 'sodomy', and the brutal denial of rights, and even life, to 'homosexuals' in much of Africa. A Zimbabwean delegate attended at the peril of his life. However, as Desmond Tutu was fond of referencing, in the *kairos* tradition of liberation theology, 'We must read the signs of the times' (Matthew 16.3). For some who attended, the signs were bodily stigmata. But read them they did, and that reading constituted the Event.

The Purpose and Context

My purpose was intellectual. An ideological formation, the new South Africa, was taking shape under our eyes, and it deserved scrutiny. My purpose in setting up the Event stemmed also from the intellectual duty I felt, as Dean of Arts, to open up disciplinary enquiry. I imagined the Event as an opportunity to synchronize the *aggiornamento* of the country's laws with scholarly innovation.

Regarding the wider institutional context, as is often the case in similar postcolonial societies, intellectual life took place in and around the universities. No intellectual life took place outside. However, some campuses were, under apartheid, the locale for theorizing white supremacy as much as they were the hotbed of Black, and white, resistance to apartheid. Outside campuses, unlike in Continental Europe, or Latin America where intellectual life evolves often in its own sphere, there was no autonomous praxis for intellectual, scholarly debate. It is still the case.

For the purpose of the Event such closure was paradoxically beneficial: it ensured support from within and outside UCT, for reasons of public prestige and political identity. The Event received support from a host of organizations or programmes, academic or learned societies, gay and lesbian, in France, Australia, the Netherlands and the United States, and a prominent South African publisher not immediately known then for its progressive mindset printed the programme booklet, for free. It features a Q, hand drawn with gusto by South African poet Joan Hambidge. The UCT Vice-Chancellor placed the Event under his aegis, which helped secure the help of grant committees. In short, the Event illustrated the ability of a university, under an enlightened leadership, to seize an opportunity to help expand scholarship, much against resistance of departments that, at least then, were focussed on their sacrosanct, and haphazard, 'canon', an elegant word to qualify tunnel vision. Gay colleagues privately scoffed at the project, either because it smacked of trendy 'theory', or simply because being 'out' was still seen as somewhat vulgar for academics.

This rallying secured, however, the participation of some of the sharpest minds in the developing field of what was already labelled 'queer studies'.

The localization of the Event carried a certain ethos. UCT, an English-speaking university was then, by tradition and mission, and in a utilitarian sense of strategic foresight which tempered the ideological gesturing of a dissident institution. Her hallmark was the obstinate rejection of the effects of apartheid legislation in tertiary education. It was South Africa's, and arguably Africa's, most advanced university in terms of scholarship and science, in spite of years of relative isolation and thanks to a disorderly boycott. Afrikaans-speaking universities had been, by contrast and true to their own tradition and mission, the harbingers and propagators of apartheid ideology. One exception was the University of the Western Cape (UWC), a creation of apartheid to cater for Coloured students who, incidentally, mostly had Afrikaans as an L1. Finally, geography was a factor: Cape Town was, and is, the legislative capital of the country, which lends any intellectual show of ideas an edge, and guarantees exposure, especially before the development of the internet.

However, the intention of this academic gathering, the first ever in Africa and, to date, the only one of such scope, was misunderstood.

The Event highlighted three 'taken for granted', as we call them in critical rhetoric, that is three sets of public tropes with regard to what it is to deliberate. I call them 'misunderstandings', with the full force of the prefix 'mis', that is not merely not-understanding, but missing the point as to why one refuses to understand, or disdains to apprehend.

This First Misunderstanding Had to Do with the Academic Idiom of Apartheid Intellectual Life

For a brief moment we had feared that a perception would cohere, that the Event was to be 'another liberal' academic venture, with the usual result that Afrikaner academics would stay away, partly due to their often staunch Calvinist values, or due to a fear of reprisal by their own institutions (and denial of travel funding to attend), or their apprehension of being turned into objects of opprobrium or ridicule by political opponents on their campuses.

This turned out not to be the case. One reason for this fortunate situation was that some Afrikaans universities had in fact been at the forefront of the rise of 'French Theory' in a few academic circles. A detailed history of censorship of the intelligentsia under apartheid remains to be written: repression was not monolithic and many Afrikaans university lecturers were not monolingual, unlike most English-speaking academics. Quite a few had competence in foreign languages, and local African languages too. They read widely. For some two decades some Afrikaans university departments had innovated by running courses that exposed students to the latest theoretical trends in Continental Europe (structuralism, narratology, semiotics, the works of Barthes, Lyotard, Foucault, Habermas) whilst English universities remained wilfully ignorant of such intellectual developments, or brushed them off, while counting iambic pentameters. One exception was the Comparative Literature programme of Reingard Nethersole at the English-speaking University of the Witwatersrand, the erstwhile College of Mines. That pioneering programme was closed down later. Of course, isolated, English-speaking academics read Theory but isolated they remained. I recall my colleague, the future Nobel laureate J. M. Coetzee, drawing on a blackboard the well-known paradigmatic and syntagmatic axes, with a desultory look on his face. That was as far as Theory was tolerated. From the mid-1990s the intellectual landscape slowly changed.

In this regard the Event eroded the frontiers between innovative Afrikaans academics engaged in theory, and their English-speaking colleagues who ruminated in isolation, if not ostracism. The Event helped erase some of the misunderstandings, prejudices really, fed by ideology and politics. It brought together promising young, public intellectuals who, in the context just described, were lacking a commonality of speech. Let me name just four: Vasu Reddy, who later created a Deconstruction Studies Centre at UWC, and brought Jacques Derrida to the Cape. John Higgins who, single-handedly, introduced Continental criticism to generations of UCT students. Pierre de Vos, whose performance at the conference was his first public lecture on gay rights – an academic coming out, that took some courage. He is now South Africa's leading constitutionalist. Aubrey Theron, from the staunchly Afrikaans University of Pretoria, delivered a criminologist groundbreaking analysis of anti-gay hate crimes.

From a different angle, in terms of intellectual breadth, the Event provided for the first time a platform for dissident views, inspired by Continental philosophy, stemming from Theory and not solely embedded, as was the case then (when it happened), in the social sciences. The revolution that had taken place in Europe a good twenty years before, whereby sociology lost its reigning status, began to happen, in South Africa, at the Event. In fact, except for a couple of papers, in themselves laden with pertinent views, ideological sociology was markedly absent. The 'scientificity' of sociology had been in favour with the technocratic apartheid regime, while progressive sociologists, mostly English-speaking, responded in kind – but often in complete ignorance of the way in which the works of Bourdieu, for instance, had displaced sociological discourse. A history of the strategies of subversion developed within sociological disciplines considered as 'scientific' by South African officialdom at the time, is also still to be written. Again, it is in such an intellectual context and its tensions that the Event located itself. The Event was an occasion for showcasing new discourses about 'the social' and 'the political', and to project from within the *langue* of academia a new *parole*, to put it in Saussurean terms.

Taking all that into consideration, the opening keynote, delivered by the renowned American language ethnographer William L. Leap, hit the right chord: a foremost anthropologist, author of *Words' Out: Gay Men's English* (1996), and leading figure of the annual Lavender Linguistics Conference, Leap was able to show how various strands of spatial anthropology, discourse analysis and social performances of gay *parole*, harnessing traditional field questionnaires, could form a unitary object for queer studies. It was, for many attendees, a eureka moment.

To summarize, the Event was climacteric: Theory moved to the fore and exploded an intellectually depleted academic culture, bringing concepts and methods that are now hackneyed, or reduced to platitudes, but were then innovative, revolutionary even. A quick look at the Event booklet is revealing of the scope of the proceedings.

The Second Misunderstanding Was About the Deliberative Nature of the Event

In 1995 South Africa was still immersed in a strong, pervasive, liberation era praxis, whereby activists often took the initiative or leadership of public debates, asserting their prerogative. They understood public deliberation as an appendage to 'the struggle' against apartheid while, after the regime change, the concept of 'deliberation' itself was framed by 'constitutional development', regulated processes for 'public participation' preceding the drafting of legislation. Activism then, in relation to gay rights (as it was commonly called), hinged on AIDS and marriage rights. The perception activists had of the Event carried a twofold questioning.

First, how could a university initiative evolve outside the precinct of activism, without first deferring to the latter's self-appointed leadership whose credentials were activism itself. This was, at best, a tautological self-determination, activism never being defined beyond being activism. Second, why was the Event not pinned on the two points of their own compass, over the map, as it were, of their political territory: AIDS, marriage rights? Theirs was a reluctance to imagine and a resistance to accept, that public deliberation was being reshaped in new rhetorical ways, detached and independent from the stolid Marxist-Leninist concept of centralized debate, which activists had employed successfully up to then, and wanted to deploy after the regime change. In critical rhetoric such sustenance of a rhetorical model for agency, after the ground has shifted, is quite well-known. It consists in preserving rhetorical modes that initially facilitated access to power, and hereafter to try and keep them alive, this time through what Althusser called 'repressive apparatuses' (controlling education, for instance, and in this case, an attempt to control an intellectual event). Thus, activists misread the purpose of the Event. In terms of ethos, it appears that the 'hero-ization' of anti-apartheid activism, that was not exempt from a low-intensity form of personality cult, found it difficult to inscribe itself in an open field of equal voices, where all qualified voices had a fair share, and norms and forms of debate were thrown open. The Event's deliberative ambit was not predetermined by a set political agenda and the qualification to address gay and lesbian concepts was intellectually mediated by a wide range of ideas and methods.

In the end, among the some 300 contacts that were made in preparing the Event, activists did attend. Activists may have discovered what is meant by 'deliberative' practices, a different form of activism rooted in the actioning of concepts and methods. They misunderstood what the Event was performing. It was performing liberating discourse.

By contrast, gay and lesbian students' societies from several universities (Namibia, South Africa, Zimbabwe) sent speakers, and this was not an easy personal undertaking. Nor was it for speakers from Black universities. Equally important, a Constitutional Court judge, Edwin Cameron, chaired a key session. A jurist-activist and courageous public intellectual he had broken ranks with the stale *esprit de corps* of the judiciary, still laden with apartheid tropes, to rise to the apex court, a defender of equality of rights for all citizens under the law and within the rule of law, and a prominent figure in the AIDS debate. He did not misunderstand what the Event was meant to perform: opening up public deliberation by having it translate for, and transfer to, South Africa, concepts and ideas elaborated outside the apartheid autarky. The Event truly was a 'transition' of sorts, towards freeing debate.

The Third Misunderstanding Was Related to Commodification

The 1990s discovered the 'pink dollar'. Gays and gay goods were now becoming marketable. In a way the commodification of lifestyles is, as long as one accepts capitalism, a natural thing to happen, and Mandela's government, in spite of its communist roots, embraced it wholeheartedly: capitalist commodification brought wider acceptance of new lifestyles, created apposite goods, secured also, through goods, acceptance of people who, until then were seen as exotic consumers. South Africa moved overnight from a closed economy to an open one. However, the downside was the intrusion of gay start-ups and entrepreneurship that saw the Event as an 'opportunity'. It was an interesting misunderstanding.

The Event was not meant to attract market-related funding, to create opportunities for business, to be, in other words, an occasion for making 'pink money'. The economic activists were not concerned primarily with the intellectual purpose of the Event, but with its derivative products: for example, we were presented with an unprecedented budget to host an exhibition, we were coaxed into support for a film festival. Those events took place as 'off events', interesting in themselves and offering to the numerous international participants a cross-section of gay and lesbian art and culture. How they related to the deliberative pursuit of the Event remains unproven – though perhaps not for the art exhibition. It falls outside of the scope of this chapter, again, a study of art and entrepreneurship at the time from the angle of the 'falsification' of liberation art and its discourse remains to be investigated.

Gay and Lesbian entrepreneurs conceived public deliberation as merchandise and a commodity, a neat case of 'linguistification' as per Groys' (2009) analysis of postcapitalist language in the *Communist Postscript*.

Yet, one artistic event stood out for its generosity and topicality, and refusal of commodification: award-winning young director Geoff Hyland staged a play, produced for the Event, *Deathwatch*, drawn by Jean Genet from his *Our Lady of the Flowers*, with a cast of senior drama school students, and in tandem with one of South Africa's most controversial and successful producers, Marthinus Basson. In its stark eloquence the play itself, which was preceded by a lecture by Genet scholar Gisèle Child-Olmsted (from Loyola, Baltimore), displayed deliberative scholarship as performance. As it took place at one of the University theatres, in the heart of Cape Town, it focalized public attention on the Event.

Rhetorical Stakes and the Legacy

Notwithstanding the three misunderstandings mentioned, whilst they were revealing of a naïve or ideological or venal conception of public deliberation and intellectual transaction, the Event produced what Hegelians call an *Aufhebung*: it produced, from misunderstandings, a new state of discourse, what, in critical rhetoric, is called '*stasis*' (hence 'state', 'standing').

Regarding the first misunderstanding, the presumed lack of common deliberative ground amongst academics from different sides of the linguistic, and cultural, divide, proved to be non-existent. Speakers from Afrikaans universities, historically Black universities and traditionally English universities proved, from the first session, that they spoke a common language. Our own preconception that outsiders, from America, France, Mauritius and Australia, would play the role of rhetorical shamans, as it were, turned out be naïve. A shared idiom existed, and foreign participants, from academic environments where 'gay studies' were already fully fledged (if under suspicion or attack), fulfilled a performative function: they operated, as we say in rhetoric studies, epideictically, that is their papers, as scholarly as they were, served to extol concepts and methods, to address values and frame them in analytical discourses. Foreign speakers displayed gay studies, and played a key role: Bill Leap, already mentioned, Charles Nero of Bates College, William Spurlin then of Columbia, Wolfram Hartmann from Namibia, amongst others, were outsiders to the academic Afrikaans/English divide and *au fait* with the latest development in G&L studies. This *Aufhebung* was the most rewarding of all.

The speakers cited above were pivotal in building a common ground for intellectual debates.

In the second case, the political activists' misunderstanding of public debate as solely an extension of grassroots action, was confronted with different rhetorical practices based on thoughtful exchange of opinions, and not the apologetics of positions. In the third instance, the tension between our project, to debate, and the prevalent ideology of 'communicating' gay commodities, or gay commodities as communication, eventually taking over the need to have ideas, was left unresolved as a novel form of capital accumulation.

To sum up, the Event worked from a different deliberative, 'rhetorical', angle. The articulation of the Event with rhetoric was not fortuitous, and this held true in two respects.

First, until the protection of gay and lesbian citizens was enshrined in the new constitution of South Africa (May 1996, a year after the Event) gay rights were a point of great contention between the African National Congress (ANC) and the Democratic Party, on the one side, and African Christians and the National Party (ex-apartheid party), on the other. First mentioned in the interim constitution of 1993, non-discrimination on the basis of sexual orientation saw some of the speakers at the Event, Judge Cameron, publicist Mark Gevisser, lawyer Kevan Botha and Colonel Juan Nel of the South African Police, bring to the proceedings a sense of legal urgency, and an awareness of arguments that were exchanged in public fora, in order to secure the sexual orientation provision in the Bill of Rights – a first in any constitution worldwide.

This convergence of deliberation, outside and within the Event, was, possibly, an eye opener for foreign speakers and participants: they witnessed public deliberation and academic deliberation converge, 'rhetoric' in its primordial sense.

Second, a year before the Event another breakthrough conference had taken place: the First African Symposium on Rhetoric, which drew a large international cohort of rhetoricians, who did not think of themselves as intersectional in their practice, but as merely doing what the new tradition in rhetoric set in motion in the 1970s had done, outside the limited confines of literature: to study persuasion as tools of power, and reclaim Aristotle as the mainstay of their project. Not Aristotle the logician dear to English philosophy, not the skeletal Aristotle still enjoying some currency in literary analysis, but the Aristotle who had devised, in one single daring gesture, a framework for understanding social deliberation, harnessing emotional reasoning and deploying practical justice.

Some of the international speakers at the Symposium on Rhetoric did return for the Event, applying critical rhetoric to gay studies, and agitating successfully, and against opposition, for 'queer rhetoric' be included, for the first time, in the programme of the International Society for the History of Rhetoric world congress held in Canada in 1997. Anthropologist Bill Leap, again, returned as a fellow of the Centre for Rhetoric Studies, on pioneering research in queer discourse. The *Encyclopedia of Rhetoric* (2001) went further and reflected this expansion of scholarship by including a detailed entry on queer rhetoric (Sloane 2011). At the same time, UCT introduced a course on gay and lesbian studies, within an innovative cross-departmental major in Theory of Literature, where queer studies, under the aegis of Joan Hambidge, cohered with offerings that tried to prise open the departmental, inward-looking straightjacket of disciplinary foreclosure. The emancipation of queer studies from sociology or psychology held hands with the emancipation of rhetoric from outdated mindsets. In June 1996 one delegate at the Event, Chris Dunton (then at the National University of Lesotho), authored with Mai Palmberg *Human Rights and Homosexuality in Southern Africa* (1996), and with Ingrid Fandrych subsequently convened in Lesotho the biannual Conference of Rhetoric in Southern Africa.

The Event, and the Symposium, set in motion a series of smaller international conferences in South Africa, on themes such as Truth, Dissent, Rights, Diversity. Collaborative networks sprung up in Miami (with Ralph Heyndels, the Barthesian scholar, who organized cross-cultural events over the years in South Beach); in Australia – some of the participants to the Event contributed articles to the Routledge twin volumes *Who's Who in Gay and Lesbian History* (2001) *Who's Who in Contemporary Gay and Lesbian History* (2002) co-edited by Robert Aldrich (who spoke at the Event) and Garry Wotherspoon; in Holland, the journal *Thamyris* (1997); in France, the Foucaldian *Cahiers Gay-Kitsch-Camp* of R. Mendès-Leité (present at the Event), also specialized in publishing nineteenth- and early twentieth-century rare texts on the subject matter. And *Rue Descartes*, the journal of the Collège international de philosophie (1997), founded by Derrida. These are some examples of the Event's intellectual legacy.

The Event had also an immediate impact in the media, amongst gay organizations and various international ventures at the time, such as the Magnus F. Hirschfeld Centre for Human Rights, the *Zeitschrift für Religion and Homosexualität*, the *Harvard Gay and Lesbian Review*, inter alia. The Event was not an ivory tower: a formal letter of protest was sent to the Director of the United Nations Information Centre in Harare questioning an award made in recognition for her 'efforts in promoting human rights' [*sic*!] to a virulent opponent of gays and lesbians in Zimbabwe.

The long-term legacy of the Event, beside the academic developments I have mentioned above, is difficult to determine. As a scholar I do not believe in perennial academic concerns, but, clearly, the 1995 First Colloquium of Gay and Lesbian Studies in Southern Africa did open tracks for young academics, has left memorial traces and found its place in the development of a field of studies which at the time was at best a conundrum, at worst an *aporia*.

One singular disappointment was a protracted exchange with a leading South African theory journal, which resulted in a failure to publish the transactions of the Event. The handling of the process was disingenuous, but it cast a harsh light, in my view and I believe, that of Marianne de Jong, my co-editor, on the innate and prejudiced resistance of some South African academics to a field of studies taking shape under their own eyes. The universities' divide mentioned earlier on, that had been placed under erasure by the intellectual acumen, and courage, of speakers from English, Afrikaans, Black, Coloured, Indian, white universities (I use those terms because they meant something specific then), surged forth, with a vengeance. After two years of being subjected to obfuscation, De Jong and I withdrew the planned volume. This book, today, would be an extraordinary testimonial to the state of gay and lesbian studies, across a broad spectrum of South African scholarship, at a crucial moment in the intellectual life of this country, and Southern Africa; a lost memorial to different, yet congruent to the *kairos* of liberation theology, 'Signs of the Time'. Let us recall that in the Bible a telling sign of the times to be fulfilled is … a rainbow.

References

Aldrich, Robert and Garry Wotherspoon, eds. 2001. *Who's Who in Gay and Lesbian History*. London: Routledge.

Aldrich, Robert and Garry Wotherspoon, eds. 2002. *Who's Who in Contemporary Gay and Lesbian History*. London: Routledge.

Dunton, Chris and Mai Palmberg. 1996. *Human Rights and Homosexuality in Southern Africa*. Uppsala: Nordiska Afrikainstitutet.

Groys, Boris. 2009. *The Communist Postscript*. London: Verso.

Leap, William L. 1996. *Words' Out: Gay Men's English*. Minneapolis: University of Minnesota Press.

Sloane, Thomas O., ed. 2001. 'Queer Rhetoric', in *Encyclopedia of Rhetoric*, 649–54. New York: Oxford University Press.

Chapter 11

TRANSAFRICA: JOAN HAMBIDGE TO CHANTAL ZABUS

Joan Hambidge

To: Chantal Zabus
From: Joan Hambidge

Thanks for your invitation to participate in your book *TransAfrica: The Languages of Postqueerness*. I am uncertain how to address the 'languages of postqueerness' and have decided to write an email to you instead of writing a theoretical analysis. A blend between theory and practice: theorist versus poet.

Gender has been my basic field of interest and when we met at the ICLA (International Comparative Literature Association) conference in Korea in 2010, I was always impressed with your awareness of how problematic binaries are. Then we met in Paris a year later for a seminar on postcolonialisms at the Sorbonne. An inspiring conference on 'the empire writes back', organized by you.[1]

After this a reunion in Vienna in 2016, Freud's city and currently a book on Freud (and Women) is another project with Jane Gallop, Shoshana Felman, Luce Irigaray, Julia Kristeva, et al. and their ventures in psychoanalysis.

Forty Easy Steps to Remembering

In 2000, I completed a second PhD on gender at the University of Cape Town: 'Gender-konstruksies in die Afrikaanse letterkunde: 'n Ondersoek in kultuurstudies, literêre teorie en kreatiewe skryfwerk.'

A blend between culture studies, literary theory and creative writing. Mostly researched in 1999 at Harvard University during a sabbatical.

My poetry reflects a gender awareness. The poems are primarily written in Afrikaans and mostly translated by myself. Here are some of them.

One night-stand

The scène is always the same:
intro-drink-seduction-bed.

The next day constantly a mind fuck:
guilt-silence-longing
and regret.

To fall in love is like placing a bet.[2]

Writing as fucking

To write a sapphic verse
close before midnight
leads to many problems
(ignoring 'vicious mathematics' …)
to find a non-off-beat image
for our for(ever)ness:
the pen is mightier than the sword:
does not work; too phallic, sexist,
sounds like penis-envy …
when two lips speak together:
does not reveal much of our softness/tenderness;
rubyfruit jungle:
is false, fruit-
less romanticism;
dark labyrinth:
too desperately literary;
bitter lemons:
cute poetic cunninglingus.

To write a (love)poem
like this, creates
coldness/logic/guilt
about that which merely is.[3]

T. M. T. ♡ *T. B. M. G*

There's more to love
than patterns: boy meets girl,
buying a Sterns ring etcetera.
There's more to love

than boy meets girl.
Both of us refuse to accept this.
Oh, meeting at first (call it exposition)
always rather briskly spills over
into the highlight.
(i.e. climax or
coming without qualms). Both trapped.
Who wants to hazard a further guess?
So what goes up, must come down.
Ecstasy only lasts as long as flowers
give off scent
or the sweet deceit of romance.
Dénouement: vide the glossary, an 'unknotting
of complication'. A discovery that passion
– by one? or both? – is running out.
Our dénouement: discovery of your deceit.
There's more to love
than girl meets girl,
investments in love, togetherness, understanding.
There is more to love
than a beginning, middle or an end.
But you (and I) are caught up in symbols.[4]

Tierra del Fuego

In the sauna of the PanAmericano hotel
the fires of remembrance burn, an enduring hell.

In the sauna of the PanAmericano hotel
I experience loss and there's no one to tell

In the sauna of the PanAmericano hotel
I sit alone, *para solo*, only with a towel.

In the sauna of the PanAmericano hotel
I count my lovers from paradiso back to hell.

In the sauna of the PanAmericano hotel
I realise in this art it is only loss and tell.

In the sauna of the PanAmericano hotel
everything becomes Tierra del Fuego, a lasting hell.[5]

The original versions are anthologized in Joan Hambidge, *Die Buigsaamheid van Verdriet* (2004).

Look Back in Anger (John Osborne, 1956)

My youth was maimed by depression: side-lined, Othered, a voiceless person.

Being gay in the 1970s in South Africa was a non-event. You had no voice, no friends and no support system.

I became openly gay and vocal as a young student at Stellenbosch University because of the abuse in my youth.

I started wearing male clothes: bow-ties with male blazers. The freedom was to be male and aggressive. As an open woman-identified-writer I stated boldly:

   I don't only write gay-texts – I am also gay.

A long trajectory of criticism and defiance until 1994, when South Africa embraced a new constitution with gay rights.

Finally, the nom-du-père was overturned and same-sex marriages permissible.

The Afrikaans Church (like the Catholic Church in your country) with the community of elders had to face a new reality.

In the new timeline (as of 2023) gender positions fluctuate. The binaries are constantly deconstructed.

I endorse **LGBTQIA+**

We experience transgender operations or so-called gender reassignment opens a new brave world.

I have four friends with children confronting their biological sex and changing into the real person.

Come Back to the 5 & Dime, Jimmy Dean, Jimmy Dean (Robert Altman's film from 1982 based on Ed Graczyk's 1976 play) analyses the impact of a gender change.

The new gender awareness with yet another politicised position: maybe a New Stonewall?

New issues arrive: is it possible and permissible for a straight actor to portray a gay character?

Is it correct for Cate Blanchett to be *Tár* in Todd Field's film?

I think her portrayal of the lesbian director is stupendous. Is it permissible for straight male translators to translate a lesbian poet? I would think the best poet and translator should be appointed. Douglas Reid Skinner, Johann de Lange and Charl J. F. Cilliers translated my poetry. One gay. The other two hetero males.

Vladímír (2022) by Julia May Jonas deconstructs gender roles. The anonymous narrator objectifies her male colleague. The male gaze is now presented as a female gaze. The character, a lecturer, residing on an American campus addresses all the gender stereotypes and simultaneously overturns these constructs: sexual harassment, power struggles, same-sex relations.

A riveting novel for me as my campus novel *Stasies/Stations* will be published later this year.

And now? Maintenant?

You as a Belgian-born theorist impressed me with your understanding of Afrikaans.

I commenced my email to you with poetry and I will end with a poem:

Fisting-as-écriture

Moes deur baie pyn
om mens te word,
artikuleer ons digter
op die Dam; moes deur baie veg
om self te vind,
van hier tot in verre plekke
terug in die gevegsone van die digkuns
immers 'n binne-geweld wat beskut
teen buite-geweld:
ek-sing-oor-die-liggaam
se oorskot, ek lees
Eve Kosofsky Sedgwick
se *Die weer in Proust*
en elders, ja elders
is dit altyd mooi weer en warm
vir hulle gebore met regte
en voorregte,
nooit weet hoe
dit voel as jou tong

as kind uitgesny is.
Uitgeskuif, weggedruk.
Hierom die vuis-in-die-lug,
daarom die woede
by ons, 'n myn – 'n dyn,
die Afwykendes, die derde seks,
die transgender, die deviant,
smagtende na stilte
na hierdie oorlog, 'n El-Alamein.

I song the body electric; I sing the body in double speak …

With warm regards,
Joan
Pronouns: she/they
Emotionally: transgender
Fellow at the University of Cape Town

Notes

1   The 2014 Conference proceedings, celebrating the 25th Anniversary of the 1989 publication of Bill Ashcroft, Gareth Griffiths and Helen Tiffin's *The Empire Writes Back*, were published in Zabus 2015.
2   'One night-stand' from *Tachycardia* (Cape Town: JutaLit, 1990). Translated by: Joan Hambidge.
3   'Writing as fucking' from *Interne Verhuising* (Johannesburg: Perskor, 1995). Translated by Joan Hambidge.
4   'T. M. T. B. M. G', from *Kriptonemie* (Cape Town: Human & Rousseau, 1989). Translated by Johann de Lange.
5   'Tierra del Fuego', from *Verdraaide Raaisels* (Cape Town: Human & Rousseau, 1990). Translated by Joan Hambidge.

References

Hambidge, Joan. 2000. 'Gender-konstruksies in die Afrikaanse letterkunde: 'n Ondersoek in kultuurstudies, literêre teorie en kreatiewe skryfwerk'. PhD diss. University of Cape Town.
Hambidge, Joan. 2004. *Die Buigsaamheid van Verdriet*. Pretoria: Protea Boekhuis.
Jonas, Julia May. 2022. *Vladimir*. New York: Picador.
Zabus, Chantal, ed. 2015. *The Future of Postcolonial Studies*. London and New York: Routledge.

Chapter 12

Ó: AN ESSAY ON PRONOUNS AND POWER AMONG THE YORÙBÁ

Logan February

Prologue: What's in a Pronoun?

When Chris Dunton asked, in an interview, about the basis of my identifying with 'they/them' pronouns, my response – which may have been a little vague and cheeky – was, 'My main basis for this choice is really my native Yorùbá, in which the third-person pronouns and their plural forms are gender-neutral and apply to individuals in certain contexts.' In this chapter, I will try to unravel a sense of that sociolinguistic phenomenon, of which my current understanding itself remains somewhat vague. Yet, vagueness may be exactly what most interests me about pronouns.

Although I prefer to be described using 'they/them' pronouns, my identification with the pronouns is only marginally rooted. I do not say this to diminish the great efforts of sociolinguistic change or the conviction of the many people for whom those pronouns may feel essential or self-defining. My own preference of the pronouns is designated as more of a linguistic solidarity than a passionate personal cause. The distance in my relation to 'they/them' is perhaps due to this particular debate being situated within the English language, where the gender-neutral third-person-singular pronoun is not naturally inherent or generally agreed upon – thus prompting an effort within a radical (queer) collective to repurpose the neutralized third-person plural pronouns to function as gender-neutral third-person singulars. I find the effort necessary, but not quite integral to my own sense of identity.

The (Gender) Neutral Yorùbá

In my native Yorùbá language, the third-person plural pronoun is inherently capable of performing that singular function, without contest or confusion. Additionally, the language has no pronouns with any clear connotations of gender. As Augustine Agwuele describes in a survey of pronoun usage in Yorùbá, '[i]ndefinite pronouns of passive constructions by definition are silent about the identity of their subject' (2012: 195). I am myself no linguist, and I have no culturally deterministic speculations to offer. What I do know is that having grown into adulthood in a culture whose language deprioritizes gender, at least in pronominal functions, gives some room for me to understand my gender as its own sovereign and fluid identity, not meant to be summarized by a pronoun and not necessary to every reference to myself as a third-person subject. I understand the privilege of having such language in this age when the specifics of gender-queer identity continue to be hotly debated and increasingly policed. My own sense of pronouns fundamentally sees their imprecise mechanism as a casting of multifunctional, reusable and evermore elastic nets. For me, the ideal pronouns leave enough room for an understanding between speakers to create the latent meanings they share, so the notion of their being 'silent' about my identity is not unappealing.

The singular and plural third-person subject pronouns in Yorùbá are *ó* and *wón*, respectively. Their functional overlap occurs when any element of hierarchy is present in the context of the utterance, with the number/plural feature of *wón* becoming neutralized in service of recognizing the position of the superior. Thus, in an honorific capacity, the third-person plural will take on a singular function (replacing *ó*) in the standard, most common dialects of Yorùbá. A young child reporting back from a market errand, for instance, might be (speculatively) translated into English as saying: '*They* asked me to buy oranges, but *they* did not say how many.' In such a case, 'they' (*wón*) would very likely refer to a single older person who has sent the child on such an errand. It should be noted that, despite the absence of gender markers in much of the Yorùbá language, the contemporary culture still maintains a largely binary male-female world-view – the child in the above example is probably fully aware of the sex or gender of the superior subject they refer to. This use of the singular 'they' is not necessarily in reference to a gender-queer adult – in fact, the child in question would most likely have meant something closer to 'he' or 'she' even though the sense of them is neutralized in the utterance. Rather, the singularization of this 'they' is associated with the individual's higher social place or power. Describing the fundamentals in recognizing the Yorùbá social hierarchies, Michael A. Abíódun writes:

> Bases for power in the social setting of the Yorùbá include age, wealth, education, institutionalised role in the state, etc. Anyone who holds power as defined above is considered superior while others are subordinate. The superior, because he has access to power, can bring to bear on the subordinate and his conduct various methods of social control that include instruction, advice, persuasion, reward and punishment (Fadipe [, *The Sociology of the Yorùbá*,] 1970). In actual fact, the superior is looked upon with awe, and is treated with deference.
>
> (Abíódun 1992: 105)

Abíódun further contextualizes the non-reciprocity in the honorific use of *wón*, since it is most often based on unidirectional forms of power. However, the non-reciprocity is not fully inherent, as the third-person plural may work reciprocally as an honorific singular when the speaker and their referred subject share relatively equal positions, such as being age-mates. The show of mutual recognition of equality is a social courtesy, which is another highly cherished form of etiquette.

My Age, My Language

I have a fraught relationship with the honorific third-person singular 'they' and this hierarchical basis of social power in Yorùbá culture. Although I share the essential value of a society that privileges the elderly and whatever wisdom comes with age, I am also a younger sibling to three older ones, with the smallest age difference being a six-year gap. Any chance of mutual courtesies or reciprocal respect was already forfeited in the context I was born into. Whereas my native culture privileges me to take an unspecified gender for granted within the bounds of language, I am conversely burdened with complexes and traumas rooted in an ageist upbringing which disempowered me as a young person in larger society, and relatively, even in my own family. To begin with, the traditional Yorùbá language has no specific words for 'brother' or 'sister'. Rather, the words for siblings refer to older (*ègbón*) and younger (*àbúrò*) ones – where the specification of their genders is relevant, the words for male or female are added as qualifiers. As such, instead of having gender as a core categorization in my upbringing, my age and position in the birth-order were of great essence in the assignment of my place, what respect was due to me, and what power I could claim and use. Suffice it to say, being an *àbúrò* to three elders, there was not a great amount of legitimate power at my disposal.

In instances like that of the earlier-mentioned child, the assignment of such errands and chores obviously would go towards the younger and/or less powerful members of the group, provided they are reasonably able to carry out the tasks. Such a norm might constitute a nuisance to the younger sibling who perceives themself being constantly relegated to positions of service and subordination with seemingly no logical reason besides birth order and age difference. Growing up, those inequalities of labour were a lesser inconvenience to me, compared to the deeper psychological effects of enduring that hierarchical bias, especially in cases of conflict resolution amongst siblings.

My adolescent experience as an *àbúrò* was tinged with hard feelings of censorship and silence. It was not uncommon for simple fraternal disagreements to escalate into heated altercations which would, in turn, be treated with the unilateral, respect-based reparations. I got used to going unheard, having my complaints dismissed in favour of the *ègbón*, almost by default. Protesting mistreatments put me in the wrong; it was expected that I apologize to my *ègbón* before I got a say. My word was easily superseded, never holding the requisite weight. To speak with passion or act in defence of myself could signal an unacceptable disrespect, provoking punitive and, at times, abusive consequences which were ultimately tolerated. 'In the social structure of each Yorùbá dialect community, power is not only recognised, it is revered' (Abiọdun 1992: 108).

It should be noted that the stratification of these values – social position, power, respectability – is not limited to the Yorùbá tradition alone. Across the cultures of Nigeria, respect for elders and superiors tends to be an enforced measure of etiquette and honourable upbringing. My first year of secondary school was spent at a military school, one of the Nigerian 'unity' schools (a project of large, government-subsidized comprehensive schools aimed at a postcolonial integration of the various national tribes by creating a kind of cultural melting pot). In my brief experience at that school, seniority served as the fundamental mechanism of social hierarchy. The inequalities were aggravated by an added emphasis on rank in the school's military setting. In fact, the many dimensions of social power were in full play amongst the students: pervasive bullying of underclass students by seniors in prefect positions; uneasy dynamics between students of various economic backgrounds and pedigree; even ethnicity-related tensions, despite those efforts to foster the contrary. I, unlike my older brothers, implemented a strategy to avoid spending my entire secondary education at that school, having perceived the layers of social norms that facilitated the indelible divides and dis-identifications between myself and them. Those alienations have taken considerable efforts to repair in the following years. A hierarchy of power grounded in sociolinguistic codes, in conjunction with formative influences of patriarchy and the military, is difficult to unlearn, heal from and transcend.

The Yorùbás do have an innate familiarity with – or at least, a sensitivity to – the broad burden of living in subordination and fear of external powers. One alternative usage of the third-person plural *wọn* relates to superstitious beliefs about unknown, malevolent forces of the spiritual and immanent worlds, notions which are widely common across religious groups, social classes and literacy levels. Used in this context, *wọn* refers to *àwọn ayé*, which might loosely translate into 'the world' or '*they* of the world', a Yorùbá sense of the evil eye, which may belong to an individual or a collective. Since this is one of the core beliefs informing the Yorùbá subject's relationship to destiny, prosperity and ill-will, much of the cultural values are designed around the avoidance of *àwọn ayé*, the containment of their influence, and the fortification of oneself (through ritual sacrifice or right living) from those attacks of 'the world'.

> *Wọn* in Yorùbá language use and thoughts reminds Yorùbá people of the lurking presence of the unknown. It forces them to pay attention to the power of the hidden, and consequently, the need to always be protected. Yorùbá people are constantly at war, they fight enemies in order to fulfill their destiny; they battle the world to wrestle from it a place of honour and dignity. [...] *Wọn* is the euphemism for these nefarious forces and enemies against which Yorùbá people contend.
>
> (Agwuele 2012: 200)

I highlight this as a loose parallel between the oppressive forces of this malefic 'they' and the power-based, honorific singular 'they' of Yorùbá social convention. Both represent categories which cannot be taken for granted by those at their mercy, the vulnerable outsiders and lessers; categories that may create a framework of respect often enforced through fear, intimidation and social pressure, with the lesser often being stripped of confidence and full agency. Just as dignity is only gained as a result of contention with 'the world' in traditional mystical conception, the honour of a lesser-status or younger individual in social settings must also be earned from gradual processes of recognition and rites of passage.

The Fugitive Sound of Ó

The Yorùbá norm of an honorific singular 'they' is, however, not dialectically universal. Sociolinguistic research explores the restricted spread of this particular pronoun. In the dialects of the Ondo, Owo and Oyi (an amalgamation of the Owe, Yagba and Ijumu dialects), as well as 'two languages that are genetically related to Yorùbá – Itsekiri and Igala' (Abiọdun 1992: 109), it is noted that the honorific feature of *wọ́n* is either absent or lost. The scholarship thus surmises that the honorific feature is possibly 'an innovation restricted to those dialects that display it' (109).

Further references include the review of Yorùbá oral literatures, which are considered 'a reliable source of linguistic research in a society where written literature is just developing' (Abiọdun 1992: 109), a rightful observation of the fact of Yorùbá only becoming a language of written script in the last 200 or so years. In oral literary artefacts such as the *oríkì* (poems of praise or mourning directly addressed to a subject) and *ẹsẹ̀ ifá* (narrative verses which make up the comprehensive corpus of literature in the Ifá belief system), as well as records of popular Yorùbá musicians, there are several instances in which the honorific subjects are referred to, *not* using the honorific third-person singular *wọ́n*, but the standard third-person singular pronoun *ó* (a gender-neutral equivalent of 'he/she/it'). These imply a potential for flexibility in the linguistic rules of social convention, suggesting that a symbolization of hierarchy may not always be universally applicable. It is also known that, informally, a superior or senior subject may be referred to using the standard, non-honorific singular *ó*, provided that they are absent from where the speaker is, and that no other enforcing entities are present. In this sense, the linguistic agency of the subordinate speaker is only policed and prescribed in social performance, not subjectively stripped from them.

Similar to the issue of a limited dialectal incidence of the honorific 'they' is the question of the pronouns' underlying form. Besides both being third-person pronouns, *ó* and *wọ́n* are similar in their sonic/tonal nature. So long as they occupy the subject position, both are pronounced as high-tone syllables, as opposed to low- or middle-tone sounds. Some scholars have argued that these third-person subject pronouns have no essentially specific form barring their high-toned identity. This is especially true in the case of the standard third-person-singular (3psg) *ó*, which is a distinct morpheme. In speech, it may not always present as *ó*, but in less generic dialects, with an *í* or *ú* sound, so long as the alternatives are also pronounced with the raised tone. Comparative and historical psycholinguistic scholar Boluwaji Oshodi reports:

> [T]he *ó* with a high tone is what writers like Bámgbóṣé ([*Fọnọlọjì àti gírámà Yorùbá,*] 1990) and Ọládèjì (['Àròkọ Awóbùlúyì,'] 2003) take to be the 3psg short subject pronoun in standard Yorùbá. Stahlke (['Pronouns and Islands in Yorùbá,'] 1974) on his own part believes the *ó* with a high tone is not the 3psg short subject pronoun but concluded that the 3psg short subject pronoun in standard Yorùbá has no specific form. Awóbùlúyì (['Aspects of Contemporary Standard Yorùbá in Dialectological Perspective,'] 1992, ['Arópọ̀-Orúkọ Kúkurú Ẹni Kẹta Ẹyo Aṣolùwà,'] 2001, and ['Ó kìí ṣe Arópò-Orúko nínú Èdè Yorùbá,'] 2006) supports the claim of Stahlke that the morpheme *ó* is not the 3psg subject pronoun in Yorùbá but opined that the 3psg short subject pronoun has as an underlying form which is always covert in standard Yorùbá but overt in some Yorùbá dialects.
>
> (Oshodi 2018: 4)

Another formal feature of *ó* is its versatile capacity to be elided in colloquial speech and writing, being typically assimilated into the last syllable of the noun phrase to which it refers. In this covert state, the high-tone syllable takes on the dynamic and syntactically essential role of linking a subject noun phrase and a verb phrase in the third person. Without a high-tone syllable succeeding it, the subject noun phrase can only relate to its neighbouring verb phrase in the form of a second-person address. In the scholarly controversy, it is further speculated that the high-tone syllable may function grammatically, in various dialects, not just as a third-person pronoun, but also as 'a tense and aspectual marker in Yorùbá' (Oshodi 2018: 8). As Oshodi's report concludes:

> the underlying form of this morpheme is simply a High tone (bearing in mind that the high tone is the most restricted of the three tones in standard Yorùbá) which is then supported by default vowel features in most cases [*í*] as a matter of abstract form which is irregular and dialect specific but which fails to show up overtly in this position in standard Yorùbá due the fact that it is usually underspecified in certain positions in standard Yorùbá but shows up in Àkùngbá, Ọ̀wọ̀, Òṣogbo, Ìlọrin and Ọ̀yọ́, which are all established dialects of Yorùbá.
>
> (Oshodi 2018: 14)

These ephemeral, auditory qualities of *ó* are the source of my mystified curiosity about the pronoun, and perhaps, the indefiniteness of pronouns in general. Its covertness and dissolution into the surrounding language turn its sound into an invisible but necessary presence, a fluid marker of temporal relations. As a younger and, thus, less respectable member in a typical Yorùbá setting, this sense of the pronoun due to me – the standard, non-honorific third-person singular – allows a subversive identification with another, softer kind of power. *Ó* and its fugitive nature give me the gift of a negative space in which my being can remain multiple, ongoing, inconspicuous and inapprehensible. Though it may remain silent about the specifics of my identity, this pronoun is one that sings in its own subtle tone.

To conclude, I have composed a short 'Ode to the Lesser High Tone'.

Epilogue: Ode to the Lesser High Tone

Beginning at birth, which is *ó*,
    the hot plains of living, each one
ó, outstretched sea, azure
    assembly, the wave, the wind it is
wounded by. *Ó* is forest and pseudo
    -night, shaded green, lone starling.
And the O.O.O of object-oriented
    ontology is *ó*. A pregnant dog, of
course, and her foetus, each as *ó*
    as I could be. More than ever I am

ó in rooms I stand absent from.
    Any voice swimming as such I would
insist is *ó*. Can a name, in itself,
    be *ó*? A neighbour, a question,
a long-lost key – all keenly *ó*.
    Blood, *ó*, as any lost dialect.
Ó, the bomb, the borrowed land.
    Blame allotted in advance. A glance,
touch, *ó*, elided violence. A brother is,
    at the end of the day, another *ó*.

What grows away a younger heart
    must be *ó*, somehow, early on but
more so now. And the heart, I
    confess – *ó* – when I am quiet enough
to hear. Again, this voice, the humming *ó*.
    Sterling silver, salt, *ó* – forgiving
unnameable life, the lie of myself.
    Every last of these trinkets, every
secret song. *Ó*, my fortune, to be held
    in their ripe and obvious privacy.

References

Abiọdun, Michael A. 1992. 'On the restricted spread of the honorific pronoun in Yorùbá: a case study of Ondó, Òwò and Òyì dialects', *African Languages and Cultures* 5 (2):101–11. https://doi.org/10.1080/09544169208717749.

Agwuele, Augustine. 2012. 'Indexicality of wọ́n: Yorùbá language and culture', *Journal of African Cultural Studies* 4 (2): 195–207. https://doi.org/10.1080/13696815.2012.697310.
Oshodi, Boluwaji. 2018. 'The Underlying Form of the Third Person Singular Short Subject Pronoun in Standard Yorùbá: A Structural Motivation from some Yoruba Dialects', *Nordic Journal of African Studies* 27 (3): 1–17.

Chapter 13

AFTER QUEER, AFTER DECRIMINALIZATION:
BOTSWANA; JOHN MCALLISTER AND KATLEGO
K. KOLANYANE-KESUPILE IN CONVERSATION

John McAllister and Katlego K. Kolanyane-Kesupile

John McAllister and Katlego K. Kolanyane-Kesupile have been friends and colleagues for more than a decade and have collaborated on scholarly, activist and creative projects on African queer identities, cultures and activism going back to 2014. Their different social and educational backgrounds, ages and positionalities have added spice to their collaborations. John knows Botswana well, though from a relatively privileged white expat standpoint, having taught at the University of Botswana from 2000 to 2015. Katlego is based in Gaborone but travels frequently and widely as a much in demand speaker and consultant on trans and other issues.

Botswana is often framed by outsiders as a rare bastion of democracy and stability in Africa. Botswana's leaders and elites like to frame it this way too, and many ordinary Batswana pay at least lip service to this self-image; it connects readily with the traditional African ethic known in Botswana as *botho*.[1] John and Kat – and Botswana's activist community generally – know that this 'official' image does not correspond very well to the realities on the ground, especially for marginalized identities – ethnic minorities, rural communities, the poor (especially poor women), people living with HIV or AIDS and queer Batswana.

John retired to Canada in 2015, but he has followed developments in Botswana closely since then. He came to Botswana in 2000 after eleven years in Kenya, and first got involved in queer activism while writing and editing training manuals and public information materials for the Botswana Network on Ethics, Law, and HIV/ AIDS (BONELA). LeGaBiBo, Botswana's only LGBT rights organization at the time, having repeatedly been denied legal registration by the state, operated as a BONELA 'project', and John also began writing and editing for them.

In 2010, LeGaBiBo sued the Registrar of Societies in a case that would take six years to succeed. The case got only limited coverage, but it was the first time LGBT issues had got any serious public attention in Botswana since the scandalous Kanane criminal case in the 1990s.[2] Registration enabled LeGaBiBo to raise its own funds and expand its work beyond quiet lobbying within the Ministry of

Health around access to HIV/AIDS prevention and treatment programmes. Other organizations also started to come up, beginning with Rainbow Identity, the first trans rights group to be registered in Botswana, and a year later its director, Tshepo Ricki Kgositau, won her case to allow transgender Batswana to have the correct gender markers on identity documents.

Decriminalization was the movement's obvious next target, and in 2019, with assistance from the Southern African Litigation Centre (SALC), the so-called sodomy statutes were challenged on constitutional grounds as a violation of freedom of expression and denial of the right to privacy. In November 2021, after we succeeded in the High Court and the state appealed, the Court of Appeal, the final arbiter in Botswana, ruled in our favour, effectively nullifying the statutes.

While all this legal manoeuvring was in process, gradually opening up space for increasing public awareness of sexual and gender identities and rights, Katlego was establishing her public presence in Botswana as one of the first unambiguously 'out' queer and trans performers with her band Chasing Jaykb and as a solo artist. In 2013, after graduating from University of the Witwatersrand, Johannesburg, in Dramatic Arts, she founded Queer Shorts Showcase, the first explicitly queer-themed theatre festival in Botswana. After three instalments of the festival, Katlego went to Goldsmiths, University of London, as a Chevening Scholar, and returned to Botswana in 2018 with a master's in human rights, culture and social justice. Since then, she has become a well-known figure in national, regional and international forums as a presenter and consultant.

To prepare for their dialogue, John and Katlego developed a set of research questions to guide conversations with a cross-section of Setswana queer activists and artists around the impacts of decriminalization and the future of queer politics and culture in Botswana. The interviewees included pansexual, nonbinary, bisexual, gay, lesbian, queer and transgender persons. Katlego's conversations with them in May and June 2023, were recorded and transcribed. John and Katlego then sat down (online) for a conversation of their own on what the interviews suggested about the direction that queer and postqueer activism and culture may be heading in Botswana in the wake of decriminalization. What follows is a condensed text of that conversation edited down from a two-hour recording.

***

> John: It's now just short of two years since the Court of Appeal ruled that Botswana's old colonial homophobic laws were unconstitutional. The ruling, at one stroke, removed the main legal threat that had hung over queer Batswana, but has it had an effect beyond that yet? Since we're mainly concerned here with the queer community's perceptions, what did the interviews suggest, first of all, about how people's self-understandings of their queer identities are changing as a result of decriminalization?
>
> Katlego: There *have* been some significant changes in our self-understandings – and our hopes or expectations for the future, but we need to trace them back to before decriminalization, in particular to the decade or so leading

up to the court ruling. The registration case, which went on for six years, remember, and Ricki's case right after that got straight people in Botswana thinking, if not necessarily talking publicly, about queer rights for the first time in a sustained way. This was a point that several of the people I interviewed stressed. At a procedural level, I don't believe that Letsweletse [Motshidiemang][3] would have been able to sue the state if LeGaBiBo had not been registered. The first ruling in his case in 2019 was surprisingly swift, but when the State appealed – which we knew from inside sources was mainly for form's sake – that got the case onto the front and op-ed pages almost continuously for more than a year.

John: Yes, the Attorney General appealed because the government wanted to *look* like it opposed decriminalization. For years, both President Mogae [1998–2008] and President Khama [2008–18] had hinted that they did not personally oppose decriminalization but that 'the country' wasn't ready. After he was safely retired, Mogae even claimed he had secretly ordered the police not to enforce the law!

Katlego: By 'not ready' they meant they were scared that decriminalizing would lose them votes. Our ruling party,[4] as you know, depends heavily on conservative rural voters and, in the towns, on the traditionalists and religious right. *Those* voters are *still* not 'ready'.

John: As the recent protests showed.

Katlego: Yes, but the interesting thing is that there was no pushback after the ruling, only when politics came into it. Earlier this year, the government proposed a bill to formally repeal the sodomy statutes, and that's when some of the smaller Evangelical Christian churches organized protests and—

John: But didn't the Court of Appeal's ruling automatically nullify those statutes for once and all?

Katlego: Yes, of course. The bill, which for some reason the government didn't get around to for almost two years, just tidies up the statute book. It's copy editing; it doesn't change anything substantively. That didn't stop those churches from trying to rile people up, claiming the bill would open the 'floodgates of immorality', as one over-heated preacher put it.

John: (*laughs*) Did the protests get support apart from members of those small churches?

Katlego: Hardly at all. There was one poorly attended march in the centre of Gaborone and a couple of others elsewhere that got some sensational press coverage, but you know that Batswana generally shy away from street demos; they are not part of our harmonious self-image. In any case, the mainstream denominations all spoke out against the protests, and the whole thing was incited and funded by evangelical missionaries from the United States; it wasn't a local, organic reaction.

John: It gave the government cold feet though.

Katlego: Sadly, yes. Just a few days into the protests, the bill was 'withdrawn for consultations with stakeholders'.

John: Yet President Masisi met the LeGaBiBo leadership shortly after the
ruling and publicly pledged to respect it, saying he expected all Batswana to
do the same, and even told the queer community, 'You are fully embraced!'

Katlego: Sure, but the backtracking didn't surprise us. We've always had
leaders more concerned with advertising their tolerant, democratic
credentials than living up to them. All the same, we're not worried.
The ruling is final, and the proposed bill would have changed nothing.
The 'floodgates' cannot be closed. (*Laughs.*)

John: I'm more interested in the floodgates of queer activism and cultural
expression. Activists have been the boldest members of the queer
community, I suppose. Has decriminalization emboldened others to also
speak out or present more openly?

Katlego: The artist side of me can testify that there's been quite a remarkable
flowering of openly queer voices in the performing arts and the fashion
and photography scenes in the past couple of years. Some of these new
artists are getting popular with straight audiences too, young straight
audiences especially. For the moment anyway, decriminalization seems to
be having more of an effect on the cultural side than on activism as such.

John: Did you explore the reasons for this with the people you talked with?

Katlego: I did, and the consensus was that after decriminalization activism
needed to pause, in a sense, to strategize, have conversations with the
broader community, and develop more contacts and resources for
the way forward. I think we'll soon see some very interesting initiatives
in the media and education sectors in particular. Meanwhile the cultural
flowering is building confidence and pride in the queer community
generally and more acceptance among straight and 'questioning' youth.

John: So can one say that decriminalization is opening up space for the queer
community to move closer to the larger community?

Katlego: The fact that more conversations and interactions with other
Batswana are now able to take place, and *are* increasingly taking place,
suggests a movement towards a concept of 'communal development', for
lack of a better term.

John: And even perhaps a reorientation towards a more indigenous Setswana
concept of human rights as a matter of, I don't know, belonging?

Katlego: Not a 'return' to something from the past but more like an updating
of something that's always been there. Most of the activists I interviewed
were familiar with the term *postqueer*, only a few of the artists seemed to
be, but among those who knew the term, there was a lot of variety and
even uncertainty. What emerged as we talked was very interesting – a
definite tendency to associate *queer* with life before decriminalization
and *postqueer* with after, and specifically with the new space for self-
expression, with being able to present as who they really were, that
decriminalization has opened up. Everyone I interviewed who associated
postqueerness in Botswana to life after decriminalization also linked it to
freedom of expression.

John: So being able, thanks to decriminalization, to express their queerness was the consensus of what *post*queerness meant? For me, that's odd as well as interesting. I associate the term queer mainly with the new wave of activism in the West in the late 1980s and the 1990s, with a post-HIV/AIDS desire to 'reclaim' a word that had once been used to shut us up in order to speak openly about ourselves. It was part of the radicalization that the crisis phase of the HIV epidemic created. In Botswana, I don't think queer as a pejorative ever had any currency, and I didn't start hearing people use queer in a positive sense until around the time that activism started to go more public in the 2010s. Even then, it was used mainly by activists returning from 'SOGIE' workshops and other trainings outside the country. It didn't seem to reflect radicalization or 'acting up' but rather the idea that queer was a more useful umbrella term than the ever-expanding initialism.

Katlego: *Umbrella term* was, in fact, what several of those I asked called it. But yes, *queer* was an import from Western activism but hardly used here in the sense it had in the West, though I'm not sure how much of that 1980s radical sense, or the spirit behind it, has survived over there. Anyway, all our terminology for modern concepts of sexuality and gender identity are imports from the West. *Gay* and *LGBT* and *trans* all originated over there and like queer were all 'naturalized' by us. The difference with queer is that, in the West, it's a term associated with the coming of age of the movement, with the freedom to speak out and 'act up', while here it's a term that most of the people I interviewed associated more with the opposite, with a time of having to keep quiet and behave discreetly.

John: Even by the time I left Botswana towards the end of 2015, queer Batswana were still talked about, when talked about at all, in relation to HIV/AIDS and so-called MSM and WSW. The terms we used among ourselves were almost unmentionable in the media or in 'polite' company.

Katlego: Yes, and outside our own circles, though there was nothing like the persecution or violence in some other countries, we got by thanks mainly to the traditional Setswana respect for privacy and family reputation, which required 'looking the other way' and pretending not to know about things that would be embarrassing or socially disruptive if brought out in the open.

John: That traditional reticence or selective ignorance must have got a lot more difficult to sustain after 2016 as the movement diversified and the court cases started to get headlines.

Katlego: Yes, and that coincided with a strategy shift in activism from mainly talking with high-level stakeholders out of public view to moving into the public square, so to speak. Visibility and its possible consequences became a concern too. As the traditional avoidance strategies got harder to use, we started to hear or read more and more excuses like 'we don't have a problem with your lifestyle except when you try and shove it in our faces', all that kind of thing.

John: In Canada in the 1970s, decriminalization for a while actually seemed to increase homophobia. It certainly seemed to make the police, for example, more ferocious. Even by the late 1980s when I left for Kenya, they were seizing books and raiding bathhouses using other old sumptuary laws[5] that had not been repealed, but so far that kind of backlash doesn't seem to be happening in Botswana.

Katlego: I don't foresee that kind of backlash happening in Botswana. As you know, we have a dual legal system. We have indigenous customary law, which was formalized for the 'natives' by the colonizers, and over top of that we have the Roman-Dutch law brought in by the same colonizers but originally reserved for whites. What may seem strange is that although Batswana have a strong attachment to customary law, it's the Roman-Dutch system that has the prestige and respect. It's a difficult contradiction to explain.

John: Is it perhaps the difference between fondness and reverence?

Katlego: Batswana are very proud of the power of the stable, peaceful postcolonial state we've built, and I suspect it has to do with that. I mean that keeping the colonizers' legal system and placing it above our indigenous system is a way of showing that we have turned colonialism on its head. A system we were excluded from when we were 'natives', we have taken ownership of for ourselves as free citizens. So I wasn't surprised when several people told me that having the protection of the Roman-Dutch law made them feel 'respectable' and 'valued' – as Batswana – in a way they had never felt before. One even said that the 'shield' of the law had given them 'dignity' for the first time in their life!

John: One of the things that struck me about Botswana when I came down from Kenya was what seemed to me at first to be a trivial preoccupation with being 'recognized', for lack of a better word. A foreigner feels it most immediately in the expectation to formally greet people before you say anything else to them – and in the offense taken when a newly arrived Westerner just goes straight to a request or question. But, of course, it goes much deeper than etiquette.

Katlego: It goes very deep. We are a modern, Western-influenced society in all kinds of ways, but we are still very rooted in the traditional idea that other people make us who we are. That's why we are so concerned about belonging. In that context, the difference between queer and postqueer isn't about who you are in a relationship with or who you are having sex with but the idea that decriminalization has created space for fuller, more social expressions of who we are.

John: As soon as I started to get involved in LGBT activism in Botswana, I worried about what seemed to me an over-reliance on Western concepts and terminologies. Not only did it make the movement vulnerable to the 'un-African' canard, but I thought it would prevent the development of distinctive, organic Setswana understandings and ways of being queer. Perhaps I needn't have worried.

Katlego: If my conversations accurately reflect community opinion, the emerging local sense of postqueerness, in its concern with social dignity, respect and belonging, with participation in the larger culture, does reflect a distinctive, organic Setswana way of interpreting the term even if postqueer remains another term imported from the West. It's still an open question, of course, whether decriminalization really will enable us to achieve full dignity and belonging in the larger community, but remaining 'queer' – in the literal sense of the word – seems, almost by definition, unlikely to do that.

John: The earlier terms – gay, bisexual, lesbian, LGBT and so on – were incorporated into the discourse in Botswana, in both English and Setswana, in more or less their Western senses, weren't they? In my experience, 'gay' Batswana defined and presented themselves, from 'butch' to 'femme', in ways that, to me, often seemed indistinguishable from the gay world I had known in Canada before I left for Kenya. What people were telling you in the interviews suggests that queer is still read as more of a pejorative, or at least, an exclusionary term rather than one 'reclaimed' and repurposed as a sign of pride and a marker of liberation from precisely that older sense of the word.

Katlego: The introduction of *gay* into the discourse happened here first from a point of violence. It was used to protect morality and heteronormativity rather than to identify someone as an equal or partner in citizenship. That's not to say it has lost its sharpness in some people's mouths. But as some of those I interviewed pointed out, the time of silence, of hiding and hoping that others would look the other way, overlapped with the reclamation of the term in the West. Keep in mind, though, that the people I interviewed were all multilingual but, beyond primary school, had mainly been educated in English, and the interviews were also in English. This may have blurred the lines of when queer became a word that could be used 'naturally' in Botswana, that is, without thinking about where it came from – the point when it acquired a local patina, so to speak.

John: So, from what the interviews revealed, how does that adoption or adaptation of *queer* into Botswana's postcolonial hybridity tie in with how the people you talked with view *post*queerness?

Katlego: First of all, I have to say that it was clear in many of the interviews that people have not thought all that much, or systematically, about postqueer.

John: It's a much newer term in Botswana than here, and there's still a lot of debate, or confusion, about what it means here, so that's not surprising.

Katlego: Yes, and it also means that if I were to interview the same people again in, say, five or ten years, their ideation of both queer and postqueer, even their memories of how the words have been used, could be quite different. But going back to your question, let me start with what one of the interviewees said when I asked them what postqueer means in Botswana: 'postqueer if we get there will not necessarily be a utopia, because we'll

always have something to fight for and against, but I'd like to see it as a time
when everyone has access to being queer without feeling or being seen as if
they have to prove a point. When we can just be'.

John: When being queer becomes a non-issue? You mentioned when we were
arranging the topics for this conversation that several people used that
term when you asked what postqueer meant to them.

Katlego: Yes, in the sense that *queer*, for most of those I talked with, refers
to classifications that cluster LGBTQI+ identities under a terminological
umbrella as a form of shelter but in the process fix them in a kind of eternal
opposition to the identities that drove us under the umbrella in the first
place. Besides providing shelter, this has enabled us to fight collectively, and
thus more effectively, for our rights. But at the same time, it undermines
the ideal that, as Batswana, we share with the larger community—including
our haters—of society as the harmonious, organic whole that *botho*, our
traditional communitarian ethic, envisions. So, though the classifications
serve a purpose in terms of activism, people feel that at some point they
need to be dissolved and become 'non-issues'. One of the best-known of
the new wave of post-decriminalization artists told me that ideas of gender
normativity and gender queering and what category within the queer
community they belonged to had never been things they thought about,
whatever others might think watching them on stage. They see themselves
as a traditional Motswana and their categorization as queer by others as
spoiling that.

John: Does it all come down to words, then?

Katlego: (*laughs*) Well, questions of language and indigeneity are our shared
fascination, so of course I had to ask people if they felt that English
suffices as a tool for queer expression or if indigenous terms need to be
reappropriated. Most cited the potential harms of reappropriation since,
they claimed, Setswana is slow to develop, so they worried that trying to
indigenize the discourse – beyond just naturalizing the English terms –
would arm the haters. And with the globalization of the English terms in
the media and social health programming as well as through the worldwide
reach of activism, thanks to ILGA World and other transnational
organizations, many felt that tweaking the pronunciations and using
traditional forums to propagate and 'indigenize' the English terms will be
a swifter, and a more controlled, means of educating and sensitizing the
wider community. The consensus seemed to be that if the international
English terminology can be made to feel 'local' to all Batswana, as it already
does in the queer community, and thus isn't rooted in othering, this will
lead – now that decriminalization has made us feel protected and able to
speak out and interact more openly with others – to a culture in which
being queer is a non-issue while also not being erased.

John: That seems to be a good place to wrap this conversation up. The
conversation on queerness and postqueerness in Botswana – and how
those concepts interact with ways of self-actualization and in relation to

botho – will obviously keep developing. It's still early days, and there's an awful lot to do to get to that vision of a postqueer, inclusive community.

Katlego: Yes, and that vision may also change as we go forward. What is clear, I think, is that for the queer community, nurturing a sense of localized ownership of our words and self-concepts needs to lead to an emancipation from being defined by external actors and ideas. The most important finding from our interviews may be that, even when approaching an issue that is new to them, queer Batswana of different generations and backgrounds are looking for tools that can serve the whole Setswana community as well as themselves. So, I would say, based on what I learned from my generous interlocutors, is that postqueerness in Botswana will be about social and cultural wholeness and the *botho* ideal of a harmonious, unified Setswana social fabric.

John: And with the inadequacy of traditional, indigenous categorizations of genders and sexualities at the local level aiding that process?

Katlego: Yes! Because that lack, if you like, enables – compels – queer artists and activists to create our own tools, and that's true even if we start with borrowed English terms. Our own culture and circumstances will always bend those words into local senses, as the interviews show is already happening with postqueer.

John: That seems like an excellent note on which to end (for now). Thank you, Kat, for all your hard work organizing and interviewing and transcribing. I've really enjoyed this chance to catch up on developments in Botswana, a place I'll always miss.

Katlego: It's been a pleasure.

Notes

1   Better known by its Nguni name, *ubuntu*, the principle that a person is a person on account of other people.

2   See https://www.icj.org/sogicasebook/kanane-v-state-court-of-appeal-botswana-30-july-2003/

3   The named complainant in the constitutional case.

4   The Botswana Democratic Party (BDP) has been in power continuously since independence in 1966.

5   Sumptuary laws are of ancient origin and can be traced back to ancient Greece and ancient Rome. They usually refer to prohibitions such as attending drinking events, owning an extravagant house, using currencies in other metals than, for example, iron; they also restricted the type of materials used for the making of clothes, or the number of guests at entertainments, especially in ancient Rome. The Editors.